CHARLESTON'S GHOSTS

CHARLESTON'S GHOSTS
HAUNTINGS IN THE HOLY CITY

By JAMES CASKEY

Copyright © 2014 James Caskey

All rights reserved. No part of this book may be reproduced or transmitted in any form or by any means, electronic or mechanical, including photocopying, recording, or by any information storage and retrieval system--except by a reviewer who may quote brief passages in a review to be printed in a magazine, newspaper, or on the Web--without permission in writing from the publisher. For information, please contact Manta Ray Books LLC, 510 East 64th Street, Savannah, GA 31405.

Although the author and publisher have made every effort to ensure the accuracy and completeness of information contained in this book, we assume no responsibility for errors, inaccuracies, omissions, or any inconsistency herein. Any slights of people, places, or organizations are unintentional.

First Printing 2014
ISBN: 978-0-9882529-8-1

All photos courtesy of James Caskey, and the
Library of Congress, pages 12, 18, 23, 87, 111, 114, 116, 118, 119, 121, 125, 148, 151, 154, 174, 191, and 259.

Cover Design by Liz Wiglesworth

Map Design by Amanda Marks

Printed in the United States of America

Acknowledgements

To write this volume, I leaned heavily on the talents of many people. This book would not have been possible without the invaluable help of Charleston authors, historians, tour guides, and many people who own or work at the establishments described within these pages. I'd like to thank authors/tour guides Mark Jones, Rebel Sinclair, and Bruce Orr; tour guide Ginger Williams; Fort Sumter historian Rick Hatcher; owner of the Tavern, Gary Dow; Tony Youmans, Director at the Old Exchange and Provost Dungeon; Christopher Parham, the Managing Director of the Dock Street Theatre; and to everyone else mentioned in this volume who offered their time and technical expertise.

I'd like to offer gratitude to my pre-readers, who offered valuable advice and suggestions for some thorny, in-progress conundrums, and Liz Wiglesworth, the owner of Manta Ray Books, who shepherded this project from the very beginning.

Table of Contents

Charleston-Why So Haunted? 11

The Whistling Doctor (Thomas Rose House) 27

Lavinia and John Fisher 37

Mad River Bar and Grille 53

Pirate Treasure at 'The Bosoms' 56

Apparition at the Battery 60

Blind Tiger Pub 71

Ruth Lowndes Simmons Gateposts 77

Book-Loving Ghost at the Hannah Heyward House 86

Children's Cancer Thrift Store 90

Spectres at Southend Brewery 94

Francis Marion Hotel 101

The Old Jail 106

Poogan's Porch 127

The Tavern 132

Bocci's Italian Restaurant 143

Fort Sumter 147

The Dare at St. Philip's Churchyard 156

Old Exchange and Provost Dungeon 159

Battery Carriage House Inn 169

Madame Talvande and the Sword Gates 177

82 Queen	187
Charleston Orphan House	190
Dock Street Theatre	195
Duelists at St. Michael's Rectory	203
The Old Citadel	208
Aiken-Rhett House	211
Gullah Culture	215
USS Yorktown	227
Old Charleston Ghost Shop	236
The Ghost of Annabel Lee	238
Andrew Pinckney Inn	241
1837 Bed and Breakfast	244
The Mills House	246
Jasmine House Inn	248
Husk Restaurant	250
Phantom of the Bridge	252
Meeting Street Inn	254
Coda	256

Haunted Map of Charleston

1. Thomas Rose House
2. Philadelphia Alley
3. Mad River Bar & Grille
4. "The Bosoms"
5. 21 East Battery
6. Blind Tiger Pub
7. Ruth Lowndes Simmons Gateposts
8. Hannah Heyward House
9. Southend Brewery
10. Francis Marion Hotel
11. Old Jail
12. Poogan's Porch
13. The Tavern
14. Bocci's Italian Restaurant
15. St. Philip's Churchyard
16. Old Exchange and Provost Dungeon
17. Battery Carriage House Inn
18. The Sword Gates
19. 82 Queen
20. Charleston Orphan House
21. Dock Street Theatre
22. St. Michael's Rectory
23. The Old Citadel
24. Aiken-Rhett House
25. The Old Slave Mart Museum
26. Old Charleston Ghost Shop
27. Unitarian Churchyard
28. Andrew Pinckney Inn
29. 1837 Bed and Breakfast
30. The Mills House
31. Jasmine House Inn
32. Husk
33. Meeting Street Inn

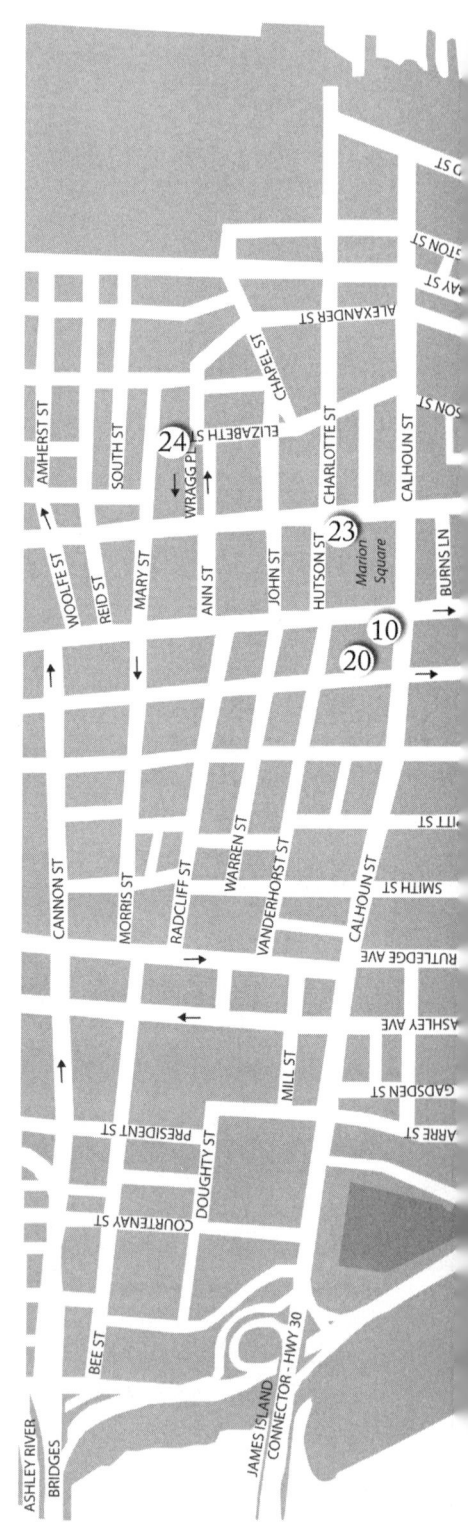

Charleston: Why So Haunted?

"South Carolina is too small for a republic, and too large for an insane asylum."
—James Louis Petigru, former South Carolina Congressman and Attorney General, December 1860

Charleston, South Carolina is a ghost storyteller's paradise, full of unrequited love and noble tragedy. Simply by walking down by the waterfront or through the palatial mansions of the peninsula, one can *feel* the crackling passions of this sultry, romantic city. The Palmetto City is so gorgeous that many of its inhabitants have simply refused to depart, despite the fact that they have left this mortal coil. A lot of visitors describe a feeling of being 'tuned into' the vibe of the city, and that they can get a sense of the inner workings of this unique Southern town.

You should always be aware, however, that Charleston does not give up her secrets so readily. It is quite easy to be sucked in by the siren's call. Many people, after spending a long weekend being stealthily seduced by this grand dame of the South, mistakenly think that they have gotten to know her: they believe (in error) that after a long stroll amongst the rustling palmettoes and gas lamps, a couple of sumptuous meals, and a tour or two, that they have discovered everything there is to know about this seemingly genteel, elegant city. But like any great seductress, Charleston presents a careful veneer of half-truths and outright fabrications, and it lets you, the intended conquest, fill in many of the blanks. Seduction, after all, is not true love, nor is it a gentle act. She whispers stories spun from sugar about pirates and patriots and rebels, about plantations and traditions and manners and yes, even ghosts; but the entire time she is guarded about the *real* story. Few tourists ever hear the truth, because at the dark heart of Charleston is a winding tale of violence, tragedy and, most of all, sin.

Never, ever forget while you are hearing these alluring stories of Charleston, that although this town has been nicknamed the Holy City,

Ruins of Circular Church, Charleston, S.C. Obtained from the Library of Congress Prints and Photographs Division.

her history is anything but virtuous. Author Maggie Davis once described Charleston's history as "not only bloodstained and wicked but continuingly unrepentant." There isn't one Charleston, but in fact two of them, and this paradox of duality has been with the city from the very beginning. I'll go into more depth on this subject in a moment, but first we need to examine the grim early history of this grand Southern city by the bay. Most theories which attempt to explain why certain locations are haunted (while others are not) center on the extreme tragedy which has occurred there. After all, with no ill-fated deaths, there are very few ghost stories to be told. If that "tragedy equals hauntings" theory is correct, Charleston's narrow historic peninsula might very well be the most haunted spot in North America.

Sin, Slaves, Pirates and Disease

The average person, when asked about the most tragic thing that has ever happened in Charleston South Carolina, invariably replies with some variation of: "The 1861 Confederate bombardment of Fort Sumter." I mean, if everyone knows about it, then that must be the most awful thing to happen in the city of Charleston, right? Well, no. The symbolism of starting the War Between the States was much more terrible than the actual attack, and had awful, far-reaching implications for the rest of the country; but the actual firing on the fort took zero lives, neither Union nor Confederate. Charleston has endured some horrific ordeals, but the shelling and reduction of Fort Sumter wouldn't even crack the top twenty. That event, I humbly submit, was not even the most tragic occurrence to happen to the city of Charleston in the calendar year of 1861. Let's backtrack to the beginning of the colony, however.

Charleston's masterful deceptions start early. You will find the founding date of 1670 displayed proudly all over town, but please be aware that the Charleston peninsula where the Historic District now sits (then called Oyster Point because of the plethora of oyster shells lining the bank) was not formally settled until ten full years later. Prior to 1680, the settlement was located at Charles Towne Landing, located across the Ashley River to the east. This means that even cultured Southern dames like the Palmetto City will occasionally lie about their age (prior to the American Revolution, the colony was referred to as 'Charles Town,' and was not formally abbreviated to 'Charleston' until our successful uprising against the British, post-1783. I have followed suit in this volume for consistency's sake, so please be aware that any reference to 'Charles Town' means that the period in question refers to when we were still subject to the English Crown).

The new colony's connection to sin started early, as well: the city's namesake was English King Charles II, a man who was famously addicted to visiting brothels. It was said that he was "the father of his people, or at least a great many of them." King Charles II had at least fourteen illegitimate children. A top advisor to Charles II, Anthony Ashley Cooper (Earl of Shaftesbury), was also quite fond of ladies of negotiable affections. Oddly enough, despite being a close confidant of Charles II, he was sometimes disloyal to the King. Charles even went so far as to imprison the Earl in the Tower of London for a while, yet he eventually forgave Cooper and released him. Lord Ashley Cooper was the driving force behind the Carolina colony, and honored by being the namesake for both rivers flowing by the peninsula, the Ashley and the Cooper Rivers.

The colony was settled by ninety-three passengers aboard the two hundred ton frigate *Carolina*. These British settlers sailed into Charleston Harbor in April of 1670, and must have thought they had found paradise itself: plentiful fish and oysters, and towering oaks and pines as far as the eye could see. That impression was extremely short-lived, however, since the population of early Charles Town (known at that stage as Albermarle Point) was ravaged that first warm season by fever and disease. These bouts of dysentery and other illnesses were a recurring problem for the settlers, particularly in the rainy late summer months when mosquitoes, which could spread yellow fever, bred by the millions. In fact, the location of the colony was shifted from the first location to the second (Oyster Point) because it was believed by many that the peninsula was more healthy, being described by early colonist Joseph Dalton as "being free from any noisome vapors and… refreshed with Coole breathing from the sea." The colony was relocated to what today is known as the French Quarter—so named for the high concentration of French merchants in that area—which is bounded by the Cooper River to the east, Broad Street to the south, Meeting Street to the west, and Market Street to the north (roughly the boundaries of the walled city on the peninsula). Despite the move, new colonists continued to succumb to deadly diseases in droves. The English presence was also deadly to the existing Native American population, with an English settler describing how smallpox virtually eradicated an entire nation of Indians, the survivors of which "ran away and left their dead unburied," leaving them "lying upon the ground for vultures to devour."

In September of that first year, a boat from Bermuda brought the first slaves, making the Carolina colony the only English settlement in North

"... a ghost storyteller's paradise..."

America where slaves were introduced almost from the very beginning. Soon, the English settlers were also enslaving vast numbers of Native Americans. These American Indians did not appreciate being sold into bondage, and the danger of backlash was very real. Just three years after arriving, Charles Town residents were engaged in a war with the Westoe Indians, and then faced a similar series of battles with the Stono Tribe as well. The Yemassee War of 1715-17 was particularly devastating. Over one hundred Carolinians were killed in the initial Native American raids, including one unfortunate legislator named Thomas Nairne, who was roasted alive. Victory was only secured through an alliance with the Cherokees. If not for the Cherokee intervention, the English settlers, Charles Town residents included, could have been wiped out by angry Yemassee, Creek, Choctaw and Catawba forces.

There were other threats to Charleston's very survival, the most notable being Spanish-held Florida to the south. Charles Town was attacked by the Spanish in 1686, an assault which failed in part due to a hurricane. The English colony was attacked again in 1706, when a combined French and Spanish expedition was repulsed through proper military strategy and yet

Magnolia Cemetery.

another providentially-timed storm. According to Robert Rosen's book *A Short History of Charleston*, there were other threats, too: "Pirates of various descriptions inhabited coastal Carolina before Charles Town was founded. They roamed the South Atlantic and the Caribbean, free to loot because the fledgling governments of the area were unable to stop them. In its infancy, Charles Town was constantly menaced by pirates."

Historian Carl Bridenbaugh once wrote that "Charles Town was probably the least religious of all the towns" in North America during the early 18th century. Drinking to excess permeated much of Charles Town society, and all manner of debaucheries could be witnessed merely by strolling along present-day East Bay Street, a reputation which persisted for a long time. 19th century politician John C. Calhoun was appalled at the level of lewdness and offensive behavior he observed in Charleston. He went so far as to claim that the many fevers and illnesses were a result of "the misconduct of the inhabitants; and may be considered as a curse for their intemperance and debaucheries." He might have been on to something, but he likely got the causation backwards. Surely part of this 'devil may care' attitude towards sin and vice was caused by the rampant illnesses and fevers (and the resulting shortened time frame to enjoy life's pleasures) so common to the area, and not the other way around. Yellow fever was a frequent deadly threat, and the drinking water was brackish and fouled with human waste in many instances, making dysentery a terrible problem. In 1738, a smallpox epidemic struck with such ferocity that residents began taking a mixture of cow's dung, milk, and bread, which was thought to ease the symptoms of the disease. Another supposed remedy was drinking a mixture of tar water, which became an accepted 'cure' until the man prescribing it also died of smallpox.

In 1739, the bloodiest slave revolt in colonial American history occurred about twenty miles south of Charles Town at the Stono River Bridge. A group of rebelling slaves killed over a dozen whites and looted and pillaged the countryside. The Charles Town populace was terrified of an all-out slave rebellion and war. The slaves' plan was to flee to Spanish-held Florida and freedom, but they were apprehended and executed by an enraged militia before they could do so. Over forty of the Stono Slave Rebellion leaders were put to death, and their severed heads were mounted on posts along major roads to serve as a grisly warning against slaves who might consider throwing off their chains. The following year, another slave rebellion was discovered before it happened, this time in Goose Creek, slightly to the north of Charles Town. Sixty-seven slaves were brought to trial, most of whom were hanged.

Life in early Charleston, then, was brutal for all the inhabitants of the city, regardless of class, race, or religion.

Terror Amongst the Flames

Traditionally one of the biggest fears of the Charleston populace of the 17th through the early 20th century were fires. The trepidation was well-founded: the archives are full of both newspaper reports and chilling first-person accounts of the city almost entirely going up entirely in flames. Fires threatened the city's very existence many times. In late February, 1698, fire consumed roughly fifty buildings, or approximately half the city which existed at that time. One year later, another fire burned a great portion of the walled city. One year after that in 1700, nearly every structure in Charles Town burned. Charles Town again was nearly turned into a smoking ruin in 1731 and once more in 1740. In the latter fire, citizens used gunpowder to knock down structures in the path of the inferno, thus

Panoramic view, the ruins of Charleston, S.C., Roman Catholic Cathedral in the distance, by E. & H.T. Anthony (firm). Obtained from the Library of Congress Prints and Photographs Division.

saving portions of the city.

In 1778 as the American Revolution intensified, a fire destroyed over 250 houses and an unknown number of commercial buildings. Another blaze hit the area just south of Market Street near Broad in 1796, which destroyed over 500 structures. An 1800 fire on Calhoun Street was caused by the unlikely combination of a leaky barrel of brandy, a lit candle, and a keg of gunpowder. In 1810, 194 houses went up in smoke. 1835 had not one, but two serious fires, and 1838 saw yet another large blaze just north of the Market area.

When discussing fires on the Charleston peninsula, however, most of the other blazes pale in comparison to the Great Fire of 1861. The conflagration burned 540 of the most densely populated acres of the city, fanned by strong winds that made it impossible for terrified Charlestonians to combat it effectively. Also adding to the problem was the fact that most able-bodied young men were in military service. "The fearful conflagration that has just passed over our city will cause the 11th and 12th of December 1861 hereafter to be remembered as one of those trying periods, which for the moment seem to paralyze all the long cherished hopes and bright anticipations of the future," wrote the *Charleston Courier* on December 13th, 1861. In a letter to her brother, Charlestonian Elizabeth Frost relates the events of that terrifying evening, noting that "it soon became apparent that the whole city was in danger... we saw that Broad Street was in flames, then becoming frightened we ran back to Mr. K's and got there in time to see the [St. Michael's] Cathedral spire burn and fall; it was a magnificent sight, all the intricate pieces of wood work were on fire and the cross shown brilliantly to the end."

"...In Dreadful Anticipation of Immediate and Cruel Death..."

One of the worst calamities to ever strike Charleston, at least in terms of property damage and sheer terror of the inhabitants, occurred on the evening of August 31st, 1886: the Great Charleston Earthquake. From the next day's *Charleston Courier*: "An earthquake, such as has never been known in the history of this city, swept over Charleston last night, shortly after 10 o'clock, causing more loss and injury to property and far more loss of life than the cyclone the year before. The city is wrecked... the streets are encumbered with masses of fallen bricks and tangled telegraph and telephone wires... it was almost impossible to pass from one part of the city to the other... The first shock was, by far, the most severe... the air was filled with the cries and shrieks of women and children. From every side... came the cry, 'God help us!', 'God save us!', or 'Oh, my God!'" A *Courier* writer named Carl McKinley later described the terrifying ordeal: "The floors were heaving underfoot, the surrounding walls and partitions visibly swayed to and fro, the crash of falling masses of stone and brick and mortar was heard overhead and without, the terrible roar filled the ears and seemed to fill the mind and heart, dazing perception, arresting thought, and for a few panting breaths, or while you held your breath in anticipation of immediate and cruel death, you felt that your life was already past..." On Broad Street, several forty-five ton granite blocks were heaved more than ten feet by the oscillations. Hundreds of buildings were either destroyed outright or were later judged to be so unsafe that they had to be torn down. Downtown was in ruins. Amazingly, only about sixty people lost their lives in the disaster.

A *Charleston News and Courier* article from 1986 (which marked the one hundredth anniversary of the earthquake) noted the fatalities: "People rushed from their houses in various states of dress and undress. Several of the... deaths reported that night resulted from people rushing out too quickly and being crushed by the collapsing cornices and facades of damaged buildings." The quake's effects were felt as far away as Canada, and church bells rang in New York due to the vibrations. Though it lasted only forty seconds or so, the Great Charleston Earthquake of 1886 was undoubtedly the single most terrifying event in Charleston's long history.

Tempests

Other forces of nature conspired against the Palmetto City as well. The historical record describes nearly twenty hurricanes which struck the Charleston area. In the storm of 1699, a Scottish frigate was dashed to pieces in the harbor, with captain, crew, and ninety-seven souls going down with the vessel. In 1713, several houses were swept away and close to seventy people drowned. Perhaps the worst hurricane in the area's history occurred in 1852: dozens of small craft were lost and a brig was driven up Vanderhorst Creek, coming to rest in the middle of Meeting Street at the present-day intersection with Water Street. For a thirty mile radius, the storm flattened trees and houses, and fifteen people drowned in the city.

In 1885, Mother Nature's fury struck again. Winds at an estimated 125 miles per hour created a massive storm surge which swept over White Point Gardens, submerging it under as much as six feet of seawater. Tin roofs were ripped away, slate roof shingles littered the streets by the thousands. All along the waterfront, ships, piers, and wharves were smashed to kindling. Twenty-one people died in the storm. Then in 1893, a hurricane's surge drowned nearly two thousand people along the South Carolina coast.

Amazingly, not every hurricane that has struck the Charleston area has been detrimental to the city: in 1686, a storm almost certainly saved the city from a Spanish invasion. One hundred and fifty hostile troops intent on seizing the city for Spain were ravaged by a horrific yet providentially-timed storm. The attack was called off, and Charleston was saved.

The Key to Understanding: The Dark Pre-History of Charleston

You might be thinking: *Okay, that's a lot of tragedy. But a lot of places have had tragedy, without this many ghost stories popping up everywhere. Why, then, is Charleston so haunted?* Fortunately, I have a theory.

In my previous books about Savannah, Georgia and New Orleans, Louisiana, I have explored a theory as to why certain locations in the Deep South have such a haunted reputation (I have borrowed some thoughts from those earlier volumes for this section, in the interests of full-disclosure). I believe that my premise also applies here: namely, that people who try to explain why certain locations are so haunted by citing prior tragedy do not go back far enough into the historical record. Exactly like in Louisiana and Georgia, there were Native American tribes occupying present-day South Carolina. They existed for thousands of years before Europeans settled the area. These native settlements, whose exact populations we can only guess at today, were almost completely eradicated by contact with the Spanish, specifically the conquistador Hernando De Soto and his men, from 1539 to 1541. Both conquistadors spreading violence and the missionaries spreading the gospel inadvertently introduced something else to these indigenous South Carolinians. Rather than guns or swords, the Spanish raiders' primary (though accidental) weapon against these Native Americans was a variety of diseases, for which the natives had little or no immunity. The effect was startling. According to Jared Diamond in his book *Guns, Germs, and Steel: The Fates of Human Societies*, the Native Americans who contracted these diseases died on an unthinkable scale. "Throughout the Americas," he writes, "diseases introduced with Europeans spread from tribe to tribe far in advance of the Europeans themselves, killing an estimated 95 percent of the pre-Columbian Native American population." North America, he reveals, was home to an estimated twenty million natives at the moment of contact with Christopher Columbus' expedition. "When Hernando De Soto became the first European conquistador to march through the southeastern United States, in 1540, he came across Indian town sites abandoned two years earlier because the inhabitants had died. These epidemics had been transmitted from coastal Indians infected by Spaniards visiting the coast. The Spaniards' microbes spread to the interior in advance of the Spaniards themselves." To list these sites of contact between coastal natives and seagoing Spanish explorers is to make a list of the most haunted cities in North America: Charleston, Savannah, New Orleans, and Saint Augustine, among others. Today's most haunted sites all previously had huge Native American populations, the very settlements which were eradicated by disease in one of the worst pandemics ever seen in the history of mankind. This simply cannot be a coincidence.

Those ravaging diseases, combined with the all-out war that the conquistadors waged on the native population, led to the fall of those Native American societies. The American South degenerated into what University of Mississippi Professor of Anthropology Robbie Ethridge has described as a "shatter zone," since the diseases would have knocked down the basic framework of those cultures. That, coupled with the fact that many of the young men of the tribes died in battles with the Spanish, was a blow from which those societies could not recover. The fracture of those Native American tribes into a plethora of almost disconnected subgroups ultimately made it possible for the later-arriving English to establish Charleston in its present-day location. And this was a story that was repeated, with very little variation, all over the American continent, but particularly in the Deep South. So the very existence of these Spanish, French and English seaports is due to the fact that almost a full two hundred years before their founding, there was an epidemic of disease which nearly destroyed an entire way of life. History works this way much of the time: if those Native Americans had just a little more resistance to smallpox, seaports like the present-day city of Charleston would likely not exist, since taking the American continent away from the hostile natives would have been difficult (if not impossible).

CHARLESTON-WHY SO HAUNTED?

Graveyard, Circular Church, Charleston, S.C., created by George N. Barnard in 1865. Obtained from the Library of Congress Prints and Photographs Division.

Graves at Circular Congregation Churchyard.

This perfect storm of disease cut both ways: the European settlers had little resistance to yellow fever and malaria, which were deadly tropical maladies they encountered during their explorations. Syphilis is also widely regarded as a Native American disease, which was spread back to Europe and Eurasia by returning sailors.

If the theory that one death forever psychically stains a particular location is correct, then what is the result of eradicating an entire society and culture? How can there be no repercussions for such a horrific tragedy, one which played out on such an unimaginable level? Consider that the Spanish settlers introduced catastrophic disease, and put many of the surviving Native Americans to the sword. The later-arriving English slaughtered and enslaved the random bands of natives which had withstood the earlier cataclysm. Perhaps we are seeing the consequences of this desolation.

So, Why Is Charleston So Haunted?

I've heard a lot of ideas put forth as to why Charleston is so rife with stories of the paranormal. Many people, as previously mentioned, point to the extreme tragedy that has happened from the very early days of the colony. My own idea, that the land itself was somehow 'pre-charged' to be a perfect spot for hauntings when those Spanish, French, and English explorers introduced smallpox and other diseases into a Native American culture which had no defense against those illnesses, is yet another theory, but is by no means a complete one. I have also heard it frequently said that houses could possibly store a 'dry charge' of the energy expended in the structure, much like a battery stores electrical power. This energy could be bound to the property by moments of extreme emotional distress, such as death or great sadness. Charleston, as you see in the preceding pages, has experienced an immeasurable amount of tragedy over the years. There is also the possibility that an action repeated over and over again can also have this dry charge effect, which would explain why hearing footsteps is one of the most common forms of a structure being haunted. From time to time, when conditions are right, that stored power is unleashed. Think of sound waves: energy is released in audible form, and when conditions allow, such as an object reflects the sound waves back toward the point of origin, the energy returns in the form of an echo. If energy can return in this way several seconds after the actual event, why can't psychic energy return at a later time as well, sometimes years, decades or even centuries after the fact? It is possible that the act of renovating a structure could release this energy, and the fact that Charleston's old buildings are constantly being refurbished might help explain the city's haunted reputation, as well. So the phenomena we label 'ghostly activity' may be an explainable occurrence in this way.

There is another factor to consider: many old port cities have a reputation for being haunted. Southern seaports like Charleston, Savannah, Wilmington, St. Augustine, Key West and New Orleans have garnered the reputation of having many supernatural occurrences. Perhaps it is tied in with the close proximity to the water—if ghosts are life-force energy that has not faded away, then maybe the tidal ebb and flow has somehow polarized the entire area, preserving the remaining energy and capturing it for a time when conditions are right.

So, what are ghosts? And am I trying to prove their existence in these pages? I prefer to keep these matters more in the realm of faith. You, the

Magnolia Cemetery.

reader, either already believe in ghosts, or disbelieve. So my answer to the second question is that it isn't my job to convince you, and that's not really what this book is about. I personally don't need an electromagnetic field detector or an 'orb photograph' to tell me that ghosts exist, because I have experienced them first-hand. I have seen objects moving on their own with my very eyes, and have even once witnessed the shadowy form of a person which I knew was not there, and yet I distinctly saw a silhouette step across a doorway. Recorded in this volume are encounters with the paranormal that I personally have had, occurrences which I cannot easily explain away. But let's be clear: we're talking about belief, not proof. Regardless of my assurances that I have accurately recorded these instances in this volume, belief is up to you. You as a reader may find fault with my assessment of history (it has happened), you may disagree with my conclusions (which is common for this genre), but I hope that I faithfully convey the pains I have taken to make sure that this book is honest on the subject of ghosts. I can promise you that the witnesses I have interviewed are quoted accurately, and that I've done my best to double-check facts and dates as best I can. Only you, however, can choose to believe.

The Whistling Doctor

The Thomas Rose House, 59 Church Street, and Philadelphia Alley, near 20 Queen Street

*I*n the middle of Charleston's most historic area, a beautiful yet modest home sits, giving no clue from its innocuous exterior of the violence which will forever stain its name. If the stories are to be believed, and those supernatural tales go back well over two hundred years, then the Thomas Rose House is regularly visited by the crackling anguish of a friendship gone terribly wrong. This story of an affection which ended in brutal violence is so notorious (and the tragedy so complete) that the occurrences in 1786 have forever altered Charleston's paranormal landscape, and not only at the Thomas Rose House. There is another location, more than a quarter of a mile distant, which also feels echoes of that fateful moment.

Built in 1735, the home is indicative of the type of construction which was prominent in the city at that time period: modest two-and-a-half story brick dwellings with slate roofs (the piazza on the left-hand side was added much later, in the 19th century, when that architectural feature became fashionable). The Thomas Rose House came into existence when the city was still very young—a blushing fifty-five years old—which was a time when the City Fathers finally began thinking of Charles Town not as an armed fortress but as a proper city. The defensive walls which protected the city were still largely in place when this house was constructed, as evidenced by Herman Moll's 1733 map of the area. It is difficult, if one walks the upscale area today, to get a sense of what the area would have looked like back at the time of the house's construction. This house, built at the original Charles Town lot number 61, replaced a more modest dwelling at the same location, so this was still a working-class neighborhood for Charleston's new merchant class. A likely reason for this upgrade in living

"During moments of great stress at 59 Church Street... the distinct sound of whistling has been reported on many occasions."

quarters was that Charleston's economy experienced a huge surge in the 1730's, based mostly on rice and indigo production.

While the house will forever bear his name, it does not appear that Thomas Rose ever lived at 59 Church Street. He sold the house almost immediately upon completion to the Savage family, who owned it for the next ninety years. A little less than fifty years into the Savage's ownership, it became an upscale boarding house run by two sisters of the family.

One autumn day in 1783, Doctor Joseph Ladd arrived at the Thomas Rose House, fresh in from Rhode Island, with his newly-made Charlestonian acquaintance Ralph Isaacs graciously showing him the way. No one at that point knew of the trouble and heartache this chance meeting would later entail: almost three years later to the day, Isaacs would wind up killing his new friend, Dr. Ladd.

Love, Money, Scandal

Joseph Brown Ladd was a magnet for undeserved drama and heartache. It started early for him: his father William, a strict disciplinarian, worked the rocky Rhode Island soil on his farm, and did not understand his intellectually brilliant son. According to an 1832 biography (by Elizabeth Ladd Haskins and W.B. Chittenden) called *The Literary Remains of Joseph Brown Ladd*, despite having little access to formal schooling he immersed himself in academic pursuits, teaching himself mathematics, fluent Latin, and memorizing large passages of the Bible.

His father did not support his quest for knowledge, claiming it interfered with the work on the farm. Young Joseph had an unconscious habit of whistling, which meant that his father could always locate him even if he was not performing his chores. The son was adamantly fixed in his cerebral pursuits, however. From *The Literary Remains*: "He made no secret of his unconquerable aversion to the drudgery of agriculture, and had recourse to various stratagems to escape from it when compelled to labor by parental authority. On one occasion, he fitted up a study in a thicket of alder-bushes, in an enclosure through which he had to pass to his employment, in a manner so ingenious as to elude discovery for many months." When his secret study-hall was discovered, he was rebuked severely by his father, to which he replied, "My head, sir, and not my hands, must support me."

Disgusted at what he perceived as his son's laziness, William sent him to work at the age of fourteen at a mercantile business, a placement that was an almost immediate failure. Young Joseph then went to work at a print shop, which was a slightly better fit for the boy, but he was fired after a customer paid him to write a satirical (and scandalous) poem about a local doctor. The enraged physician dragged him back to his parents, who in a fit of desperation, asked the boy if there was any profession he would like to try. He immediately chose medicine, so William arranged for his errant son to apprentice with another doctor in nearby Newport named Isaac Senter, who was by all accounts a brilliant surgeon. Joseph, finally in his element, entered the medical field "as though sitting down to a banquet with an appetite sharpened by long fasting." Doctor Senter found him to be a veritable sponge for medical instruction, possessing a keen mind and skilled hands. His thirst for learning expanded to chemistry, languages, philosophy, physics, and the Classics.

The only thing his books and already-formidable intellect did not prepare him for was love. Nineteen year old Joseph fell madly in love with a young woman named Amanda, whom he described as being "lovely to soul and to eye." She was an orphan, but was from a wealthy family. Her money was held in trust for her by mercenary relatives, who would lose control of the rather sizeable fortune Amanda was due to inherit if she were to marry. Despite the couple's strong feelings for each other, their chances at love were thrown very much into question through a series of vicious rumors spread by these same relatives, some of whom were attorneys. They did not hesitate to ruin her happiness to serve their own selfish interests, and Amanda strongly suspected that they wished to keep her inheritance for themselves. These (unnamed) lies about Joseph's background and intentions made marriage impossible in that small community, and Ladd had no money of his own. So Joseph Ladd and Dr. Senter decided that he should go south, at the urging of a mutual acquaintance, former Revolutionary War General Nathanael Greene. The plan was that Joseph would travel south to Charleston as soon as he became a doctor, and secure a practice there in order to repair his damaged reputation. He would send for Amanda once he had saved enough money for their wedding. Even if her relatives stole the money held for her in trust, the two would still be together. Amanda and the newly-minted doctor were secretly engaged, and Joseph, now twenty, went south in 1783 to seek his destiny.

Doctor Ladd arrived in Charleston, and immediately trouble found him. At the docks he naively asked the wrong person where he should stay. An extremely nefarious individual offered to lead him to an area of town that was by reputation quite dangerous and seedy, where he would almost certainly be robbed. Another man standing nearby, hearing the very bad advice the young doctor was receiving, stepped in. "By all means, take this worthless oaf's advice, if you'd fancy to be robbed of your valuables. You'd likely get your throat cut just for straying into the area of town he is directing you towards." When the first man protested, still hoping that his prey would not get away so easily, the second man brandished his cane and gave the would-be robber a few good lashes. The man ran away in terror, leaving the two of them alone.

"My name is Ralph Isaacs," he said, grinning warmly. "I would be happy to show you to a nice boarding house run by two respectable ladies, one that's fit for a proper gentleman such as yourself." Joseph must have felt that he had found a friend for life.

Indeed, the two men became inseparable for a time, with the older Isaacs serving as tour guide and entertaining provocateur to the good doctor's 'straight man.' A man of strong opinions, Isaacs was willing to argue just about anything, whether it be a new piece of local legislation or a restaurant's bill, with equal conviction. Some people in Charleston, especially those in the upper echelons of society, found Ralph Isaacs too coarse and opinionated for their tastes. He also had the reputation of drinking too much. Dr. Ladd was loyal to his new friend, however, reasoning that the man had saved him some rough treatment when he arrived in town. Joseph, with the help of his landladies, the two Savage sisters, and his letter of introduction by war hero Nathanael Greene, very quickly established a successful medical practice, and was noticed as a rapidly rising star in Charleston's social scene. The good doctor's habit of whistling while he worked proved to be an endearing quality for the Charleston elite, and even earned him the nickname 'The Whistling Doctor.' The Savage sisters also loved the whistling, believing that it brightened up the mood in their home.

Doctor Ladd remained constant to his beloved Amanda, writing her love letter after love letter. She especially enjoyed his poetry (he often referred to himself in these poems as 'Arouet,' which was the real name of his idol, French essayist and philosopher Voltaire). As much as he liked his newfound popularity, his idea of a perfect evening would be to never leave his room at the boarding House on Church Street, writing words to his beloved, and then later falling asleep while reading books on philosophy or medicine. He cared little for the social engagements and party invites which flooded in, only entertaining notions of expanding his practice to the point that he could send for Amanda. They were only a means to an end, he confided one evening to his best friend on earth, Ralph Isaacs.

Ralph teasingly chided his doctor-friend's jam-packed social schedule, but also pointed out that he himself had not been invited to these same parties. Shouldn't he be more grateful? Joseph, not picking up on the subtlety of what Isaacs was really saying, complained openly of the constraints of his time and the exhaustion he felt attending endless social galas. All he wanted, he asserted, was enough money. Which, he didn't feel he needed to add, would secure him the hand of his lady love, Amanda. Ralph Isaacs' gaze at Joseph, his younger and infinitely more popular friend, hardened for a long moment before finally looking away.

The two began to spend less time together. Dr. Ladd's increased social obligations and workload took a toll on their friendship, and Isaacs' jealousy flared dangerously bright towards his seemingly ungrateful friend. Isaacs' opinions grew unflinchingly sterner, especially where Doctor Ladd was concerned. Things grew worse, not better, when they attended the theatre together for a performance of Shakespeare's *Richard III*. The doctor had acquired two exceptional tickets through his connections with the Charleston elite, and hoped his gift would sooth his friend's ever-darkening mood. When they arrived on the night of the performance however, the usher revealed that there had been a mix-up; the play had been oversold, so only one of them would see the play from the rarefied air of the luxurious box-seats. Joseph was about to offer to take the less prestigious standing-room ticket in the pit below, but before he could, Ralph Isaacs flew into a rage. He was positive that this perceived slight was on purpose. "I showed up expecting actors only on the stage, not the orchestrations of an invented doctor! Go ahead, sit with your new cronies and guffaw at my expense. I shall attend the play with my own kind, the rabble and the peanut-chewers down below!" He stomped off, leaving a stunned and embarrassed Doctor Ladd wondering how his kind gift had gone so terribly wrong.

After the performance, the two met at the carriage. Isaacs was still incensed. Dr. Ladd attempted to turn the subject toward something lighter, such as the actor's performances; surely Mr. Isaacs had enjoyed the performance of a local actress, who had played the role of Lady Anne. "Pure rubbish," Ralph asserted. "I was much more interested in the theme of the piece. Or did you miss it, giggling up above me with your new benefactors? Well, let me enlighten you: the play details a scheming man, who rises to power through cunning and back-stabbing. It has a happy ending, however: he dies!" Ralph Isaacs stormed off angrily, preferring to walk alone in darkness. As bad as that was, the next day was worse. Isaacs had apparently gone to several drinking establishments favored by Doctor Ladd's new friends and had made some extremely damaging statements about Joseph, calling him a social climber that cared only for money, a quack, and a turncoat friend. The terrible stories spread like wildfire. It seemed to Dr. Ladd that the awful events which had caused him to leave Rhode Island in disgrace were happening all over again in his new city.

When Isaacs' smear campaign intensified, friends counseled Ladd that he must defend his honor. Remembering from his Newport days that a non-response did him no good (and in many ways seemed to confirm the rumors), Dr. Ladd finally printed a reply in the local newspaper, the *Charleston Morning Post*, to his former friend on October 12th, 1783, ending with the line: "I account it one of the misfortunes of my life that I ever became friends with such a man."

Isaacs responded in print on the 16th with equal fury: "I dare affirm that the event of a little time will convince the world that the self-created doctor is as blasted a scoundrel as ever disgraced humanity." He even insinuated that Doctor Ladd had become infatuated with the actress in the play! A *Charleston News and Courier* article published on June 7th, 1942 detailed the escalating trouble, stating: "…Dr. Ladd learned too late the unwisdom of bandying expletives and epithets with a street gamin… As was at the time inevitable, honor demanded satisfaction," meaning settling the affair over smoking pistols.

In those days, dueling was not only accepted as a means of resolving disputes, it was somewhat expected in circumstances such as these. Dr. Ladd, had he allowed comments like these to pass without addressing them, would have suffered humiliation and lost business. Joseph, despite not inviting this trouble with Isaacs, could not simply ignore his former friend's taunting, because to do so might disrupt his growing practice and thus ruin his dreamed-of future with Amanda. Locked into a certain narrow course of options by the very society whose business he was courting, he did the only thing he could to save his reputation: the Whistling Doctor challenged Ralph Isaacs to a duel. His former friend quickly accepted.

He spent a long, sleepless night before the duel writing a letter to Amanda. It contained a poem, which was later published in *The Literary Remains*:

Death, friendly death may soon relieve my pain.

Long, sure, he cannot be implored in vain.

Soon, the grim angel will restore my peace,

Soothe my hard fate, and bid my sorrows cease

And tear Amanda's image from my breast.

When deep oblivion wraps my mind in night,

When death's dark shadows swim before my sight,

Will, then, Amanda? Ah, she will, I trust,

Pay the last tribute to my clay-cold dust.

Will, sighing, say there his last scene is o'er.

Who loved as mortal never loved before.

O'er my lone tomb oh, yield that sad relief,

Breathe that soft sigh and pour out all your grief,

Or, shed one tear in pity as you pass,

And just remember that your Arouet was.

Day of Destiny

Philadelphia Alley runs between Cumberland and Queen Streets, very close to Church Street. The location was formerly known as Cow Alley, but local residents renamed it after the city of Philadelphia sent assistance following a devastating fire. Regardless of the charitable renaming after the City of Brotherly Love, it had acquired a reputation since Colonial times for being an ideal spot where men could settle their differences. According to a January 7th, 1894 *New York Times* article, it was where Revolutionary War General William Moultrie "pinked his man" in a duel with swords, against an unnamed opponent. The number of duels actually fought in the Alley has no doubt been greatly exaggerated over time (and in fact most of the duels in Charleston were fought at other locations entirely, such as on present-day Line Street or near the old racetrack), but there were apparently enough combatants in the narrow lane over the years that the nickname 'Dueler's Alley' stuck.

The two men met at dawn. A slight fog obscured the ground, adding surreality to the scene of former friends loading pistols to use against one another. Doctor Ladd, whistling lightly to calm his nerves, had the honor of the first shot. They paced off an appropriate distance, giving Joseph time to really think about his friendship with Isaacs. He began to have doubts about whether the duel would truly resolve anything. Wouldn't they have been both better served if they had sat down over a coffee and hashed this disagreement out? When it was time to fire, he turned to see the form of Ralph Isaacs obscured slightly by the mist, and shuddered at thoughts of

"People have also reported the sounds and sights of a duel in Philadelphia Alley."

harming his friend. *No*, he decided, *I am better than this*. He discharged his gun straight up in the air, hoping this could end the troubles between them.

Isaacs, due to the fog, heard rather than saw Doctor Ladd fire. "Hah, you missed!" Ralph exclaimed, and aimed low at his target. Ralph squeezed the trigger. Joseph Ladd was hit in the knee by Isaacs' pistol shot. He fell immediately, clutching at his shattered leg in agony. According to the aforementioned 1942 *News and Courier* article, "Isaacs escaped unhurt, and for three or four days lay hid in the thatched roof of Milligan's Tavern, to escape the vengeance of the friends of Dr. Ladd."

Doctor Ladd was carried back to his room at the Thomas Rose House. Doctors were at first hopeful of saving him, but he very quickly took a turn for the worse. The wound became infected, and he lapsed into a delirium fever as it turned gangrenous. Despite the fever dreams, he never stopped asking for his beloved Amanda, but due to the great distances involved it is doubtful she even knew of his injury before he died. He expired in very early November, 1786. The 1942 article goes on to note: "The unfortunate young physician-poet was buried in St. Michael's churchyard; but the record of internments is lost, and no stone marks his resting-place. Somewhere within that acre of the dead his bones return to the dust from which they came, without a broken shard to record his passing."

Whistling Presence

It is said that the spirit of Joseph Ladd, the Whistling Doctor, never left the home. During moments of great stress at 59 Church Street—they are few and far between, but all houses, regardless of their history, know conflict—the distinct sound of whistling has been reported on many occasions. Great storms, disagreements, and other moments of disquietude seem to produce this effect equally: any stressful situation causes this phenomenon. Perhaps this is the good doctor, ever mindful of the far-reaching effects that even the simplest conflicts can have, trying to sooth tempers before they boil over. The duelist has become peace-maker. His footsteps and whistling are frequently heard on the stairs, going up to his third-floor room, probably filled with thoughts of his dearest love Amanda, forever and ever.

People have also reported the sounds and sights of a duel in Philadelphia Alley. It is less clear if this is the psychic echo Dr. Ladd or Ralph Isaacs, or if these are other, anonymous spectral duelists, seemingly locked forever in a recurring affair of honor. The only thing we are certain of, really, is that the first shot is discharged into the air, but the second shot, sadly, finds its mark. More than one person, however, has reported hearing faint whistling in the moments before the duel commences.

Lavinia and John Fisher

The Legend of the Six Mile Wayfarer Inn

If you were to take a ghost tour in Charleston, the one story you would undoubtedly hear is the tale of Lavinia and John Fisher. You might hear that the pair ran a charming little 'Bed & Deadfast' in the wilderness outside of town in the early 19th century, killing (and robbing) those unwary and unwise travelers who tried to stay the night at their cottage. However, thanks to a very special cup of bitter tea allegedly supplied by the Lady Fisher, many of these journeyers wound up overstaying their intended check-out times, instead falling into an eternal slumber. The duo supposedly murdered upwards of one hundred people this way (and John had a much more brutally direct approach to dispatch those targeted patrons who did not drink tea).

Justice eventually caught up with the pair, the tour guide will tell you, and will save the most shocking bits for the very end of the tale: how Lavinia insisted on wearing a wedding dress to her own execution, asserting that she was about to be married to the Devil himself in the fiery depths of Hades. She even offered to carry messages to Lucifer, should any of the stunned crowd wish to send a piece of express mail to Hell.

How much truth is there in the outrageous legend of Lavinia and John Fisher? First let us start by examining the legend, and determine what you'd likely hear about this unholiest of women in the Holy City. I have assembled this narrative piecemeal, combining the accounts from several tours, books, and websites into one story.

The Bride of Evil

In the early days of Charleston's history, there was no railroad or interstate highway system linking the seaport with the interior of the state. Rather than shipping containers being moved by rail or semi-truck, the majority of goods moved by wagon, both to and from the docks located downtown. These roads were not paved, so movement was extremely slow and difficult, and travel was extremely dangerous due to robbers and highwaymen. Dotting the road were a number of small hamlets or inns where the traders could rest and relax along the way, or even spend the night.

The further you got from Charleston, the further you were from what passed for law and order in the city proper, so most traders armed themselves to guard against outright attack. Much more difficult to guard against, however, was a clever Lowcountry thief who disguised him- or herself as a legitimate innkeeper, offering a place to sleep as they (or members of their gang) robbed you blind.

It is here that Lavinia and her husband, John, enter the story. Around 1819, the two ran a modest dwelling which catered to these merchants along an otherwise forbidding stretch of road which connected Charleston with trading posts all over the Southeast. They ran the Six Mile Inn, which was located, appropriately enough, six miles from Charleston. To our 21st century ears, six miles sounds like a very short distance, but in those pre-paved highway and telephone days it was quite a long distance, and very isolated.

John Peoples was one such merchant, moving south towards the city with a large wagonload of furs and other valuables. He got a late start and his rate of travel was slower than he anticipated, so he grew more and more nervous about being out alone on the road so close to dusk. He had heard many stories of fellow traders who had wound up missing along this very stretch of lonely dirt track, and he began to pick up the pace as he thought about the way the stories always ended: the goods, the wagon, and the man all vanished, without a trace. It was a moonless night, and there were no lights on the wagon—that was too dangerous, since it marked him as a target. The inky darkness seemed to swallow him. Peoples gripped the reins tighter and pressed on, urging his horse to go even faster.

He saw a flickering light in the distance. Fearful of an ambush, Mr. Peoples drew his knife from behind the seat and placed it beside him. As he drew nearer, he began to make out the outlines of a house in a clearing ahead. It was some sort of lodging house. A lantern placed right off of the porch seemed to beckon to him. He breathed a sigh of relief, and decided that if the owners were willing, he'd pay whatever the going rate was for a room and continue on to Charleston in the morning. Pressing his luck further in the darkness was just plain foolhardy.

He noticed a woman in her mid-twenties on the porch. She stood motionless, watching his approach impassively as if she had somehow known he was coming. John found that somewhat unsettling, as well as the fact that she offered no im-

mediate greeting. Even though it was a chilly evening, she was dressed in a thin chemise and little else. He was struck by her intense beauty, the kind that could make many a man forget about his wedding vows. Mr. Peoples twisted his wedding band nervously once that wagon had come to a stop, and finally ventured asking whether there were any rooms for rent.

"Of course," said the woman. She finally smiled, a dazzling, radiantly warm grin, and added, "I am Lavinia Fisher. Welcome to Six Mile House! You look famished! Let me prepare you a special meal, and please let John, my husband, tend to your horse and wagon." Mr. Peoples couldn't help but flinch, because he hadn't seen or heard anyone else, yet somehow Lavinia's husband had appeared right at the opposite side of the wagon and seized the reins. It was unsettling how someone so large and powerfully built could move with such speed and silence. Fisher said nothing, a trait that Mr. Peoples could not help but find distressing. It would not be the most disturbing thing about the Fishers, as John Peoples would learn later that evening. But at that moment, the weary trader was just grateful to be off the road, so he dismounted his wagon, and followed Lavinia inside.

Peoples found his room to be very small, yet adequate for his purposes and clean. It looked barely used, having just a narrow bed and a chair. Once he rejoined his host and hostess at the kitchen table for the meal that the beautiful woman had promised, he asked about the rate for the night's stay. Lavinia laughed, a giggle that turned into a deep guffaw, as if he had told a particularly funny joke. If anyone else had laughed at an innocuous question as she did, the effect would have been deeply troubling. But somehow it was easy to overlook such odd behavior in Lavinia because of her stunning beauty. She glanced at her husband, who still said nothing. "Oh, the rate is very affordable," she said. "We are willing to take much less than the usual lodging fee, because you might find the bed a trifle uncomfortable." She laughed again, as if this were a sly allusion he wasn't privy to. Her husband did not return the laugh, continuing to glare sullenly at Mr. Peoples. He found the pair odder and odder, and he was surprised to find himself wanting to leave this inn and his strange innkeepers. But the lovely Lavinia insisted that the uncomfortable meal continue.

Lavinia served them all equal portions of a delicious smelling stew, but something was amiss. John Fisher continued to glare ominously. Peoples was suspicious, but did finally consume the meal when he saw them eat from their bowls first. It all came from the same pot, so poison was unlikely, he decided. "This is good," Peoples offered, hoping to break the awkward mood at the table. "Is this pork?" Lavinia giggled again, her only answer. Perhaps they are not good at socializing, the trader decided. However, a tiny alarm went off in the back of John People's mind when she served him (and him alone) a single serving of piping hot tea. They instead drank water with the meal, and the brew that she served him smelled slightly off. After pretending to sip it out of politeness, he abruptly stood up and announced that he was very weary, and needed his rest. Just touching that tea to his lips had left a very bitter taste in his mouth, and his lips began to tingle and go numb.

He extinguished the light in his room, and sat down in the chair, considering. He did not want to spend the night here, and he was growing more and more distrustful of his innkeepers. Their odd behavior made him nervous, and the fact that many travelers had turned up missing on this very stretch of road weighed heavily on his mind. As he sat, trying to figure out a graceful way of extricating himself from this possibly dangerous situation, he heard low voices from the kitchen.

"Let me do it," a distinctly male voice rumbled. "I will fetch my axe and finish him now."

Lavinia's voice resisted. "No, John, let the tea do its work. He did not have much, but it may be enough."

The male voice protested, wanting to make quick work of him. Lavinia's voice took on a chilling edge when she responded. "I know you like to do it quick, but slower is always easier, and less messy. Just flip the switch in a while and we shall be done with it. Those hides and sundries he's carrying will fetch us a pretty penny."

John's voice growled: "He didn't drink enough. And if he didn't, then the switch won't do the job and he might escape."

Lavinia considered, and then agreed. "Okay, I will wait for you to go into the basement, and I'll flip the switch. When he falls into the pit, finish him." She laughed, a haunting sound. Peoples heard the front door open and close.

John Peoples had little time to wonder what they were talking about. He heard a mechanical groaning sound, and the bed in his room suddenly fell away with a crash, leaving a gaping hole in the floor. The bed had been a trapdoor! He bolted from the room, coming face-to-face with a startled Lavinia. "John," she screamed. "He's up here! He's escaping!" Mr. Peoples tried to run towards the front door, but he could hear John Fisher's heavy boots stomping towards the front door to cut him off, so he turned around to race out the back exit. It was then that he was smashed nearly senseless by Lavinia, who had picked up a piece of firewood. She rained blows down upon him with one hand and choked him with the other. Her sweet countenance had become frozen into a vicious sneer, and a steady stream of vile curses issued from her lips. Bloodied, Peoples regained his feet despite her savage strokes with the log, and ran like a scalded jackrabbit for the back door.

Peoples raced to his wagon and leapt aboard it, the murderous pair hot on his heels. John Fisher carried a wicked-looking axe. With a frantic lash of the whip, People's horse lurched to life. He roared away at breakneck speed, rattling the springs of his wagon in a desperate attempt to get away. He did not stop or even slow his pace until he reached Charleston, and he raised the alarm to the authorities.

An angry mob formed, determined to put a stop to the lawlessness on the roads around the city. They quickly marched out to the Six Mile Inn and surrounded the house. John Fisher and a few members of his gang meekly surrendered, but a cursing Lavinia resisted, fighting her captors tooth-and-nail. Eventually she was physically subdued, but the verbal assault continued. She provided a steady stream of profanity all the way back to the Charleston City Jail, located on Magazine Street.

Once the pair were arrested, the authorities searched the grounds of Six Mile House, and began to find body after body. Most of the dead were found buried in the basement, which was the scene of truly horrific slaughter. Some skeletons were contorted, as if spasming from being poisoned, but others had been chopped with an axe. A couple of the corpses appeared to be expertly butchered, with the choice cuts of muscle removed (when John Peoples heard this grisly detail, his horrified thoughts turned to the mystery meat in his stew). A few other bodies were buried in a heap of ashes behind one of the outbuildings. The authorities could only identify two out of the hundred-plus bodies that were discovered. The men, sickened by what they had found, burned Six Mile House to the ground.

Back in Charleston, the pair were officially charged with murder, assault, highway robbery, and attempted murder, and quickly convicted. Both were sentenced to death. A local man of the cloth reached out to the pair, but John simply sulked, refusing to talk to anyone. When the minister would come by to talk to Lavinia however, she would go wild, spitting and swearing vile curses. She saved her worst language for the South Carolina governor for not pardoning her for the crimes. She refused to believe that the state would hang a lady, especially a married woman. There was a law on the books which stated that a married woman could not be hanged, even for capital crimes, and so she believed that she would be allowed to live.

February 18th, 1820 was the date of their execution, which took place in the yard of the jail. On that day Lavinia requested to wear a wedding dress to further demonstrate to the governor that she was married. A large crowd gathered at the gallows behind the old City Jail, cheering and jeering. John went willingly, praying and begging forgiveness, but Lavinia had other ideas. She had to be dragged to the platform, kicking and screaming, spewing profanity the entire way. The governor got around the prohibition of executing a married woman easily; he had John Fisher hooded and hanged first. After his execution, that meant that she was a widow in the eyes of the law, and could be legally put to death. When Lavinia figured out that the governor skirted the law in this clever way, she went even wilder. It took several bailiffs to hold her on the platform. When they slipped the noose around her neck, however, she went strangely calm. "I am about to be married again," she told the crowd. "I'll soon be married to the Devil himself, in Hell!" An eerie stunned hush fell over the crowd. She continued: "If anyone has a message for the Devil, give it to me, for I am about to meet him!"

The hangman approached with her hood in his hands, but Lavinia met her end on her own terms with a vicious feral smile on her lips. She took her captors by surprise when she darted forward, leaping off the scaffold platform. The crowd gasped. Lavinia had opted to kill herself rather than giving anyone else the satisfaction. She dangled, not through the trapdoor, but at an awkward angle off of the stage, near her still-twitching husband. The sneer never left her face. The prison officials let their bodies hang for a solid week as a warning for anyone else attempting robbery and murder on the trader's road. The only graveyard that would accept the bodies was the Unitarian Church Cemetery, located on Archdale Street, where the two were buried separately, and in secret.

It is said that Lavinia and John Fisher still haunt the Old City Jail on Magazine Street, which stands to this day. People report seeing a beautiful woman in white in the windows, but she laughs in a mocking way. Many have also claimed to have seen her in the yard of the Old City Jail, patiently awaiting a pardon from the governor—one which will never arrive. Lavinia's spirit does not rest easy, because she has also been reportedly seen in the Unitarian Churchyard, looking for her husband who she spurned on the scaffold. Others have reported seeing her in the same burial ground, but she is dancing on the grave of the judge that condemned her.

How Much Of This Is True?

There has been enough material written about these supposedly murderous Fishers that it could fill a large book, all on its own (in fact, there is a book specifically devoted to the Fishers, by Bruce Orr). This story shares a lot in common with a famous New Orleans tale, namely the exceedingly cruel Madame Delphine LaLaurie and her mansion on Royal Street (for a recounting of the myths and horrifying reality of Madame LaLaurie, please check out my earlier book: *The Haunted History of New Orleans: Ghosts of the French Quarter*). The similarities are downright eerie: both stories deal with the dreadful actions of a married couple, yet focus most of the attention on the actions of the female. Both stories have a strong basis in reality, but in both, the legends (and the body counts) have been exaggerated into something else entirely, rendering the actual events almost unrecognizable. Also, both stories have become, for their respective cities of New Orleans and Charleston, *the* definitive tale of the ghost-tour trade.

The legendary version of the story does get the beginning of the tale exactly right, including the dangerous wagon trade situation, and the prevalence of robberies occurring in and around the various inns dotting the trade-route road heading north out of Charleston. Today, this road still exists as Rivers Avenue (Highway 52). Charleston's shipping trade in general was experiencing all sorts of problems, including a lack of access to the interior of the state in these pre-railroad days, and piracy on the Atlantic (most famously, pirate Captain George Clark, who raided the American coast during this time period with his vessel, the *Louisa*). Here is what the wagon trade was like, according to Bruce Orr's fantastic book on the subject, *Six Miles to Charleston: The True Story of John and Lavinia Fisher*:

It was not unusual for hides, cotton or tobacco to travel three or four hundred miles… to reach… Charleston. The trips were long and tiresome. Horses wearied and so did their owners. Teams of six to eight horses were needed to pull the loads to market. They needed places along the route to stop and rest and receive water. These places took form in the stage taverns or inns known as "Houses" that dotted the roadways on the outskirts… These inns were usually designated by the distance from the appointed destination. The stagecoach taverns or houses were not what we imagine an inn or tavern to be today. [They] were more social centers for the countryside.

Many readers, no doubt, are picturing the small towns/trading posts that sprang up along wagon trails all throughout the Old West in the latter half of the 19th century, and are quite correct to do so. The analogy is perfect.

Some of the other details in the 'legendary' narrative are right, too, such as a man named John Peoples being robbed of his money. But he was not the first victim of theft, nor did his robbery incite the rest of the story. There had been many robberies in the areas around Five and Six Mile Houses (the latter of which was located very close to the present-day intersection of Rivers Avenue and Dorchester Road, near today's Charleston Naval Clinic). There had been so much lawless activity in this area that the crimes provoked a group of average Charlestonians to invoke what is commonly known as Lynch's Law. Lynch's Law (which is where we get the modern term *lynch mob*) is the formation of an angry mob, which in the absence of local law enforcement would dispense justice as they saw fit, despite having no legal authority to do so. This is precisely the sort of crowd, roughly thirty men in all, which departed Charleston on horseback and headed up the northern trade road on February 18th, 1819. When they arrived at Five Mile House, the angry Charlestonian mob demanded that the occupants of the house depart. There was some dissent from the criminals in residence, so the angry mob wound up burning Five Mile House to the ground. The criminals fled into the woods, but rather than pursuing them, the Lynch mob rode further north, to Six Mile House, and repeated the demand: leave the area, or else. This time, the criminals quickly agreed, perhaps correctly interpreting the smoke from the nearby burning inn as proof of the mob's serious demeanor. The occupants peaceably departed. The lynch mob left behind one of their own to stand guard, a young man named David Ross, and rode back to Charleston. They must have felt very confident, as they galloped past one abandoned inn and another on fire, that they had solved the robbery problems north of the city. However, they could not have been more wrong, because David Ross was savagely attacked the next morning. His sworn deposition, given on February 20th, 1819, reads like a forensic study of how to best beat a man into submission:

David Ross… deposeth that on yesterday about the hour of nine [in the morning], William Heyward came to Six Mile House… accompanied by another person. Heyward cursed him, collared him violently, and pushed him out of doors. The deponent then again reentered the house, and asked to take away the few articles that belonged to him; Heyward put his hand to his bosom [implying he was armed], and said you damned infernal rascal, if you lay your hands on anything, I will blow your brains out. By this time Fisher and his wife Lavinia Fisher came up, with two other men… Lavinia Fisher laid violent hands upon him, choaked [sic] and boxed his head through a pane of window glass... Heyward and Fisher beat him unmercifully, with loaded whips aided and assisted by the other two men... there was also another woman, who aided and assisted [in thrashing him], whilst they were beating him, the deponent leapt out of the piazza... but just as he had entered the woods, they fired at him... Fisher exclaimed several times, you damned infernal rascal if I ever catch you, I will give you a hundred lashes.

This report alone would have been enough to alarm the authorities. However, around that same time, John Peoples, a wagon trader, also had an encounter on the same stretch of road outside of the city. According to Mark Jones' amazing 2005 book, *Wicked Charleston: The Dark Side of the Holy City*:

Peoples arrived at the Six Mile House [around 11 a.m.]. He had finished his business in Charleston and had stopped to water his horses on his way back to Georgia. A young boy was filling a bucket so Peoples waited. A drunken man stumbled out of the house and told the boy, "Give me that bucket." The man lunged at the boy and Peoples, in an effort to protect the boy, flicked his whip at the man... [who] flew into rage, screaming and shouting. Almost immediately nine or ten persons, including a woman, poured out of the house, armed with clubs, pistols and knives and attacked Peoples. In his affidavit Peoples claimed "most active" in the brawl was the woman. She attacked Peoples with a stick, cutting his face. But as suddenly as the attack commenced, it stopped. Everyone stomped back inside. Peoples decided not to water his horses... [but] as he was pulling away two men ran out of the house. They pulled pistols and hopped onto the wagon. They robbed him of forty dollars.

Clearly, the gang had chosen to ignore the earlier warning by the group of concerned citizens from Charleston, and returned to harass travelers on the road. The sheriff, Colonel Nathaniel Greene Cleary, quickly organized a large party of armed men which surrounded the Six Mile House. Despite the fact that the gang holed up inside of the house had up to a dozen muskets and adequate black powder, they almost immediately decided to surrender to the authorities. Most accounts claim that John Fisher did not wish to see his wife Lavinia harmed, and it was he who talked the rest of the robbers into giving up. The gang was loaded into a large iron paddy wagon, and Six Mile House, like Five Mile before it, was burned to the ground.

It is important to note how the legendary version deviates from the actual, documented history. There was no trapdoor, no poisoned tea, and no basement full of a hundred graves. In fact, this is a story as yet without a single dead body. In addition, John Peoples never stayed the night at the Six Mile House, and not one, but two men were severely beaten by Lavinia Fisher. But the most surprising part of the story is yet to come, and is one of omission. This part of the documented story left out by modern folklore storytellers shows a deep, abiding love between two people that are largely, and perhaps even a little unfairly, labeled as monsters today.

John and Lavinia: Incarcerated, and Infatuated

For people who are only familiar with the legend and not the documented facts of the case, the absolutely most shocking thing about the arrest (and ultimate conviction) of Lavinia and John Fisher is that the only crime the duo were ever charged with was highway robbery, not murder. Highway robbery, like piracy, was a hanging offense during this time period. Why weren't they charged with murder? Lack of proof appears to be the reason. Two bodies (not ten, or a hundred, like the legend states) were indeed found buried in a grave on the property near Six Mile House's charred foundation, along with damning evidence of another. One of the bodies was only identified as a female slave, and the other body found was of a white male with long gray hair. While the male showed evidence of having been shot to death, there was no way to identify his body. He appeared to have been killed a week prior to being discovered. He might have even been a member of the gang, shot in a robbery-gone-wrong. And that damning evidence of a third body? That was the hide of a cow, which had up until recently belonged to Stephen LaCoste but had been reported stolen.

Remember, this is a time before modern forensic investigative techniques. Crime labs did not exist. There was no team of highly trained scientists combing the area for DNA, blood spatter and dental records, because that technology was centuries away. This case had coroner Jervis H. Stevens, walking around the property, looking for obvious signs of misdeeds. His forensic tool was a shovel, which he used to dig up the bodies. But just because his tools were crude doesn't mean that he would have missed a basement full of easily-discovered bodies. Also, if you'll pardon the terrible pun, the part of the legend that dealt with a trap door and a basement full of decaying bodies never quite passed the 'sniff test' with me, even before I knew the truth. The storytellers spinning yarns about moldering corpses underneath a house have obviously never caught a whiff of even one dead body, because the odor of a decaying corpse is overwhelming. A charming inn with dead bodies littering the basement would smell absolutely stomach-clenchingly awful. Even the most naïve and weary traveler would shy away from a lodging house which literally reeked of death.

The witnesses, Ross and Peoples, identified the perpetrators, which included Lavinia and John Fisher. What crime were they accused of? It was for the offense of robbery, not murder, that Lavinia and John Fisher were cast into the terribly forbidding Old City Jail on Magazine Street (for more information about this remarkable building, please see the chapter devoted to it in this volume). They were given a cell together, but it would have provided only a little comfort for the couple; the experience would have been agonizing. The lower levels, where the Fishers were initially held, were considered the worst in the prison.

On May 27, 1819, John and Lavinia were brought to trial at the courthouse. During the trial, John displayed no emotion, while Lavinia wept openly. Her fear was understandable: conviction meant a death sentence. They were found guilty of highway robbery by Judge Elihu Hall Bay, and their lawyer petitioned for an appeal. A stay of execution was granted—an eight-month temporary reprieve.

During the months of their incarceration, the pair conspired to escape the dungeon-like prison. Because of their married status, the Fishers had been moved (conveniently, for them) from their hellish cage in the bowels of the jail to a top floor cell designated for debtors. The two were not content to simply wait for their execution, so they hatched a plot, along with fellow gang member Joseph Roberts, for a bold escape from the jail. They made a hole under a window which was wide enough to squeeze through, and, using a rope made from blankets, attempted to lower themselves to freedom. The two men successfully descended, but the rope snapped, leaving Lavinia behind, alone in the jail. John Fisher and Joseph Roberts, free men on the ground, looked up at a still-imprisoned Lavinia.

It was at this moment that a remarkable thing happened: John Fisher, so often portrayed as a butchering monster in the folklore versions of the story, was unwilling to leave his wife behind. The love between John and Lavinia must have been powerful, and it is easy to see why this action by John is omitted in the folklore tales: his loyalty humanizes him. The two men stayed in town, seeking a way to free Lavinia—perhaps by bribing a guard—until the pair of men were recaptured. In fact, when they were pulled from their hiding place underneath a small overturned boat on present-day South Battery, the two men had gold coins and several pocket watches on their person. They had almost certainly gone on a robbery spree to raise funds in order to pay off a prison official. John was devoted to his wife, but he was still a petty criminal, after all. With their jailbreak attempt a total failure, they were reunited together in prison, and placed under heavy guard.

No Salvation

John and Lavinia received bad news in January, 1820: the appeal for a new trial had failed, and the judge set their execution date for February of that same year, less than a month away. Every day prior to their execution date, Baptist Reverend Richard Furman visited the couple in prison. He found John Fisher very receptive to his visits, and reported that John converted religiously before his date with destiny. Lavinia, however, was another matter. She was seemed interested in one thing from the good reverend: news of a pardon from the governor. When Reverend Furman would tell Lavinia that no, there was no news of any pardon, she would rattle off a string of vile curses and spit at him. It is possible that her year spent in captivity might have caused Lavinia to become mentally unstable. Or, considering how she choked David Ross and attacked John Peoples with a stick, perhaps she always was tinged with madness beneath her beautiful visage.

The *Charleston Courier* ran a notice on Friday, February 18th which announced their execution later that day:

EXECUTION—The awful sentence of law is this day to be carried into effect upon John Fisher, and Lavinia, his wife, who were sentenced to death, at the late sitting Constitutional Court, for the crime of highway robbery. We understand that they are to meet their fate just without the lines, on the Meeting Street Road, between the hours of 12 and 4 o'clock.

(Author's note: the phrase "just without the lines" in the Courier article refers to the general vicinity of present-day Line Street, which at the time was the line denoting Charleston's city limits. It is very close to where Interstate 26 loops through and meets Highway 17 today.)

Again, it is interesting to note the stark differences in the documented history with the tour story legend. The execution did not take place at the Old City Jail, it occurred nearly two miles from the spot named in the legend, outside of town. It is also quite interesting that John's religious conversion is neatly excised from the legend. The real person we meet in the history books is unrecognizable from the bloodthirsty killer whispered about in the folklore version. And yet another major difference in the accounts is all about wardrobe. On February 18th, 1820, the date of the execution, Lavinia indeed wore white to her execution; but it wasn't a wedding dress. John and Lavinia both wore the traditional garb of the condemned: loose white robes. She did not present herself as the bride of Satan, which is an obvious invention added after the fact.

At a little before 1 p.m., John and Lavinia were ministered to by Reverend Furman. John prayed, but Lavinia began shrieking in a very unnerving way. Matters did not improve when the pair were led out of their cell and met the person who would very shortly execute them: the hangman. According to John Blake White, writer and attorney, the hangman was a terrifying creature. He described, in an 1830's essay, meeting him in a visit to the jail just prior to the Fisher's execution:

The door being unbarred and opened, we beheld, stretched upon the floor, a being that appeared to be rather [inhuman]. Haggard, pale, emaciated, it began, slowly, to rise from the floor, growling like some glutted hyena at being roused from his lair... Here then, stood before us, in unsophisticated reality, the murderer of state, the pensioned cut-throat, the day laborer of death, one who did his work for pay with fidelity and skill, and all by virtue of law and under the sacred sanction of justice... Again and again, he entreated us to be supplied with liquor, which was positively refused, though with the assurance that, after the execution, if well performed, he should have as much drink as he desired. A transient, but ghastly smile flickered for and instant on his cheek, when the door to his cell was again closed and bolted.

Executions were a major spectator sport in cities like Charleston, and a special draw for this particular event was seeing a true rarity: a woman was to be put to death. A large crowd turned out specifically to see Lavinia Fisher, who was not just a female but an extremely attractive one. Indeed, John Blake White describes the rabble: "It was a melancholy, though novel sight, to behold a female led out into execution, and it attracted an immense concourse of spectators... of both sexes, and of all ages and conditions!"

When the couple disembarked the coach, John mounted the scaffold first. Lavinia, still resisting, struggled with her captors below, so John took a moment to address the crowd. He protested his innocence to the end.

Lavinia, shrieking an inhuman wail when she was not cursing the governor's name for daring to hang a woman, was finally dragged, kicking and screaming, to the top of the platform. John turned then to his wife and pleaded with her to make peace with God. She seemed to listen to him, but still looked anxiously for a pardon from the governor. The haggard executioner, described by White as "hovering like a vampire," readied their hoods.

Reverend Furman urged her at that moment to address the crowd and repent, but Lavinia suddenly smiled wickedly, and spoke the words which catapulted her to instant infamy: "Cease! I will have none of it. Save your words for others who want them. But if you have a message you want to send to Hell, give it to me; I'll carry it."

The couple were then hooded, and the lever was thrown which sprung the trapdoor from beneath their feet. They died together; first Lavinia, who seemed to expire right away, and then John, who took several minutes to die.

From the *Charleston Courier*, February 19th, 1820:

THE EXECUTION of John and Lavinia Fisher, for Highway Robbery, took place yesterday, in the suburbs of the city, agreeably to their sentences. They were taken from the jail about a quarter before 1 o'clock, in a carriage in which, besides the prisoners was the Rev. Dr. Furman, and an officer of the police. They were guarded by the Sheriff of the District, with his assistants, and a small detachment of cavalry. Arrived at the fatal spot, some time was spent in conversation and prayer.--Fisher protested his innocence of the crime for which he was to die to the last, but admitted that he had lived a wicked and abandoned life. He met his fate with great firmness: and expressed his obligations to the new Sheriff for his kindness and humanity. His wife did not display so much of fortitude or resignation--She appeared to be impressed with a belief, to the last moment, that she would be pardoned. A little past 2 o'clock the husband and wife embraced each other upon the platform, for the last time in this world, when the fatal signal was given--the drop fell--and they were launched into eternity. She died without a struggle or a groan; but it was some minutes before he expired and ceased to struggle. After hanging the usual time, their bodies were taken down and conveyed to Potter's Field, where they were interred. The concourse that attended the execution was immense. May the awful example strike deep into their hearts; and may it have the effect intended, by deterring others from pursuing those vicious paths which ended in infamy and death.

Deconstructing Facts and Fantasy

So we know from the article that the story of Lavinia's ghost being seen in the downtown Unitarian Cemetery must be false, because neither she nor her husband were buried there—their remains went to Potter's Field (a place for burying indigents, vagrants and criminals, who could not afford proper burials), as the *Courier* article states. A Unitarian Churchyard Committee member who I asked stated firmly that the executed pair were not buried anywhere within the Unitarian lot. In addition, if tour guides are correct when they say Lavinia's ghost is seeking the grave of the judge who convicted her (presumably to tap dance on his grave), then Unitarian Churchyard is, again, the wrong spot for her. Judge Elihu Bay Hall did not belong to the Unitarian faith; he is buried in St. Philip's Churchyard, which is an Episcopal burial ground.

So where are their bodies? Potter's Field was located at that time on the western-central area of the peninsula. That plot of land is now, according to Bruce Orr's *Six Miles to Charleston*, part of the complex dedicated to the Medical University of South Carolina, near the present-day intersection of Ashley Avenue and Doughty Street. Many 1820's-era bodies have been found there whenever construction takes place, specifically in 1968, but as recently as 2001. Whether the remains of John and Lavinia Fisher, perhaps Charleston's most infamous couple, still reside there is anyone's guess.

Have the ghosts of either Lavinia or John Fisher been seen at the Old City Jail? Opinions vary greatly on the subject. There have been many reports of strange phenomena at that location, and I explore it all in detail in a chapter in this volume.

What ultimately are we to make of this tale, one which seems an equal blend of verifiable, documented history and a generous heaping of sensational storytelling? What can we take away from the two vastly dissimilar versions? I believe this is one instance where the legend is actually preferable to the documented events, from a strictly storytelling perspective. The true story of what happened along that lonely trade road is one which would be difficult to tell effectively. It involves robbery, and the only human bodies in connection to the actual happenings were never positively identified or attributed as having a tangible connection to the case at all.

I am bothered greatly, as a lover of correct history, when an innocent person's name is wrongfully tarnished, but honestly I do not believe this to be the case with John and Lavinia Fisher. It appears at least on the surface that their executions were rightfully justified under the existing South Carolina laws at that time. There's no proverbial 'smoking gun,' but after nearly two hundred years enough smoky suspicion remains that I am satisfied that they were bad people that were doing evil deeds. Robbery during that time period, be it on a dark lonely road or on the high seas, was a capital crime. The basic facts are true: they committed serious infractions, got caught, and paid with their lives. The legends, while at times wildly inaccurate, streamline the events down to an easily relatable narrative, and add entertainment value. John and Lavinia Fisher may or may not have been monsters; it is impossible to determine given the scant evidence either way. But they showed an intriguing human side which is missing in the legend.

While I enjoy knowing the truth, namely that Lavinia and John Fisher were not serial killers with a basement full of victims, I still very much relish hearing many different storytellers relate their own version of the terrible events in 1819 and 1820. The legend is a captivating story, as is the documented history, but for very different reasons. Holding these two contrasting versions up for a side-by-side can be worthwhile all on its own without casting judgments or getting bogged down about whether past authors and tour guides were right for changing the legend. From the Wicked Witch to Madame LaLaurie in New Orleans and yes, to Lavinia Fisher, we as a society seem fascinated by tales of evil women doing very bad things.

Mad River Bar & Grille

32-34 North Market Street

On the eastern edge of Charleston's unique and historic shopping experience, namely the City Market area, there sits a building which is completely out of place and yet at the same time completely apropos in the Holy City. To stand outside the edifice in question, one is likely to hear the same question asked over and over again by tourists, namely: "Is that a *restaurant* inside that church?" The answer, naturally, is 'yes,' that is precisely what is located at 34 North Market Street: a building which used to serve communion wafers is now slinging heavenly, delicious crab cakes in the same space. You can chow down on a scrumptious burger in a structure which is lit, still very much cathedral-like, by beautiful stained glass. For those who have ever felt that their cup of communion wine was a trifle too small may be relieved that this building's wine service is now blessed with a 'heavy pour.'

One might reasonably ask: *Why is there a church here, and why is it dispensing shrimp po' boys instead of Scripture?* Well, the beautiful brick Gothic style structure was built in 1916, and was dedicated to be a chapel for mariners and sailors. Originally named the Church of the Redeemer, it was intended as a place for idle sailors, who had no other place to go, to gather and receive Spiritual instruction. The interior smartly retains many of the original 'sailor' touches, such as a pulpit in the shape of a ship's prow. The building ceased to be a charitable structure in the 1960's, and rather than demolish the lovely vacant church, the restaurant owners decided to repurpose the structure into a commercial space, thus contributing to the movement to rehabilitate and conserve older historic buildings rather than destroy them.

Exterior of Mad River Bar & Grille.

Exodus... Because of a Haunting?

The converted church is now afflicted by a different kind of spirit than the Holy variety. More of a mischievous nuisance than an unfriendly haunting, the ghost at Mad River Grille once committed what is considered a cardinal sin in the food and beverage industry: it began breaking bottles of liquor. According to Denise Roffe's 2010 book, *Ghosts and Legends of Charleston SC*, several staff members who worked late and had an early shift decided that they might as well sleep at the restaurant, sleepover style, complete with sleeping bags (a lot of churches have youth lock-ins, after all). There was the expected amount of good-natured shenanigans of any small gathering of twenty- and thirty-somethings. The employee slumber party was interrupted in the middle of the night, however, by the sound of bottles breaking. A few brave souls who investigated confirmed that liquor bottles were leaping from behind the bar by themselves and smashing against the floor. Needless to say, the employee sleep-over was abruptly canceled, and the bottle-smashing likewise came to a sudden stop as well. It was the inevitable conclusion of Mad River staff members that the spirit who inhabits the former church simply dislikes horseplay.

One former server described her own experiences, mostly odd happenings involving the television or audio system. When I suggested that perhaps the cause might simply be the system being wired up incorrectly, she gave me a funny smile and said, "Oh, so you think you can clear up a badly wired stereo system by asking nicely? Because that is what I had to do, on more than one occasion. One year on Super Bowl Sunday, I had to politely ask the ghost to stop messing with the speakers. The interference stopped immediately, but only after I said 'please.'"

Sunday Service Industry

I dropped in for a late lunch at Mad River Grille one day, and had no trouble locating someone willing to discuss the paranormal. A current employee confirmed that the trouble persists, usually on the first day of the week: "On Sundays we'll have a lot of trouble with electronics: the registers occasionally, but usually it's the lights, which will flicker, or the TV, which will go out for no reason. We've had electrician after electrician in here, and a couple of audio-visual technicians too, but they all say the same thing, namely that there's nothing wrong with any of the wiring."

When I asked him what he thought the cause was, he voiced precisely what I was beginning to suspect. "I think the day of the week is the reason, quite honestly. Almost all of the stuff we notice in here happens on a Sunday, and this is a former church, so there's definitely a connection. Maybe the spirit is a little perturbed over the fact that we are open for business on that day, or it could be the fact that the ghost is still coming here on Sundays because that's what he did during life? I don't know, but a lot of Sundays we'll get something strange that will happen."

His theories sound pretty logical. The staff at Mad River seem to have decided that peaceful coexistence is more important than anything else, and have accepted that one member of their congregation can get a little boisterous at times. "He never hurts anyone," one bartender said, "and he livens up the place sometimes." When asked, I usually espouse a 'live and let live' policy with the ghosts, but at Mad River, it sounds like I might be preaching to the choir.

Pirate Treasure at 'The Bosoms'

37 Meeting Street

On the southern end of Meeting Street, a house with an unusual addition to its floor plan has garnered an even more unusual nickname: the house in the middle of the block is informally named 'The Bosoms.' Any eleven year old boy could tell you how the house achieved this moniker, unless he's too busy snickering into his own hand to do so. The 1840's addition of rounded bays to this circa 1760 house make the home appear to be a rather well-endowed lady, if you catch my drift. The twin-turret protuberances would make any runway model at the Victoria's Secret fashion show green with jealousy.

All jokes aside, the stately building has seen some incredible history during its time. Built by James Simmons, the home has seen occupants flee not once but twice due to enemy action. The house was the property of South Carolina Governor Robert Gibbes, who was forced to abandon the home during the British occupation of Charles Town during the Revolutionary War. Gibbes returned to find his home heavily damaged. In the 1840's the edifice belonged to hotelier Otis Mills, who owned the Mills House Hotel on Meeting Street. Then in 1862 it became the headquarters for Confederate General Pierre G. T. Beauregard, the commander of Rebel forces at Charleston, who had to abandon the house due to the Union shelling of the city. He shifted his headquarters to a less vulnerable position at the northern end of town. The house was then bought by Congressman Michael P. O'Connor in 1876, who still owned the property when it was damaged in the Earthquake of 1886.

The Bosoms on Meeting Street.

Talk of any old building in Charleston inevitably turns to ghosts, and 37 Meeting Street is no different. A *Charleston Evening Post* article by Jack Leland which appeared in 1969 states:

It has a pirate legend, usually not believed by its owners but of great influence on children and servants… The house was built on the south portion of Lot 278 of the Grand Modell of Charleston, an area that was a sort of knoll with the marshes and waters of Vanderhorst Creek making it a… peninsula at high tide. And that's all it took to get a pirate treasure-trove story started, one that had very little if any basis in fact… A pirate crew was supposed to have buried some loot on the knoll. Returning to their ship, the chief buccaneer found one man missing. He hurried back to the knoll, surprised the wayward pirate digging up the gold, shot him and left him there with the loot. According to Miss Caroline Connor, her brother, the late Henry W. Connor, used to dig in the back yard when he was a child. He never found any treasure, but the children and the Connor servants sincerely believed in the pirate ghost and didn't wander outside after dark.

A version of this story was faithfully repeated in a *Charleston Home Magazine* article by Carey Nikonchuk which appeared in the Spring 2006 issue: "According to legend, a band of pirates buried their treasure in this knoll. Following a dispute over the goods, one was shot on-site; the story holds that it's this pirate's ghost who still haunts the yard at night."

So this story has been reported in two separate news sources over a span of almost forty years. Is there any truth to it? I will venture that it is likely just a legend. Despite what fictional books and movies will often claim, pirates did not make a habit of hiding their loot in treasure chests. Pirates were much more likely to spend their ill-gotten money as quickly as they could. A pirate's life in the 17th and 18th centuries was, to paraphrase English philosopher Thomas Hobbes, "nasty, brutish, and short." A swashbuckling buccaneer during that era did not generally have a retirement plan or a list of long-range goals. These were criminals whose almost solitary motive was profit and pleasure; thus hiding a secret cache of loot would be contrary to their lifestyle. The history books reveal only a few documented instances where pirates hid treasure: the most notable of which was Captain Kidd, whose motivation for hiding his loot was that he was attempting to prove that he was innocent of piracy (Kidd didn't bury his haul, either. He handed it off to a friend for safekeeping). The romantic idea of following a treasure map and finding a chest bursting with gold or silver is exactly that, namely a naïve, romantic fantasy.

This means that the fun pirate's gold tales at 37 Meeting Street should be taken with a grain of salt. Besides, a chest full of ill-gotten plunder buried at the Bosoms would be illogical, since it is common knowledge that pirates prefer booty!

One More Story

In the course of doing research for the pirate plunder legend, I came across one other ghost story involving this notable house at 37 Meeting. In July of 1941, an article appeared in the *Charleston News and Courier* which contained the following tidbit:

At the back of the garden, which is partly sheltered from the north by the servant's quarters, built of brick like the house, long ago. The garden, as well as the house, is said to have been haunted by the ghost of an old lady in gray. She was always a decorous, unobjectionable specter, and has not been seen for some thirty years.

Even though the story of the 'gray lady of 37 Meeting Street' did not mesh with the pirate story, I decided to include it. My reasoning is that while the tales do not overtly complement each other, it just goes to show that many of these old historic buildings on the peninsula play host to more than one ghost. We are left with a puzzle: just who was the female ghost to which this article so casually referred? And why did she appear up until 1910 or so and then fade away? It is but one more unsolved mystery neatly contained in the enigma that is Charleston.

Apparition on the Battery

Near 21 East Battery

*R*achel was excited as she hurriedly got into her costume after work, hoping the evening would be as magical as she dreamed. She had transferred from a university near her family home in Vermont to attend the College of Charleston the year before, but had worried many times that she wasn't fitting into the Southern social scene as well as she'd hoped. Moving across the country like she did, she perhaps had an overly idealized image of Charleston at first, with her future days and nights envisioned as being full of glamour and sultry romance. She wound up getting a job at a very elegant restaurant as a hostess and server, and thought that she was well on her way towards fulfilling her daydreams. "But more often than not, I found myself getting off of work at the restaurant, going home and watching late night T.V. in my pajamas rather than attending lavish parties," she said. "I wasn't fitting in, and I started to worry that I'd made the wrong choice in moving here."

She began a secret romance with one of her supervisors at the restaurant, an entanglement of the heart which was seriously frowned upon by upper management. In fact, people had gotten fired for just that sort of affair at that venue in the past, but to Rachel, keeping their trysts a secret made it all the more exciting. "He was from a wealthy Charleston family—I won't name them, but they've been here for over two hundred years, and there's a street named after them—he only worked at the restaurant because his parents encouraged him not to be idle. Even though he was a bit of a careless boy, I guess I liked the *idea* of dating him more than I liked him personally. I could see it all laid out: the fine dining, the wild whirlwind romance, the wedding, the country club and the white picket fence. Sad to say it, but I was almost sucked in by that illusion."

Rachel had been invited by her secret lover to a costume party on New Year's Eve down on the South Battery. She saw this as a step forward in their relationship: here he was announcing their attachment to his friends,

APPARITION ON THE BATTERY

The East Battery.

and perhaps even his family. She agonized over which costume to wear. An outfit that was too revealing meant that she might meet with disapproval, and too dowdy or silly might mean that she might not be taken seriously. She decided to go all-out with a costume depicting a well-to-do Southern lady from around 1800. Her roommate was a theatre major and had access to a costume from the wardrobe department, complete with shawl, ruffled top and a frilly hat. So this is how she found herself making her way down the East Battery on an unseasonably chilly New Year's Eve wearing her borrowed outfit, eager to meet her love at the costumed ball.

"I was walking south down by the seawall, pretty much lost in thought, when I encountered another woman in costume, standing at the railing and staring out into the harbor. My first thought was that I was actually disappointed, because it looked like she was going to the same costume party I was, except her outfit, which was similar to mine, was spectacular. Mine was kind of nice, but it was still just a props department costume rigged to fit me with velcro and safety pins; hers, though, looked like the real deal, as if she had hired a costumer. Her outfit was all dark greens and browns, silks and lace, and very elegant. I thought my outfit was going to be unique, and yet I was going to be a second-rate imitation. I'd look like a dog at a pony show, standing next to her.

"But as I approached, the woman said nothing, and continued to stare out at the sea, as if waiting for something. I decided to be friendly; I mean, I had no reason not to be, right? So when I got close to her I asked if she was going to the same costume party I was. I remember thinking that it might still be funny if we walked into the party together. Well, the woman definitely heard me, and glanced a little bit in my direction, but her focus was definitely still on the water. She gave me a fractional negative twitch of the head, almost like when a child bothers a mother in church or something, and the mom doesn't take her attention from the sermon, just gives a stern head shake.

"I tried again, telling her that I loved her costume. But as I was speaking, I wondered about her outfit, because I was practically freezing, with those ridiculous ruffles flapping in the stiff breeze. But her outfit was much more revealing, and she didn't have layers on. Her skin looked so pale and *cold*, it was practically blue. And—although this didn't hit me until later—her outfit didn't blow in the breeze. I almost lost my hat twice, and she's standing there without so much as a stitch of clothing moving in that heavy wind.

21 East Battery.

"She looked so sad, so my next thought was that they were filming a movie or doing a photo shoot or something. I glanced around for any signs of a camera crew or photographer, but I didn't see anything like that. You need to understand, there were only a few feet between us at this point; we were almost touching. I asked her something else, I don't really remember what it was exactly, except I was concerned for her. I think I asked if she was okay. She shook her head, finally turning to face me for the first time, and I realized that she was not as old as I originally thought she was. She was just a few years older than me, and very pretty, but looked like she had been crying. She shook her head 'no' once again, and glanced over my shoulder at a house on the Battery. I turned to see whatever she was looking at, but I didn't see anyone, or anything amiss. And when I turned back to her a split-second later, the woman had completely vanished! I was so startled that I think I might have screamed. I recall looking down into the water, thinking that she might have jumped in, like a suicide or something. But there was no one in the water, and no one near me on the Battery."

As Rachel talked about her bizarre incident, I began to get a creeping feeling that I might be able to actually shed some light on what happened to her, and I even might be able to venture a plausible guess as to the identity of the ghost that she had seen. "Where were you, exactly, when this incident happened?" I asked. Rachel did not hesitate: "I was walking down East Battery, just past Atlantic." I pulled out my phone and pulled up a map which showed a view of the street. "You were right here at 21 East Battery? Are you absolutely positive?" She was. "Rachel, I think you might have had an encounter with Theodosia Alston. Does that name ring any bells?" It did not. But Rachel definitely recognized Theodosia's father's name: but then again, most people recall the name of Aaron Burr. He's the only sitting Vice President to ever kill a man.

The Sad, Mysterious Tale of Theodosia

Theodosia Burr Alston was born in 1783 in Albany, New York. Her father, Aaron Burr, was a lawyer and politician, most notably reaching the Vice Presidency under President Thomas Jefferson. He only served a single term, however, since he was dropped from the ticket in 1804 after killing political rival Alexander Hamilton in a duel. Young Theodosia was a vociferous defender of her disgraced father's name.

Theodosia was highly educated and spoke three languages. She achieved this advanced level of learning through the constant encouragement of her father. Theodosia married South Carolinian Joseph Alston in 1801, when she was seventeen. Some have speculated that the pair were an arranged marriage, at least on the part of Theodosia, who married into an extremely wealthy Southern family. While it is true that her father had money troubles, by all written evidence the union between Theodosia and Joseph was very warm and loving.

Aaron Burr, with the help of some investors, explored the possibility of starting his own independent nation in the center of the present-day United States in 1807. Burr was arrested on charges of treason by President Jefferson, but the former Vice President was acquitted of the charges. Burr left for Europe following his acquittal, where he remained a political and social exile. Theodosia hoped to salvage her father's tarnished reputation, but he stayed in Europe for five long years.

It is difficult to overstate just how turbulent the year of 1812 was for Theodosia Burr Alston and her husband. She engaged in letter-writing campaign to numerous members of higher government, begging for a smooth and safe return to America for her father, a process which, though it must have been humiliating for her, was ultimately successful. Tempering that fruitful strategy was the fact that her and her husband's ten year old son died in June that same year of a fever. This threw Theodosia and Joseph both into a deep depression. A heartbroken Theodosia wrote her father: "A few miserable days past, my dear father, and your late letters would have gladdened my soul; and even now I rejoice at their contents as much as it is possible for me to rejoice at anything. I have lost my boy. He is gone forever. He expired on the 30th of June. My head is not sufficiently collected to say anything further. May Heaven, by other blessings, make you some amends for the noble grandson you have lost."

Despite this awful setback, Joseph managed to become elected governor of South Carolina in December. He assumed the mantle of leadership right as hostilities commenced between the United States and England in the War of 1812. It was a difficult time to be in a position of authority, but his regime was complicated even further by the fact that it was a war largely fought through shipping, with each country struggling to ensure the safe passage of their own vessels while raiding the commercial fleet of the opposing nation. Alston governed a state which depended heavily on getting their crops to international buyers. Making Joseph's job even more difficult was the fact that the largest shipping port in his state, Charleston, had suffered a major fire in October of 1812, a blaze which reduced nearly two hundred houses to a smoking ruin. The city would be quite a prize if the British decided to invade the South, so there was much to do.

And then, right as 1812 rolled over into 1813, came arguably the most mysterious occurrence in Charleston's long history. In the midst of all this turmoil, Theodosia decided to visit her father for the first time in half a decade, despite her ill health. She embarked a very fast New York-bound ship named the *Patriot*, along with a family friend, on New Year's Eve, 1812. According to a *New York Times* article which appeared on January 12th, 1913 under the headline 'Mystery of Aaron Burr's Daughter Baffles a Century':

In her grief, she prepared to come to New York to greet her father. And now we come to the mystery. Theodosia started on her journey to New York with a desire to reach here shortly after New Year's Day. In the company of Mr. Timothy Green, a friend of her father, she set sail on the pilotboat Patriot, en route to New York. Mr. Green had warned her father by letter that he would find her looking very thin and feeble, and suffering from an almost incessant nervous fever. The Patriot had the reputation of being a fast sailing vessel, and was expected to make the journey in five or six days. Here the veil of mystery falls over the scene.

She never reached port. She was never sighted again after leaving the shores of South Carolina. It is heart rending to read the almost-frantic letters that passed between the distracted husband of Theodosia in Charleston and the grief stricken father in New York.

When Burr became convinced that Theodosia was no more, he preserved an outward sense of serenity, but, as he told his son-in-law, he felt "severed from the human race." He rarely mentioned her name. He put out of sight such objects as were especially associated with her.

But the world could not and would not forget Theodosia. It talked and conjectured, it strived and searched, it refused to give up hope until the silence told its own story, and then it began to try to solve the mystery. And it has never abandoned hope of at least a solution. So it is, on this anniversary of the problem is again on the tongues of the people: what happened to Theodosia?

The mystery over her fate has persisted for over two hundred years. Many theories have sprung up which attempt to draw back the veil of what ultimately happened to Theodosia, Timothy Green, and the rest of the passengers on that voyage. Like so many historical riddles which invite speculation, some of these hypotheses seem plausible, while others seem to stretch credibility to the breaking point.

One highly entertaining blog (which I hope is written firmly tongue-in-cheek, but I have my doubts) claims that Theodosia Burr Alston and the rest of the folks on the *Patriot* sailed into the Bermuda Triangle, where they were possibly abducted by aliens. The writer of this blog apparently cannot read a map or simply does not care that to come close to entering the Bermuda Triangle, the *Patriot* would have had to have sailed nearly seven hundred miles in the wrong direction.

An 1872 novel by Charles Etienne Arthur Gayarre, titled *Fernando de Lemos: Truth and Fiction: A Novel*, contains an account attributed to legendary pirate Dominique Youx, who in a deathbed confession claimed that he captured the *Patriot* and murdered Theodosia Burr. "She stepped on it and descended into the sea with graceful composure, as if she had been alighting from a carriage," Gayarre wrote, claiming that it was dictated by the pirate. "She sank, and rising again, she, with an indescribable smile of angelic sweetness, waved her hand to me as if she meant to say: 'Farewell, and thanks again'; and then sank forever." Gayarre wrote the book as a mixture of fact and fancy, however, and Dominique Youx was a legendary teller of tall tales (for more information on this fascinating pirate-turned-patriot-turned-politician, please see my 2013 book, *The Haunted History of New Orleans*). We must consider that, even if Youx made a deathbed confession to Gayarre, it might not be true to begin with, since Youx made up most of his pirate stories. Also, he died in 1830, and Gayarre's novel was not published until forty-two years had passed, making the story's veracity seem less than credible.

Another theory states that the *Patriot* was intentionally lured to her doom. Legend states that on stormy nights in the North Carolina Outer Banks, unscrupulous inhabitants would hobble a horse, tie a lantern around the animal's neck, and walk it up and down the beach. Sailors at sea, who were not able to distinguish the bobbing light they saw from that of a ship which was anchored securely, sometimes steered toward shore to find shelter. Instead they ran aground and broke apart on the banks, after which their crews and passengers, if they survived the sinking, were murdered. The criminals would then salvage the cargo of the vessel. It is unlikely (although not impossible) that the *Patriot*'s captain, who was extremely capable, would fall for such a ruse.

The book *Graveyard of the Atlantic: Shipwrecks of the North Carolina Coast* (1972) by David Stick offers several suggestions, including a recounting of an "1833… Alabama newspaper, the *Mobile Register*, reported that a man 'residing in one of the interior counties in this state' made a deathbed confession that he had participated in the capture of the *Patriot*, the murder of all those on board, and the scuttling of the vessel 'for the sake of her plate and effects.'" But Stick's book doesn't stop there with admissions: it also states that another confessed pirate made an almost identical deathbed confession fifteen years later. This pirate claimed that one of the passengers was named "Odessa Burr Alston," and when the lady in question was given the option of sharing the cabin of the pirate captain, she chose death instead.

Stick's book also has perhaps the best retelling of a story I have found in several texts. An unknown female portrait, first described in 1869, which depicts a woman who looks very similar to Theodosia Burr Alston. It was presented, in lieu of payment, by a very old woman to a doctor named William Pool in Nag's Head, NC. The old woman claimed that the portrait had been a gift to her by her first husband, sometime during the winter months during the War of 1812, and that he had acquired it while removing plunder from a ship which had run aground nearby. The ship, which was in rough condition, was supposedly completely deserted. According

"And when I turned back to her a split-second later, the woman had completely vanished!"

to Richard Cote's book, *Theodosia Burr Alston: Portrait of a Prodigy* (2002), relatives of Theodosia were unable to confirm that the 'Nag's Head Portrait' was an exact likeness, and no painting was ever referred to by Theodosia prior to setting sail.

According to sources at the time, a powerful storm did enter the area between South Carolina and New York during that timeframe. In fact, the blockading British fleet referred to a strong storm which would have affected the area directly in the *Patriot*'s path. It is a logical theory that the *Patriot* and all her passengers and crew might have perished in this storm sometime right after the New Year.

These theories only increase the mystery of what happened to the Governor's wife, Theodosia Burr Alston. Her ultimate fate, regardless of how it actually occurred, is a stark reminder that the deep Atlantic Ocean does not give up its secrets so easily.

Rachel, Post-Ghost Encounter

Rachel's eyes grew wide as I told her the sad tale of the doomed Governor's wife, especially the date of her departure: New Year's Eve, the same point on the calendar as her encounter. When I showed her a confirmed portrait of Theodosia Burr (believed to have been done by painter Edward Malbone sometime between 1801- 07), she shivered the moment she saw it, and said quietly, "That was her. That was the woman I saw on the Battery." Rachel was not done with her stirring tale, however.

"I went to the costume party, but I was too shaken up by my experience to really enjoy myself. I tried telling the guy I was dating what I had seen, but he actually wound up announcing it to all of his friends, and they openly mocked me. I left the party in tears, but it was due to their cruelty, not the vanishing lady I saw.

"Amazingly though, that awful night was one of the best things to ever happen to me. I broke off my affair with that guy, and got my life in order. I wound up getting my degree and a great job. A year or two later, the ex-boyfriend had an auto accident after drinking too much, and the girl he was seeing at that time was killed in the crash. He recovered, but I understand that it affected him greatly. I remember thinking back then that it could have been me, riding next to him; so in a very weird way, seeing that ghost on New Year's Eve saved my life."

As befitting a tale which involves Theodosia Burr Alston, we are still left with a multitude of unanswered questions. For instance: why would her spirit come to Charleston in the first place? She lived in Georgetown, SC at the time of her death, and although she and her husband were frequent visitors to Charleston, she never lived there. Is it because the house at 21 East Battery is named the Edmonston-*Alston* House, honoring her husband's family? Or could it be because her husband Joseph died in Charleston in 1816, tragically young (he was thirty-seven when he passed away)? And what of the eerily matching New Year's dates of Rachel's unexplainable experience and Theodosia's fateful trip? Or it is entirely possible that Rachel saw the spirit of an entirely different, yet very similar-looking woman, much like a certain portrait which figured into the story? If this is the case, then perhaps the Alston connection has been erroneously attributed.

Not all ghost stories are wrapped up neatly at the end, and tied with a bow. Sometimes all the unanswered questions, much like the story of Theodosia Burr Alston herself, make the tale even more intriguing as time goes by. All we can do is ponder why the spirit that Rachel saw on the Battery was so brokenhearted, as she looked with such longing towards the cold, dark, deep water. I am also forced to wonder whether the ghost can comprehend that she forever changed one young woman's life for the better.

Blind Tiger Pub

36- 38 Broad Street

For a place nicknamed 'The Holy City,' Charleston has certainly seen more than its fair share of sin. Residents will tell you that they garnered the 'Holy' label not from saintly behavior, but from the number of church steeples dotting the horizon in the peninsula. Much of the licentiousness can be traced to a long love-affair with strong drink, which flourished despite a strict attitude towards celebratory libations by the founders, whose distinctly Puritanical English teetotaling sensibilities were promptly ignored by many of the Charles Town settlers. More than a few of these early townsfolk originally hailed from the Caribbean island of Barbados, meaning that they had a long-standing affection with rum and sweet wines. The rugged Barbadians were not about to give up their liquor just because a dusty-wigged British bureaucrat located four thousand miles from their town frowned upon the practice.

However, this *lassiez-fair* attitude towards drinking was perhaps a bit too permissive in the early days. The colony's first Church of England clergyman, Atkin Williamson, is said to have gotten so drunk that he once baptized a live bear. Residents were required to attend church in the early days of the colony, and the language of what constituted a church service was loose enough to include a meeting "any seven or more persons agreeing in any religion." Clever Charles Town residents quickly included taverns, bars, and perhaps even brothels into this definition, making it possible to go to a local watering hole instead of a house of worship on Sunday morning. Holy spirits, indeed!

The townsfolk's love of spirits is perhaps excusable when you consider that the drinking water was so brackish in the early days that it was scarcely fit for human consumption. It was in part due to the undrinkable water that inns and taverns sprung up all over the port city. In the early part of the 1700's, the waterfront had garnered the reputation of being a melting pot of drinking, prostitution, and disorderly conduct. Sailors were such

"You will hear the distinct sound of crunching leaves, rhythmically, like someone is walking. But there will be nobody there."

contributing factors to the brawling and drunkenness that in 1703, the night watch (a citizen's police force) was empowered to question and arrest any sailor seen frequenting a "tippling house" (pub) after dark. And still the liquor flowed in Charles Town. The move from fledgling colony to the center of the Southern economy in the mid-1700's made the shipping port grow exponentially, which boosted the number of sailors in town at any given moment. According to Walter Fraser's book, *Charleston! Charleston! The History of a Southern City*, a mix of British soldiers, sailors, privateer sailors from various nations, and even the rabble from Spanish ships, flying under a flag of truce, sought out recreation in Charles Town. What they found was "gaming, liquor, and sex." Near the wharves on the bay, people gambled, drank to excess, and caroused. Even members of the night watch were caught selling booze while on duty.

A Brief History of a Blind Tiger

While all of this joyful debasement and imbibing was going on, a couple of buildings were erected, one in 1780 and the other in 1803 at 36-38

Broad Street. This pair of structures saw a number of different uses over the years, including a residence, a tailor shop, and a bank (the remains of part of that bank can still be seen in the courtyard patio today), but their connection to alcohol didn't start until the late days of the 19th century. In fact, many structures in Charleston gained more than a nodding acquaintance with strong spirits beginning in the early 1890's, because that is when "Pitchfork Ben" Tillman rose to power as South Carolina's Governor. Tillman holds the distinction of quite possibly being the most reviled person in Charleston's history, for a number of worthy reasons.

Tillman ran his political campaign on a platform of denying black men the right to vote (he was solidly pro-Jim Crow). He was quite proud of being a racist, bragging in 1900: "We have done our level best [to prevent blacks from voting] ... we have scratched our heads to find out how we could eliminate the last one of them. We stuffed ballot boxes. We shot them. We are not ashamed of it." He gained his nickname of "Pitchfork" later on as a U.S. Senator, when he announced in an 1896 Senate speech his desire to go to Washington and plunge a pitchfork into the rump of President Grover Cleveland. Tillman hated what he considered the elitism of Charleston high society, and many Charlestonians returned the bitter feelings a hundredfold when Tillman established the South Carolina Dispensary, which was a bald-faced attempt to control liquor sales through a state-controlled monopoly. The Dispensary, which existed statewide from 1893-1907, required all liquor sold in South Carolina to be bottled and sold through the state. If a county voted against the Dispensary, then that county would effectively implement self-imposed prohibition.

Charleston residents, ignoring the law, erected stills in kitchens and opened illegal bars which served only non-Dispensary booze. It is strongly rumored, though unproven, that the building which currently houses the Blind Tiger Pub was in fact being used as just such a bar during this time period. Such claims are nearly impossible for me to verify, despite finding several Charlestonians who claimed that their family lore did in fact speak of such an operation at that location. By their very nature, clandestine Dispensary-era bars did not record any documentation. These illegal bars were called 'Blind Tigers,' a term which refers to the fact that the illicit tavern owner was technically not charging for alcohol: the attendees paid an 'admission fee' to see a mythical beast, the blind tiger. The story goes that if you paid enough admission fees, one would only have to look in the mirror to see the blind tiger! This colorful, gin-soaked name of the establishment came to life again during the 1920-1933 nationwide Prohibition of the sale of alcoholic beverages (the Volstead Act). Once more, Charlestonians disregarded authority, and instead scratched behind the ears of their beloved Blind Tiger.

The Blind Tiger ownership takes great pride in celebrating the Charlestonian love-affair with spirits, offering up not only a wide assortment of beers but a nice choice of cocktails, as well. Their kitchen serves a surprisingly wide selection of food on the menu, going beyond the usual pub fare. I am usually content with a basic burger and a pint, but their Tiger Tacos (I had them with seared tuna) and fried pickles were wonderful. While I sat at the bar, talk turned to ghosts. Lisa, the daytime manager, confirmed that a customer had very recently had a paranormal experience while Lisa was on duty. The customer, who was a regular, was examining some new T-shirts on display and sensed someone approach her from behind. She felt fingers in her hair, which curled and yanked her tresses, hard. She turned around to see who had done it, and realized she was standing all by herself.

"There is a presence here," Lisa said. "Many people feel it. But you know who you should really talk to? The nighttime manager, James. He has really got some great stories!" In a matter of no time, I found myself introduced to the night manager, who at first glance is quite imposing physically. But his easy-going manner quickly dispatched any initial trepidation I might have had, and he graciously took time to tell me story after chilling story.

"These sorts of tales predate me working here, of course," James said. "The old general manager was sitting with a couple of friends, these were longtime regulars at the bar, at closing time a few years back. They're hanging out together at a table, and they are the only three people in the bar. But suddenly, chills run up and down all three of their spines when they realize that there is a woman in the bar, as well. She was wearing all black, and walked right past them, not speaking or looking at any of them. She just sort of glided past all three of them, and disappeared into the shadows, going deeper and deeper into the bar. They all three just sort of looked at each other, and all of their expressions said exactly the same thing: *Did you just see that, too?* Well, they all just stood up in unison, didn't say a word to each other, and locked the door behind them. The manager didn't count down the register, and didn't even shut off the lights; he just locked the door and didn't come back until the next morning. That's sort of a famous story. Those regulars still talk about it."

When asked if he had ever had any strange occurrences personally, James fixed me with a cockeyed expression which clearly said, 'Are you kidding?'

"I had something happen just last week," James asserted. "I was running the trash out beyond the back patio at the end of the night. Now, our lights back here are motion-activated, but it has to be something sizeable to set it off. A little tree branch blowing in the wind isn't going to do it, we don't want to aggravate the neighbors like that. It has to be something fairly big moving around back here, like a man. I've heard other staff members complain about being a little spooked when that light would go off by itself for no reason, but I always just sort of dismissed it. Anyway, I was headed back here, trash in hand, when I started to feel a little funny, you know that sensation where things are just not right? And I got suddenly cold, even though the night was pretty warm, and calm. Anyway, that light turned on by itself not once, not twice, but three times. And let me tell you, the third time it happened, I was already inside the building. I totally bolted, and am not ashamed to admit that I went back up front and told them that I was not shutting down the back area by myself. No one batted an eye, and they knew exactly what I was talking about. So I had three co-workers help me take the trash out and shut the lights out last Saturday." He laughed.

"There are other times where if you sit still long enough on that patio, you will hear noises. You will hear the distinct sound of crunching leaves, rhythmically, like someone is walking. But there will be nobody there. We heard this sound last night, like someone we couldn't see was walking around back there." James gestured to the patio area, which still contains the remains of the old bank which used to be on the property, and added, "I try to lock this place down while I still have people back here, that, or I grab a co-worker to help me. My theory is that if you're a ghost and you're coming for me, you're gonna have to take at least two of us, because I'm going have someone there with me." James' fear of the unknown is understandable, but it is worth noting that there didn't seem to be any negative entities at the Blind Tiger.

This was reinforced by one former server who had worked at the Blind Tiger years before. She was extremely sensitive to ghosts, and told me about her experiences there: "It was a great place to work, spiritually-speaking, because the ghosts were so happy there. I never got much of a sense of any angry or unhappy ghosts there, which believe me, is a real rarity in an old town like Charleston. So much murder, disease, and death has happened here that even just walking into some of these old buildings, much less

"These illegal bars were called 'Blind Tigers,' a term which refers to the fact that the illicit tavern owner was technically not charging for alcohol..."

working in them, is an ordeal. But my time at the Blind Tiger seemed to be the pleasant exception."

I pressed her for specifics, but she waved the question away. "I would catch the occasional impression of a woman who was waiting for her date to arrive, and was beginning to feel like she had been stood up, that sort of thing. But no utter heartbreak, no frightening episodes. It seems like the ghosts are happily drinking and having fun, and don't realize that they are dead. For them, the party just sort of goes on and on, which doesn't sound like a horrible way to spend the afterlife, does it?"

That really does leave a wonderful image, upon reflection: happy spirits drinking together, and not letting little things like laws or death slow down their good time? It sounds like heaven. One can easily imagine the ghosts making merriment in the afterlife, petting the Blind Tiger for many years to come.

Ruth Lowndes Simmons Gateposts

131 Tradd Street & 14 Legare Street

I was taking a rare night off from my book research in Charleston, instead choosing to spend a relaxing evening with two of my close friends. Together Mark and Rebel own Black Cat Tours, and are happily married; I had met them both several years before, and every time I would visit Charleston it seemed that they would graciously introduce me to a new, usually obscure (but always delicious), hidden gem of a restaurant. This is how I found myself sitting down with them to a great meal at the Glass Onion, which is located on Highway 17 in West Ashley, a short distance from Charleston's Historic District. All three of us were tour guides, published authors, and lovers of history, so the conversation was always lively. It suddenly occurred to me halfway through our fine meal that even though I had attended their wedding a few years before, I had no idea how Mark and Rebel met, so I asked.

"You said you were taking the night off, though, and how we met actually involves a ghost," Rebel said, her eyes twinkling. "Are you sure you want to hear this story?" You'd better believe I did.

What Mark and Rebel experienced, however, needs a bit of historical context to fully understand the significance of their paranormal event.

The Handkerchief

To exist in the upper class of post-Revolutionary War Charleston, especially for those entering marrying age, could be extremely dangerous. Reputations needed to be cultivated. Falling in love with someone beneath your station could be disastrous, and the complex dance of courtship was

77

The Gateposts at 131 Tradd Street.

fraught with peril. Even if you were to do everything properly, you might find yourself hemmed into a course of action by a rigid set of societal rules. Duels during this era were commonplace, as we see in several other stories in this volume, and often fought over completely innocent gestures. Francis Simmons did not fight a duel, but he likewise found himself locked into a certain trajectory by honor, bound to someone he did not love by the most innocuous of statements. How exactly did he find himself trapped by honor into a loveless marriage? Poor, naïve Mr. Simmons showed someone a handkerchief—the *wrong* someone, as fate would have it.

His misfortune began when Francis was restless at a summer party, growing increasingly impatient as the evening grew darker without his lovely Sabrina. He had fallen for a charming creature, and every moment away from her was like being deprived of oxygen, he lamented. *Trapped beneath the surface*, he thought wryly, *drowning in the Sea of Smalltalk*. The party had been thrown by Rawlins Lowndes, former mayor of Charleston and governor of South Carolina. The affair was well-attended by the usual upper class types, and Francis supposed that he really ought to be more interested. His law practice was barely getting off the ground, and the thirty year old lawyer should have seen everyone in attendance as a potential client. Rawlins Lowndes had made it a point to introduce him around, which should have invoked gratitude in him; but the craggy-faced old man was getting a little fuzzy-minded of late, and had introduced him to his daughter, Ruth, more than once already that evening. The last time it had happened, old Rawlins has grasped both of their hands together, awkwardly holding them together in a shaky embrace.

He had known Ruth for practically all of his life. She was good friends with Sabrina, so over the past few months he had used their friendship to his advantage, cagily spending time with Ruth to learn more information about her younger companion, Sabrina. Ruth was approaching spinsterhood, he noticed. She was his age, well past the prime years for a woman to marry. She was awkward and mostly silent around him, and Francis noted for the umpteenth time that poor Ruth had inherited her father's looks and not her mother's, especially the prominent nose. On some women a bigger-than-average nose could be handsome, but on Ruth the feature just made her seem rather duck-like. When her father had clapped their hands together, Francis noted with distaste that her hand was cold and clammy. Her mouth opened as if she wanted to say something, but she did not. He diplomatically shook his hand free and smiled at her. His mind kept returning to Sabrina. Only recently had they expressed feelings for each other, and soon he would ask for her hand in marriage.

Eventually the endless chitchat became too much for Francis. He stepped onto the piazza for a little air. He stood looking out over the garden when he realized that he was not alone. He turned, hoping that it was his love, but was disappointed when he saw old Rawlins totter out. It was an effort not to let such an emotion creep into his features. Instead, he smiled warmly.

"I'm so glad you came to my party, young man," Mr. Lowndes said. "You've always been like a son to me, and it makes me glad to see that you care enough to come to a boring old event such as this one." Francis thanked his host once again for his hospitality. "No, no, this is not some old man fishing for compliments. It is me who owes you thanks, good sir, for spending time with Ruth over these past few months. I wanted to show you my appreciation, so I had something made especially for you." The old man fished around in his inner vest pocket and produced a lovely handkerchief. It was silk, and the color of a bowl of fresh cream. Embroidered into one corner were Francis' initials, a bold 'F.S.' in a brilliant greenish blue, his favorite color.

Francis was moved. "Thank you, sir. I have never seen anything so lovely."

Rawlins leaned in. "Anything for a good friend, one that I already consider extended family. This small gift is a blessing, from me to you." The younger man was touched beyond words. The old man placed a hand on his shoulder, squeezing it affectionately, and departed.

Francis was not alone on the porch for more than a minute before Ruth stepped onto the piazza with him. "I-It's a lovely night," she stammered. "I simply adore the summer air." Truth be told, it was a stiflingly hot evening, Francis noted, but he did not disagree with her out of politeness. She stood on the porch self-consciously, and in an effort to break the awkward tension, Francis produced the handkerchief. "Did you see this gift that your father gave me?" Her eyes widened and she walked quickly to him, placing her hands around his to examine it. "No," she breathed. "It's lovely. What wonderful sewing. If only I could have these initials as my very own!"

Francis frowned at her. If she wanted an embroidered handkerchief, all she had to do was ask her father for one, correct? "If you wanted some fine initials like these, all you would have to do is say the word, and I'll discuss the matter with your father," he offered.

Her eyes widened, and her mouth flapped open and closed a few times before she said, "Francis, that—that would be lovely!" She retreated back into the house quite suddenly, leaving a confused Francis wondering: how could anyone get so worked up over some embroidered fabric?

Suddenly, he heard a rhythmic clinking sound from inside the house, like a small bell. First one, and then more, and Francis realized that he could hear a hundred glasses all being rapped lightly with silverware. He walked back into the party to see old Rawlins holding a champagne glass and Ruth beaming, with tears in her eyes. Everyone looked at the father and daughter expectantly. Rawlins quieted the crowd, and then spoke: "I have just been informed that my daughter Ruth has been asked for her hand in marriage! This grand affair just became an engagement party!" Francis looked bewildered as the old man gestured for him to step forward. A terrible realization swept over him, and he suddenly saw the events of the last five minutes from a new, horribly different perspective, all involving blessings and Ruth mooning over his initials, wishing for them. Francis was pushed by the crowd into Rawlins' tight embrace. Ruth wrapped her arms tight around Francis, too, right as he spotted Sabrina in the crowd. Sabrina's face was the embodiment of dismay.

"You have made an old man very happy," Rawlins Lowndes said into his ear, and Francis realized he was trapped.

A few days later Francis confronted Ruth. "I love another," he bluntly stated. "We will tell your father that it has all been a terrible mistake, and we will undo what has been done."

Tears welled in her eyes, and she shook her head. "But you asked me," she said, voice rising with emotion. "You asked me to take your initials! You asked to speak to Father about it! You spent months with me, spent many afternoons and evenings wooing me, confessing your desires and feelings… It is simply cold feet, my love, and it shall pass. I have dreamed of us marrying since I was a little girl." Francis was adamant that they should stop the engagement, but she would not relent, insisting that he loved her. Francis then tried to approach Rawlins Lowndes, but every time he brought up the impending wedding, Rawlins would repeat over and over how happy the engagement made him, and that they were a perfect match. He could not seem to get through to the old man.

Finally, Francis approached Ruth again. "You will get the wedding you desire, Ruth, but heed my words: unless you release me from this farce, a wedding is all you shall ever receive from me. We shall live separately, dine separately, sleep separately, and your wedding bed will grow cold in Hades before I shall ever occupy it. I am a man of my word, however twisted and mistakenly heard those words may have been. I will marry you if you force it, but you will never have children, and we will never have a life together. You will have a husband's name on a piece of paper, and that is all. I love another, and will never love you."

Ruth, for reasons known only to her, chose the loveless marriage. Their union on their wedding day was one without joy, and true to his word, Francis Simmons never once shared his wife's bed. They lived a few blocks apart, but never fraternized besides throwing the occasional party at the house that Francis had bought for Ruth right after their marriage. Her home was located at 131 Tradd Street; his was located at 14 Legare Street. When these parties would end, Francis would bow formally to his wife, and climb into his waiting carriage to take him home. Francis died in 1814, and since he was only fifty when he died, many claimed that he simply willed himself to death. His will specified that his mansion on Legare Street be given not to his widow, but instead to a family friend.

Ruth survived her husband by forty years, finally passing away in 1854. She never remarried after Francis' death.

Usually, digging into these sorts of family legends reveals that they have been exaggerated beyond recognition. Not so, in this case. A June 16th, 1941 *Charleston News and Courier* article titled 'Handsome House… Once Was Home to a Celibate Bridegroom,' backs up every detail of their bizarre marriage:

A curious story connected with [14 Legare Street] concerns the marriage of Francis Simmons to Miss Ruth Lowndes. After the wedding, at the close of the reception, the bridegroom escorted to the door of a sandstone establishment he had prepared for her. He expressed his hope that all there would be to her liking, bowed formally, and took his leave, returning to his own residence, where he continued to live… When they met on the afternoon drive around the Battery, as she rose in her carriage and curtsied, he rose in his and bowed. The reason for this peculiar situation was never made public… Even after more than one hundred years of surmise and conjecture, the true cause is not generally known.

Francis' house still stands on Legare Street. Ruth's house on Tradd Street has been torn down, leaving only the sandstone gateposts to mark the spot. Those gateposts regard each other very much as Francis and Ruth did on their wedding day: uselessly and without purpose for each other. Many longtime Charlestonians claim that if you stand near those gates at night, you can still sometimes hear the sounds of hooves and horses pass by, when no horses can be seen. These same storytellers will smile, and explain that it's just old Ruth Lowndes Simmons, driving home to her cold, empty bed.

Young Love and a Jealous Spirit

Let us return to the dinner with my two friends, and the strange story they told me which perfectly complements this tale. Over our meal, the two of them began to tell how their romantic union formed.

"We actually met eight months prior to dating," Rebel began. "That's not the good story, though. The good story is the night we became a couple. After seeing each other again, which was a chance meeting of sorts, the sparks flew and we went for a walk together. It was January of 2005, and a little cold. We strolled together in downtown Charleston, arm in arm. It was romantic. We got near Tradd Street on Legare, though, and we both got a sudden case of the chills, much more than the chilly evening warranted. It strikes me a funny now—I was then, as now, a tour guide, and I would frequently speak about people experiencing chills right before a haunting—and I failed to recognize it as it was happening to me.

"Anyway, I felt a rush of air, and smelled the very distinct aroma of horsehide. Literally, we both suddenly got a strong whiff of sweaty horses, even though there weren't any horses nearby. It was just him and I, alone on the street, with no one else in sight. We both commented on it. Well, Mark notices we're close to the spot where Ruth and Francis had their famous conversation, and points out the piazza where they would have been standing. It is a famous story, one that every tour guide knows.

"Well, the connection just hit me. I turned to Mark and said, 'I think we were just passed by Ruth Simmons' old carriage.' And Mark thought about it for a moment, and said, 'Yes, I think you're right.' And the only reason I could think that she had whisked by us like that was that we were young, and in love; we were so happy, and poor Ruth never was."

A Strange Story at 14 Legare Street

As I researched the famous story of Ruth Lowndes Simmons and her reluctant groom, I ran across yet another tale involving the home that Francis Simmons built at 14 Legare Street. The news item I found detailed a very unusual duel. The combatants opted not to meet at the traditional spots for such an activity, such as out at Line Street or in Philadelphia Alley. Instead, these two settled their differences from the windows of their own houses. Each of the men stood in their corner third-story windows across Legare Street, firing at each other from their respective bedrooms. *The Charleston Evening Post* article by Jack Leland, which appeared on Tuesday, July 16th, 1968, stated:

A fatal duel is supposed to have been fought between No. 14 Legare and No. 15, just across the way. One dueler was in the southwest third story bedroom of No. 14. The other was in the northeast 3rd story bedroom of No. 15. The one in No. 14 was killed and the bloodstains remained for many years, a sure-fire item for scaring youngsters.

Later news items confirmed the duel, stating that the two men were cousins. The exact reasons for the gunplay are shrouded in mystery. The victorious gentleman was identified as Mr. Lowndes, but clearly he is a later relative of Rawlins Lowndes and not the man himself. Rawlins Lowndes passed away in 1800 and Francis Simmons died in 1814, meaning that the duel occurred sometime after the later date.

This story goes to show that not all ghosts in Charleston are vaporous forms or phantom footsteps: sometimes the real terrors are simply family disagreements gone terribly, horribly wrong. The reasons for their deadly conflict have faded into the mists of time, but the bloodstains marking their fatal feud endure.

14 Legare Street.

The Book-Loving Ghost at the Hannah Heyward House

31 Legare Street

In 1789, a beautiful edifice was constructed on Legare Street by Hannah Heyward, who was perhaps most famous for being the sister-in-law of Declaration of Independence signer Thomas Heyward. But Mrs. Heyward was an accomplished woman in her own right, as she was a wealthy planter. Her home, a gorgeous example of a Neoclassical villa, certainly indicates the prosperous nature of her business. Most of the elegant homes in the area reflect the incredible commerce transpiring in Charleston's shipping port in the decades after the American Revolution, and the emergence of a truly elite plantation class.

The seemingly placid home at 31 Legare Street gives no clue, however, to the anguish felt there by Mrs. Heyward one cold January day in 1805, nor the curious apparition which has been seen at odd intervals ever since. Is there any way one house could contain the heart-rending emotions felt by a mother losing her child?

A Tragic Trip

Hannah's son, James, was a bright young man with a curious and sharp intellect. He loved to read in the second-floor family library, and could often be found at all hours seated there, completely engrossed in one book or another. He seemed almost addicted to reading for many happy hours in the sunlight. In addition to being well-read, he was also an avid outdoorsman, very much loving both hunting and fishing. On that very early January morning in 1805, he suited up in his favorite green hunting jacket, kissed his mother on the cheek, and promised to bring home some wild pheasants, venison, or perhaps even a boar. He left to go to his favorite

East (front) Elevation, From Northeast- Hannah Heyward House, 31 Legare Street, Charleston, S.C. Obtained from the Library of Congress Prints and Photographs Division.

hunting grounds, which were at least an hour's ride, one way, with his two faithful hunting dogs trailing behind his horse.

According to a *Charleston Evening Post* article which appeared in the early 1980's, Hannah stepped into the library that same morning, and was surprised to see James, sitting with his head down at a table. He was still dressed in his green hunting coat, and appeared to be resting, as usual, in the sunlight. As she approached him she noticed that he held his head gently in his hands, seeming lost in thought. She asked if he was all right, and wondered aloud why he had returned so soon. Rather than answer, he vanished right in front of her astonished eyes! Alarmed, Mrs. Heyward asked the servants if they had observed James returning, they all stated that they had not, and his horse, gun, and dogs were all nowhere in sight either. All indications were that he was still on his hunting expedition.

Later that same day, some friends arrived at the house, and their mournful, distressed faces told the story even before Hannah saw James' lifeless body draped over the back of the saddle. He had been involved in a terrible hunting accident. His two dogs began to violently fight with another dog and refused to answer his commands to stop, so James had used the butt of his hunting rifle to break up the fracas. He was attempting to keep all the animals from injuring each other. He had failed to remember that his gun was loaded, and after several thrusts with the butt of the firearm, the trigger was somehow pulled. The bullet traveled upwards and struck James in the head, killing him nearly instantly. The time of the senseless accident coincided exactly with the moment Mrs. Heyward had seen her son sitting in the library.

A Sunlight-Loving Ghost

James has returned time and time again over the years, always coming back to his favorite reading spot in the library. In one instance, which took place decades after James' death, a subsequent owner of the house was passing by the open door to the library when he glimpsed a seated man in that room wearing a green jacket. The man had his back to the owner. He was sitting in the sun, and appeared to be lost in thought. The owner angrily inquired what the man was doing trespassing in the library, but the man did not respond. Fearfully, the owner went and got the first item he could find to use as a weapon, which happened to be a fireplace poker. Brandishing his makeshift weapon just in case the intruder in his house was dangerous, he returned to the library and approached the interloper. As he drew near, James vanished from sight in front of the homeowner's astounded eyes.

In another instance, a family called for a doctor one bright morning to tend to their sick child. As they waited, the family butler glimpsed a man in a coat sitting in the library, and assumed it was the doctor who had arrived. He summoned the man of the house, but when the father entered the library, the coat-wearing man had disappeared.

According to that earlier-mentioned *Evening Post* article: "The ghost has not been seen for many years but it always appeared on bright sunny mornings, [and] always in the same position."

So often we, as a ghost story-loving audience are fixated on the macabre, the gruesome, or the utterly tragic aspects of the stories. But in many ways, an uplifting tale such as the one involving James and Hannah Heyward better serves to enlighten, entertain, and yes, even educate us about both life and death. We (and I include myself) perhaps spend too much time being afraid of the dark. What better way to inform us, however, of what awaits in shadowy realm which we will all eventually inhabit than to tell us that yes, we too could wind up just like James Heyward, spending decades or even centuries doing something that we love? The ghost at 31 Legare Street holds no terrors. There is neither dripping blood nor a bitter warning in this particular narrative, but maybe we should pay close attention to this spirit's message, regardless. Just like James, we should spend a long contemplative moment in the sun, pondering what fate waits for us all.

Children's Cancer Thrift Store

835 Savannah Highway

There is the occasional story, and yes this is one of those, where the hardest part of my job as the compiler of ghost tales is not finding the story or locating someone willing to be interviewed. No, my biggest hurdle is protecting the reputation of someone who is described in the tale, even if that person is deceased. Portraying someone in a negative (albeit humorous) light is not really something that I am comfortable with, especially if the person is no longer around to defend him or herself. With this particular chapter, I was faced with two options: I could either omit the salacious details—and they really are relevant to the story—or I could omit the name. I have chosen the latter. The story is a good one, and the name doesn't really matter. The man in question still has living relatives in Charleston, and out of respect for the family I will not use their good name in print. Certain dates have also been omitted in order to further protect his identity.

For many visitors to the Holy City, a truly surprising aspect of native Charlestonians is how matter-of-fact they are when their home or workplace is haunted. The city has such a reputation for ghosts that the residents frequently treat their paranormal experiences simply as part of their routine, or something to be endured. Or sometimes, a good haunting just seems to break up the monotony of the day. It was just such a series of unembellished occurrences which found me sitting with Betsy Helander one bright morning at the Children's Cancer Thrift Store, located on U.S. 17 in the Avondale area of West Ashley. The building used to be a grocery store, built back before the really big chain supermarket stores moved in. It hasn't been a grocery for many years, but the old layout is still there. Betsy, a devout woman of faith and by all indications a stable and extremely reliable witness, had worked at the Thrift Store, which was a charity benefiting the very young victims of cancer, for seven years. She related her remarkable experiences to me in a very precise, unremarkable way, which I was to find very much part of a pattern with Charlestonians who have had a brush with the paranormal.

"I started working here in 1999," Betsy told me. "I very quickly became the manager. I've actually had many paranormal experiences here. Mr. Q, who owned the store at one time but passed away a while ago, is obviously still here. He's a bit of a prankster, actually.

"My first experience with him, I was behind the counter, squatted-down. I was working with the coffee pot. The manager at that time was way down at the other end of the counter, in the office. He was one of these people who didn't like to be touched and wouldn't get close to people. Anyway, while I was squatted down, I clearly felt someone walk behind me. They brushed past my rear and then stood to my left. I turned around to see what the manager needed and realized he was still sitting in the office. I asked him: 'How did you do that?' He wanted to know what I was talking about, and when I told him, he said, 'I haven't moved.' And I could still feel someone's presence there, even though I couldn't see them. So I quickly got up and got out from behind the counter. It did scare me, a little.

Later on, other things began happening. For instance, on the stairs in the back of the store, there's a landing. I would walk by there and see a dark figure standing on the steps, but when I would turn to look directly at him, he would disappear. I started to get the feeling that this was the old owner, Mr. Q. Well, one day the man's grandson dropped by, and I got a chance to ask him whether or not he had known his grandfather. He said yes, he had. He kind of looked at me funny. And I asked if his grandfather had always worn dark clothing? Well, he really looked at me funny and said, 'Well, as a matter of fact he always wore black. Why?' I told him that I see a dark figure on the stairs all the time, and I suspected that it was his grandfather. He laughed and said, 'You don't see him. He's long-gone.' And I said, 'Yes I do, I see him standing on that first floor landing, and he's looking this way.' And at that point the grandson got very quiet, and then he said, 'My granddad used to live in an apartment upstairs, over the store. He used to frequently stand on that landing and look that direction to keep an eye on the people who were working for him.' So at that point he started to believe me."

A Fashionable Ghost?

Not all of the deceased owner's antics at his former grocery were so easily explicable: take for instance his penchant for touching ladies' dresses. Betsy describes his predilection for fondling women's apparel, which was fortunately unoccupied: "I admit that I found it funny that he liked to do that. It would happen around that first rack of clothing right up front. We always keep our clothes even and spaced, and looking nice. Well, I kept noticing that, after straightening it once, that there would be an odd space between hangers. I would straighten it yet again, and a few moments later the gap would be back in there. Well, one day, I was walking by there and a customer was walking towards me, and so I moved over. When I did, I bumped into someone with my right arm, and I turned around and said, 'Excuse me.' But there was nobody there: I had just apologized to empty air. However, there was that space in ladies dresses again. So at that point I had a little conversation with the ghost. I explained that I appreciated that he was there, but he needed to stop messing with the dresses because he was making things a little hard on us. But I guess he didn't care about that, because he became even more of a prankster. Every night before we closed we would make sure all of the hangers were even with the pants hangers, and evenly spaced, that sort of thing. Well, sometimes we would look up after we finished and there would be pants hangers sticking up all throughout the store. And I would have to yell at Mr. Q, saying, 'You've got to stop doing this!' And we'd straighten them all over again.

"He also had a thing about a clock we had up front on the counter. For some reason, he liked to flip it around backwards. He was always getting into stuff. Before the Thrift Store was in here, it was a costume shop named 'Hokus Pokus.' Well, they said that their radio was the biggest issue: Mr. Q liked to change their radio station every night, regardless of where they left it. They'd come in, and it would be on a different station.

"One day, the former butcher came in. He had worked back in the meat department there in the grocery for many, many years. I told him that Mr. Q was still here. He didn't seem surprised, he just smiled and asked if I didn't by any chance ever see a woman in a white dress? I told him that I had seen little flashes of light go by me, but I had never paid them any attention. He said, 'That would be his girlfriend.' I said, his what? He was married! The man said, 'His girlfriend, that's why he was living upstairs instead of at home.' He apparently was having a to-do with his secretary. She always wore a white dress when she came into work, the butcher said, so if you're seeing him, she must be nearby. 'They were very close,' he said.

"Well, I know it wasn't a negative haunting, but I always hated staying here late by myself. I would still get creeped out. One evening I was here by myself tallying some figures and I felt someone blowing on my neck! Well, the air conditioning wasn't on, so I went back to my paperwork. It happened again, and I just ignored it. When it happened a third time, I had to say, 'Mr. Q, I have work to do, will you please stop?' And he went away for just a very short time, but he came back that same evening. I could feel his presence moving around my office, you know, like waiting. He was there, but didn't want to bother me. He paced right behind my chair. I got goosebumps and got my work done as quickly as I could so I could get out of there!"

When I asked Betsy how she felt about her experiences there, she smiled and said, "I learned that if there is a spirit around like this one, that they just want your attention. If you recognize them, and tell them that everything's okay, they'll usually leave you alone. Now that I've had time to think about it, I'd have to say that Mr. Q would mess up the clothes near closing time because he didn't want to be left alone at night."

I reflected momentarily on Betsy's enlightened attitude. *A lonely ghost in a lonely place?* I offered. She looked at me significantly, and said, "Exactly." Betsy's attitude towards the spirit was spot-on for a harmonious coexistence with the spirits, the demeanor of 'live and let live.' Or perhaps a better description would be to let the living and the departed exist peacefully, side-by-side.

Spectres at the Southend Brewery

Wagener-Ohlandt Building

161 East Bay Street

Early one morning in 1885, a Charleston cop walked his usual beat on East Bay Street. However, when the officer reached the Wagener Building at the corner of East Bay and Queen Streets, he suddenly started screaming something unintelligible. He ran, red-faced and panicky, to a nearby eatery which was in the process of opening for breakfast. The owner of the restaurant knew the policeman fairly well and tried to ask him what was the matter, but the officer was too out of breath to form a complete sentence. All he could do was point into the fading gloom, saying between shuddery gasps, "The sidewalk… the bird… the bird on the sidewalk…!" There had already been a spectacular blaze in the harbor just a few hours' previous, when a ship loaded with cotton and phosphates had caught fire and burned brilliantly in the water. What else could go possibly wrong?

Alarmed, the restaurant owner followed his cop friend outside, and proceeded the half block towards where the policeman was pointing. There, on the sidewalk, was indeed a large bird. Specifically, it was a jet-black crow, and it was hunched down, trying to eat something it had found. Spooked by the approach of the two men, it flapped a few feet further down the sidewalk, still grasping at the small object in its scabby black claw. It shrieked a protest at those it probably suspected of trying to steal its tasty morsel. The restaurant owner noticed a few small drips of what could only be blood on the flagstone sidewalk where the bird had been moments before. Was the bird injured? And why would this so upset his

"They followed a strange sound up to the third floor of the Wagener Building, where they found a scene so disturbing that several of the men fled the scene to be emphatically sick."

friend? He approached the bird more slowly, trying to get a sense of why seeing a black bird eating something was so disturbing. That is when he finally saw the scavenger's prize clearly: clutched firmly in the crow's foot was a human eyeball, the iris of which still glittered ice-blue in the morning light.

Fortunes, Both Good and Bad

Novelist Nathaniel Hawthorne once said: "Families are always rising and falling in America." This saying, although an incomplete quote, perfectly embodies the Wagener-Ohlandt Building, located on Bay Street, very close to the Charleston docks. Constructed as a warehouse in 1880 by a wealthy German-born entrepreneur F.W. Wagener, the building illustrates Charleston's post- Civil War diversification. The structure was used to hold cotton, still then a major cash crop, but also naval stores (such as turpentine), liquor, foodstuffs, and a growing business in the postwar economy, phosphates. The Charleston area (specifically right near the Ashley

River) had a naturally occurring abundance of phosphate deposits which was discovered in 1868, which are to this day an important component in fertilizer. The curious odor emitted by mining of the profitable mineral, which permeated the air for miles around, was referred to by Charlestonians as "the smell of money." By using these deposits to full advantage, South Carolina cotton crops were some of the most productive in the South.

Wagener's lovely commercial building, mixing elements of the Romanesque and Queen Anne styles of architecture, reflects his personal success financially, and his own family's exceptionalism in other areas: specifically his brother, who served as mayor. Charleston during this time period experienced an economic downturn, but the Wagener family continued unaffected.

However, as earlier stated in the famous first half of Hawthorne's social commentary, families are always rising and falling. Wagener's financial savvy catapulted his career trajectory upward. Hawthorne did famously utter the above line, but added the following, lesser known caveat: "But, I believe, we ought to examine more closely the how and why of it, which in the end revolves around life and how you live it." And as if on cue to prove Hawthorne's words, one of Wagener's clients, George Poirier, experienced a precipitous decline during the same time period as Wagener's ascent.

The Poirier family, in the decades leading up to the Civil War, had amassed a considerable fortune. Unlike so many of their fellow aristocratic class families, however, their largesse was not destroyed by the conflict with the North. Most of these wealthy Southern families, caught up in a sort of patriotic fervor, invested their fortunes in Confederate stocks and bank notes, or in industries tied to the Rebel cause. The Poiriers shrewdly and secretly invested heavily on both sides of the Mason-Dixon Line (and even with a few European companies), hedging their bets through diversification. This meant that when the conflict came to an economy-destroying resolution, a few families like the Poiriers were perfectly poised to swoop in and buy up huge sections of Southern economic mainstays, like land and agricultural concerns. As previously stated, Charleston's economy recovered very slowly in the Reconstruction years, making this investment windfall even more crucial to the Poirier family's well-being.

Due to this cleverly-amassed enormous family wealth, the succeeding generation never had to work a day in their lives. When it came time for George Poirier to assume control of the family business in the early 1880's, he had wasted over two decades as an idle playboy, spending his time chasing women, drinking, and gambling with disreputable acquaintances. He was a poster child for bad behavior. While he was well-liked on the party scene, George lacked a good business instinct and the requisite life experience to make sound decisions in the arena of commerce and investing. Unfortunately for George, he learned the hard way that good financial sense was not genetic. In half a decade, the Poirier family coffers, formerly overflowing, had been emptied and subsequently mortgaged. His desperate attempts to reverse his ill fortune with get-rich-quick schemes had all failed, and for the first time in over thirty years, thanks in large part to George's mismanagement, the family was in real financial trouble.

This explains why George came to the Wagener Building one day in 1885, hat in hand, and explained his predicament to several associates of his who worked there. They agreed to let him invest in a ship which would shortly be transporting cotton, phosphates and naval stores to England. It wasn't a scheme: for the first time in his life, George had found a legitimate money-making operation which, if successful, could hold off the creditors long enough that he could save the family name from disgrace and financial ruin. It was reputedly George who, desperate for a bigger return, talked his fellow investors into cancelling the ship's insurance policy to save even more money.

The day of the departure arrived, and George wanted to watch his investment set sail. One can only imagine his trepidation, watching from a tall, third-floor window at the Wagener Building, as his entire nest-egg made its way out of the harbor. In hindsight, it is easy to see how poorly George had understood the lesson of his family's rise to power and wealth. His forbearers had wisely spread their money around, whereas George recklessly risked all on one throw of the proverbial dice. While the investment appeared sound, it went against the grain of nearly half a century of Poirier financial conservatism. As the sun went down behind him and the rest of the investors left to go home, he felt his apprehension ease a bit as the merchant ship steamed towards the Atlantic from the Charleston wharf.

Families indeed can rise in moments such as these, and others can fall, depending on fate and circumstance. George Poirier's life, and how he lived it, was the central issue. This desperate attempt to revive his flagging fortunes was ill-starred, and George watched in numb horror as the ship began issuing an ugly plume of black smoke. Something appeared terribly wrong, but George held out hope that it was a minor issue. It was not. A sailor on board the vessel, smoking in a forbidden area, carelessly ignited the cotton like a fuse. It burned quickly, despite the best efforts of the crew, until it reached the turpentine and phosphates. The explosive combination of these two shipments flared like a huge firecracker, and the ship blew up spectacularly. George Poirier, watching from his lone perch back in the city, literally watched his last chance at redemption burn as a false dawn in the middle of Charleston Harbor. The vessel, now reduced to a raging fire amid twisted wreckage, was completely destroyed, along with his dream of salvation.

One shudders at the images which no doubt floated through George Poirier's mind, as the dense black smoke hung like a pall over the city. His life of leisure and his family's fortune were both now irrevocably gone. His name, despite his late last honest effort to turn things around, would forever be linked to a foolishly squandered embarrassment of riches. Perhaps a man who was less dependent on family name and fortune would have recovered; but for an idle man-child like George, the idea of rolling up his shirt sleeves and carving out a different (and perhaps even somehow better) existence for himself would never have even occurred to him. George, reverting to his old ways, preferred a cowardly solution over hard work. One can picture him, perhaps steeling himself with a final drink, looking down out of the Wagener Building's top windows at the city he had always called home, and seeing not the beautiful architecture or the place of gentility and manners. No, he almost certainly saw only ruin and the coming ridicule from those he used to lord over.

Preferring death to poverty, he tossed a rope over an exposed beam, tied a noose, and positioned an old wingback chair on top of a desk. The issue was the drop: how far to do the trick? Too long of a fall can cause the head to be gruesomely ripped from the body, but too short means there is a high possibility of the neck not breaking. George chose his length and kicked the chair away, cravenly ending his life. Sadly, our failed businessman chose just a shade too short of a fall off of the chair, meaning he died of a slow, excruciating, gurgling death by strangulation. The drop was just long enough, however, to launch one of his eyes violently from its socket. It flew with such force that it arced out of the open window, and fell three stories onto the flagstones below.

After the early-morning commotion of finding a light blue disembodied eyeball on the sidewalk finally died down, the authorities entered the Wagener Building. There they found a pool of blood on the first level, and a corresponding stain on the first floor ceiling. They ascended to the second floor and found an identical scene: the blood was trickling through the floorboards all through the building's levels. They followed a strange sound up to the third floor of the Wagener Building, where they found a scene so disturbing that several of the men fled the scene to be emphatically sick. George Poirier's body, still hanging by the window, was a feast for crows and scavenging seabirds.

Spirits at the Brewery

Today, the building at 161 East Bay Street has been converted into a very prominent restaurant which also brews its own wonderful selection of beers: the Southend Brewery. The restaurant specializes in American cuisine, including burgers, steaks, chicken and fish. I have sampled the menu and found it to be very, very good pub-style food. The delicious spirits are all listed in a separate menu, but the ghosts, of course, are á la carte.

Many staff members complain of feeling a presence breeze past them, particularly on the upper floors. One former server claimed that a blurry figure knocked a food tray out of her hands (and her off of her feet) as it rushed past her. When I jokingly suggested that she might be smart to blame an incident where she was just a little clumsy and had dropped a tray of people's orders on a ghostly culprit, she asked me: "Really? Which is easier, to just apologize to the table and tell your co-workers that you slipped, or be forced to admit some sort of ghost knocked you down? I personally think it would have been easier to claim that I stumbled."

One manager reported the following incident: "A couple of years ago, we had a bartender at the end of the night who was attempting to turn off one of our wall-mounted flat screen televisions on the third floor. The remote control wasn't working, so he grabbed a pool cue from the nearby billiards table—these TV's are pretty high off the ground, understand—so he was trying to punch the switch on the side of the set with the pool cue to turn it off. Well, as he was doing this, he heard a man's voice laughing, very close to him. He whirled around but saw absolutely no one else with him there on the third floor. So he turned back around and tried to turn the set off that way again, but he heard the laughter again, and this time it was really close to him. I personally saw him come running down the stairs about as fast as I've ever seen anyone move, and his face was as white as a sheet. When I asked him what was wrong, he told me what had happened.

Then he added that for all he cared, the ghost could watch TV as long as it wanted!"

One group of tourists took a photo in the downstairs. It was intended as an innocuous vacation picture, just a snapshot where members of the party smile after a great meal. When the image appeared on the back of the digital camera, however, the woman who had been in the photograph began to gasp and hyperventilate. Pictured right next to her in the picture was the vaporous yet unmistakable image of a young child, sitting at the table right at her elbow. The child appeared to be wearing a kind of bonnet which was fashionable in the very early 1900's.

It has also been frequently said that around dusk, a strange sight has been reported by onlookers outside the building. Perhaps it is (but perhaps not) just a trick of the fading light, but many people over the years have claimed to see a corpse dangling from a noose in the upper windows. One October, a woman even marched angrily into the restaurant and demanded to see a manager over their morbidly realistic Halloween decoration which had so frightened her children. *We do not*, the manager was forced to tell her, *decorate for Halloween.*

Francis Marion Hotel

387 King Street

At the northwest corner of King and Calhoun Streets, sits a beautiful hotel, built in 1924. Named for a Revolutionary War hero who was known as 'The Swamp Fox,' the Francis Marion Hotel's elegant style and wonderful 'Roaring '20's' feel speak volumes about Charleston's sometimes overlooked significance, both commercially and socially, in the early 20th century. Touted as the city's first modern hotel, it was designed by noted architect William Lee Stoddard. After its completion, it became a center for social activities, primarily through the use of its ballroom for debutante dances and other events. But beyond the Francis Marion's reputation for elegance and comfort come other, darker rumors. It is whispered that the Francis Marion Hotel was the scene of forbidden love, heartbreak, and tragic death, the echoes of which still persist today. According to many, this is where a man named Ned Cohen plunged to his death one dark evening in 1929.

Shoes, Booze, and a Salesman's Blues

Exactly how much truth is in these stories of love gone terribly awry? Let's start by presenting the legend, precisely what you might hear if you were to take a ghost tour in Charleston:

A stunned Ned Cohen sat with his head in his hands, reading the note again. The elegant penmanship and apologetic tone provided no bandage for his heart's wound. She cannot mean this, Ned thought to himself, Evelyn cannot mean to hurt me like this. So he re-read the note yet again, as if it were some complicated contract and he was a lawyer, scrutinizing it for loopholes. But her note's simplistic denial of deeper feelings for him could not be misinterpreted. It was at this point that the wind billowed in through his room's windows at the Francis Marion Hotel, making his curtains flap like a child's wave: bye-bye,

bye-bye… Ned began to sob uncontrollably.

Just a few weeks before, his life seemed so bright and full of promise. Normally a painfully shy person, Ned was almost forcibly dragged to a nightclub by a few co-workers in New York City. Although he was very young, he was hardworking and was considered a rising star by the company he worked for, Florsheim Shoes. He recently received word that he was one of a few finalists to become a regional sales manager for the shoe company, and these co-workers insisted that he celebrate the news. "I've been told that the job is yours, Ned. The search is just a formality," one of them told him. So Ned allowed them to take him out to a jazz joint. Ned was nervous because the nightclub served liquor, and he had never indulged, but his companions insisted that it was safe despite Prohibition being in full effect. The staff did seem to be quite comfortable in selling booze, despite openly flaunting the law. It took a few minutes, despite his cohort's assurances, for him to finally relax and listen to the music. And what music! Being from a small town near Cooperstown, Ned had never heard anything like it. This was nothing like his mother's polka records. He sat enthralled by the hypnotic scene for a long time.

Another colleague leaned over and said, "Ned, you need to loosen up. Have a drink, and check out your five o'clock." Ned glanced at his watch. "What happens at five o'clock?" He asked. The co-worker had to explain what he meant: "Five on the clock face. Behind you, and to the right. That girl can't take her eyes off of you." Ned squirmed in his seat to get a look. Sitting directly behind him was the most beautiful girl he had ever seen, and she looked at him expectantly. He turned back around, dumbstruck, not knowing what to do. His friend handed him a five dollar bill and said, "Buy her a drink, Ned."

Despite his awkwardness, Ned and the young lady wound up hitting it off. She introduced herself as Evelyn, visiting from Charleston. He found the Southern lilt to her voice intoxicating, and all it took was three martinis for him to summon up the courage to tell her so. He started telling her all about his job at the shoe company, and asked what she did for a living, but she demurred. "No work talk, Ned. This evening is about pleasure." And so it was. Their night was all about passion and intensity, and Ned fell hard for the beautiful Southern belle. She seemed surprised by his naïveté and aw-shucks charm, so she agreed to see him the next night too. When he said that he loved her, Evelyn gave him a sad smile and said, "Please don't complicate things, Ned. This is fun, but we live in different worlds." She did give him her address, however.

When the weekend was over, Ned returned to work and Evelyn headed south, back to Charleston. His co-workers demanded all the salacious details, but

The Francis Marion Hotel, reputedly the scene of a tragic suicide the echoes of which resonate today.

Ned was tight-lipped about his lady-love. He was a gentleman, and didn't want to sully the honor of the woman he was madly in love with. A few days later, the new regional sales titles were handed out, and Ned was promoted. When his boss asked him which territory he would like, Ned did not hesitate: "South Carolina." A few of his co-workers exchanged a wary look amongst themselves that poor love-struck Ned mistook for sadness. They tried to talk Ned out of leaving, but he waved them away.

Ned went south a couple of weeks later. His first stop was at the Francis Marion Hotel, where he got cleaned up, and his second stop was to the address written in Evelyn's elegant hand. She was shocked to see him, to say the least, and somewhat reluctantly agreed to have dinner with him the following night. Their passion seemed to rekindle immediately, and the two wound up back at Ned's room at the Francis Marion Hotel.

Ned awoke later that evening to find Evelyn gone. A small note was on the pillow. It read:

Ned, you are a very nice fellow, but I cannot see you again. That night back in New York was all a set-up. Your friends paid me. I feel badly about you moving here, so tonight was free of charge. Goodbye forever.

Ned was absolutely devastated. He could not return to the shame of New York City: everyone would know who—what—he had fallen in love with. And every moment he spent in Charleston was a reminder of what a fool he had been. No, he thought grimly, there is but one thing to do.

Ned's shattered body was discovered shortly after midnight on the sidewalk below, very close to the intersection with Calhoun Street. He had apparently dressed himself in his finest suit, put Evelyn's note and her address in his pocket, and jumped to his doom from his eleventh story room. He himself left no suicide note or other explanation for his actions, but to the detectives investigating, it was all very clear. Poor Ned had gotten in over his head and lost his mind over the wrong woman.

Ned was buried in his native Cooperstown NY, but his spirit lives on in Charleston. Now many tour guides claim that you can still see young Ned, pacing the hallways in the moments leading up to his suicide. Others, and these are always ladies experiencing this phenomenon, claim to feel light touches on their faces, as if poor Ned Cohen is reaching out to feel an interaction—any interaction—with a woman, right before his fateful plunge.

How Much Of This Is True?

How much of this story is fact, and how much is fiction? Well, I did an exhaustive search of available records, and found that there is no record of anyone named Ned Cohen dying in Charleston in or around 1929, much less by plummeting from the Francis Marion Hotel. A death that gruesome would certainly have made the papers. In fact, I found no evidence of any suicides at the Francis Marion, ever, in its ninety-plus years of history. The lack of a death certificate or corroboration in any of the local papers from that time period almost certainly means that the story of Ned Cohen's tragic flirtations with a local gal is fiction, and nothing more.

In my research, I could find no logical explanations for any hauntings at this particular location, but this does not mean that the ghostly activity reported at the Francis Marion Hotel is bogus, necessarily. I have found that certain spots with legitimate hauntings often have colorfully fictitious folklore attached, as a way of explaining away the resident spirit. Tour guides and storytellers will often invent a captivating backstory just to entertain their listeners. Sometimes the haunting begets a story, not the other way around, and at least the tale of Ned Cohen is engaging. Who doesn't like a good yarn? And the story of Mr. Cohen, he who was too rash in his actions, serves as a perfect cautionary tale. Wearing one's heart on one's sleeve can get you hurt, or as in Ned's case, it can even get you killed.

The Old Jail

21 Magazine Street

*I*s there a plot of ground in Charleston which has seen more misery, suffering and death than the Old Charleston District Jail? To study this building's history is to uncover some of the darkest moments in this city's long narrative. Designed specifically to be a forbidding fortress, it has been home to some of the very worst mankind can offer: murderers and sadists of every sort have been stationed here, and that is just speaking of the guards at the prison, not the inmates. We have some well-known names attached (accurately or not, as we'll uncover) to this edifice, from the very famous, such as architect Robert Mills (designer of the Washington Monument in Washington, DC), to Charleston's most infamous, such as John and Lavinia Fisher, and Denmark Vesey. When you factor in both the tragic use of the land itself before the prison even existed coupled with the jail's sordidly grim history from 1802 through 1939, what we have are, quite simply, perhaps the most perfect conditions for hauntings in Charleston. One oft-repeated claim about the building is that through the years, over forty thousand prisoners died within its walls. Stories abound from eyewitnesses regarding miserable, tortured souls still trapped in this prison. It is a structure which, despite falling mostly out of use for the last three quarters of a century, still gives off an unpleasant, hostile aura.

The area was designated for public use as early as 1680. This patch of ground which saw use as a poorhouse, a public burying ground, and a hospital. As was common in English colonies, punishments for crimes initially focused on humiliation as opposed to incarceration. Punishments in early Charleston included branding, whipping, and public humiliations like being placed in pillories (stocks), where the local populace could fling vegetables, dirt and dung at the offender. The reason for public punishments this was both financial and religious: tossing someone in jail was expensive, and colonists saw crime as an extension of sinful behavior. However by the late 1790's, the City Fathers began to see a need for a centralized prison. Up until that time a variety of structures had been used, with little success.

She told me: "All my life I've been sensitive to spirits. I can hear them, usually, but sometimes I can see them, too. And this building terrifies me…"

"We were walking back past it to exit the building out the back door, and that's when something leaned around the doorway, just like it was looking down the hallway at us."

Makeshift structures were hard to maintain and easily escapable for the convicted. The new prison would have to be strong, secure, and its very appearance would need to serve as a crime-deterrent. The site in question, which had also been the location of several powder magazines (hence it being named Magazine Street), was chosen, and a simple three story brick building was constructed on the plot of ground. It measured roughly 100 x 50 feet, but the new structure was inadequately constructed. Sheriff Nathaniel G. Cleary wrote of the prison in 1812, complaining "that in its present situation and condition in points of health and security is truly deplorable and unsafe…the ceiling nearest the roof… can be cut through by prisoners and after they get through this ceiling it is a very easy matter to… let themselves to the ground and in this way make their escape."

Funds for the construction of the jail were so low that they couldn't afford a well to supply adequate drinking water for inmates, or running water for latrines. Prisoners had to utilize buckets for their waste, and were forced to coexist with the slop buckets brimming until they could be collected. Unsanitary conditions were rampant, and the jail must have reeked from over a block away.

Although the structure has been added onto many times over the years, part of this original building remains, tucked away in the center section. It had no towers, no ornate trim, and the multiple additions which would be added in stages had not yet occurred. It was this early simple rectangular prison which housed perhaps the most famous inmates in the history of the Old Charleston District Jail, namely John and Lavinia Fisher (please see their accompanying chapter). The two were convicted on highway robbery in 1819 and hanged the following year, so they spent roughly a year at this location. However, according to many tour guides, the prison allegedly had other notorious inmates.

A Man Named Denmark

Another famous supposed inmate was Denmark Vesey, who attempted to organize a slave rebellion in 1822. He was born in 1767 and originally named Telemaque. Little is known about Vesey's origins. His documentation begins when he was already a slave belonging to Captain Joseph Vesey. One plausible theory was that he was part of a shipment of slaves moved by Captain Vesey in 1781 from the Danish Virgin Islands, and that geographical reference is how he gained his new name. Captain Vesey retired to Charleston in 1783, and Denmark came with him. Denmark, who gained a reputation as a very skilled laborer, earned his freedom from slavery in 1799, when he won fifteen hundred dollars in a city-run lottery. He used six hundred dollars of his new fortune to buy his freedom, and used the remaining funds towards purchasing a home at 20 Bull Street, which is somewhat ironically very close to the building in which he would later be imprisoned.

Denmark became heavily involved in African Methodist Episcopalian Church, and became a church leader in part because he could read. He began to passionately preach that everyone deserved freedom. His philosophy seemed to be more in line with the future "by any means necessary" equal-rights leader Malcolm X, rather than the nonviolent path of Martin Luther King, Jr. Vesey began to agitate more and more for a violent slave uprising as the second decade of the 19th century drew to a close, hoping to emulate the successful slave uprising in Haiti. He began to organize an army of enslaved and free blacks, preaching that they were justified in rising up, killing their masters, and fleeing south to enjoy their freedom in Haiti.

White Charlestonians lived in terror of a slave uprising such as the one planned by Vesey. Supposedly Denmark Vesey's followers numbered in the thousands in Charleston and the surrounding Lowcountry. The date for the uprising was set for mid-July in 1822, but his plan was discovered when several slaves opposed to Vesey's scheme revealed the plot to their masters. Charleston authorities, acting quickly, charged 131 men with conspiracy, and 67 men were convicted. 35 of these men were condemned to die, including Denmark Vesey. On July 2nd, 1822, they were taken out to Blake's Land, an area close to modern-day I-26 and Line Street (where, coincidentally, John and Lavinia Fisher met their end two years' previous), and hanged. Denmark Vesey and his accomplices supposedly went to the gallows without uttering a single word, glaring at their captors in chilling, stony silence.

While it is true that Vesey was incarcerated, he was not held at the prison which exists today at 21 Magazine Street. Denmark and his co-conspirators would have been held at the neighboring Work (or Sugar) House, next door to the prison. A former slave named William Pinkney dictated his recollections of the site in 1917: "The Sugar House was on the corner of Magazine and Logan Streets… a grocery store stands on the site now. If a slave ran away or misbehaved he was put there to be sold or punished. One form of punishment was treading the wheel. If the slave fell off he broke his leg. The law allowed five paddle strokes and five cowhides. The slave was made to take off his clothes and was struck anywhere. A good many died from the effects of the whipping. Stocks were also used as a form of punishment, [and] sometimes the slaves died in [the] stocks."

It was this building, and not the main jailhouse, which was set aside for slaves and freed blacks like Vesey and his compatriots, so any stories about the spirit of Denmark Vesey haunting the Old Charleston District Jail are false. The structure in which he was actually held was long-since demolished.

Additions

It was perhaps due to the (temporarily) successful escape of John Fisher in 1819 that improvements and additions to the jailhouse were green-lighted. According to the famous architect Robert Mills in his 1826 book *Statistics of South Carolina*, he added a southeastern wing (now demolished) onto the main building. It appears that the Work House and

Third Floor, Holding Cell No. 3, View From Window. Obtained from the Library of Congress Prints and Photographs Division.

Lunatic Asylum were constructed very close to the prison walls during this same time period, making this a forbidding area, indeed. He described his jailhouse addition as "a four story wing building, devoted exclusively to the confinement of criminals." He related that it was spacious, clean, and comfortable. Even if his description was accurate at the time, by 1851, the reputation of the jail had changed radically. An investigation into the conditions at 21 Magazine Street found the structure(s) to be completely inadequate for their proscribed purpose. Despite heavy lobbying by some to tear down and begin anew, plans were made to completely renovate and refurbish the old jail, beginning with tearing Robert Mills' addition down. Architects Barbot and Seyle renovated the increasingly elderly building, adding the famously harsh Gothic façade, the forbidding towers, and a fourth floor. The octagonal cell block was also added during this time period, which originally featured a tower in the center. Supposedly this tower was used for ventilation, but it might also have been an observation post for guards, or even been used to confine prisoners. The walls were thickened and reinforced during this time as well, and the entire complex got a fresh coat of stucco.

By 1861, part of the jail served a new purpose as a military prison. Because the interior of the prison was already overflowing with common criminals, Union prisoners were housed in the jail's yard. They were exposed to truly inhuman conditions, including extreme weather, lack of sanitation, and dealing with vermin. Many Federal captives held at the prison complained bitterly about the miserable conditions they endured there, in books and letters they wrote long after their horrifying experiences at the Charleston Jail. I will not recount their letters here because they are too numerous and horrible to contemplate, but the lowlights include: six hundred officers being forced to share fifty tents, rations of rice which were infested with bugs, no way to launder clothes, and epidemics of disease and lice upon the starving men. The conditions described in these chilling accounts are positively hellish.

Receiving even worse treatment were the captured soldiers of the Massachusetts 54th, a black regiment which had unsuccessfully attempted to storm Battery Wagner (as recounted in the 1989 blockbuster film *Glory*). Some of the survivors of their gallant assault in the Confederate stronghold were sent to the Charleston District Jail yard, and were treated roughly by their jailers. They were required to do menial labor in a way never expected of their fellow white prisoners. There is no way of calculating how many of these soldiers, white and black, died at the old jail before the eventual release of the survivors at the conclusion of the war in 1865.

Earthquakes and Other Tragedies

On August 31st, 1886, tragedy struck Charleston which forever altered the jail's form. The largest earthquake to ever strike the Eastern Seaboard shook the city, collapsing buildings and houses and killing well over a hundred people. The jail did not ride out the seismic blast very well, riddling the entire structure with cracks and doing serious structural damage to the walls. The *Charleston Courier's* September 1st, 1886 article states:

The scene at the jail beggars description. When the building began to shake the prisoners made a dash for the door. Capt. Kelly, however, stood at the door, pistol in hand, and firing half a dozen shots kept the crowd back. Their shrieks could be heard for squares and many of the inmates dashed themselves madly against the bars in an effort to escape. They were kept within doors, however, and although the building was badly shattered none of them escaped.

The prisoners had to be moved to a temporary holding area while the prison was repaired. The Work House, however, was so damaged that it had to be demolished. Sometime in the 1890's, the fourth floor of the prison was completely removed, presumably for safety reasons. Also gone was the tower, which had partially collapsed in the quake.

The jail was even the scene of a shooting. In 1912, an assistant jailer named Clarence Levy drew his pistol and fired shots at Captain William Wingate of the city chain gang. Levy, who claimed self-defense, related that Wingate threatened him over the outcome of a political election. Wingate then reached for a firearm in his pocket, but Levy got his pistol out first and shot Wingate in the chest. The victim survived his wounds, and the shooter was held in the very jail where he worked before his trial. He was acquitted in the shooting by a jury.

In 1939, the hopelessly outdated structure had met its end as a useful jailhouse. The city of Charleston received a federal grant to build low-income housing, and the area adjacent to the Old Jail was selected. According to a *Charleston Post and Courier* article, the prisoners were transferred on September 15th, 1939. After that date, the building was locked up and used only as storage. After 137 years of misery, the Old Charleston District Jail finally closed. It sat vacant for six decades.

The building today is owned by the American College of the Building Arts, which purchased it from the city in 1999. The school uses the Old Jail as their main campus, providing students with hands-on training in

First Floor, Kitchen, View From North of Dumbwaiter Shaft. Obtained from the Library of Congress Prints and Photographs Division.

historic preservation. The college itself has no official position on ghosts, but a prominent member of the administration I spoke to at the college (who opted to remain anonymous) did confirm the presence of a deep spiritual side there. "Mostly for me it is just a feeling of the place being unsettled. I haven't had any experiences with seeing ghosts or anything like that. It's more subtle. For me, it's just a feeling of… I don't know… that there's something incredibly sad and—I guess 'lost' is the right word. I know some members of the faculty and even some students have felt this same sensation. Or even other, more overt things." He paused a very long time, as if pondering how much to say, or possibly wondering if he has said too much. "We don't hype it, or even like to really talk about it, because our focus naturally is on education and the building arts. But it's there. That's the reason we have allowed the nighttime tours to come in, to at least acknowledge that there is something mysterious going on inside this building that very few people understand."

At least a few of these incidents have made the local papers. A *Charleston Post and Courier* article appeared in late October 2002, which chronicled the experiences of several members of the staff. Ray Rice, a blacksmith hired by the college to help renovate the Old Jail into being a functional classroom space, was working late, all alone, to finish a project. A skeptic when it came to ghosts, Rice had nonetheless heard several stories that old inmates still haunted the building. His skepticism changed, however, when he came face to face with something he could not explain. He was walking down a hallway towards the back exit when he got the distinct impression that something was amiss.

The article recounts Rice's story: "The jail was quiet, save for the sound of his feet brushing against the cold concrete. But he was not alone. He stopped and shined his flashlight on the back door. That's when he saw him, a tall, thin man in a dark suit standing to the right of the exit. Rice stared at the man for a long moment. He seemed off somehow, Rice thought. His eyes were hollow and he had a grayish complexion. When Rice moved toward him the man disappeared, only to reappear on the left side of the door and then disappear again."

Rice quickly left, and didn't tell anyone about what had happened to him for several days. When he finally opened up, he was surprised to learn that many other workers also had experiences in the Old Jail. Some of the renovation experts had felt a sensation of someone tapping them on their shoulders, or even placing hands on their faces. The article continues: "'There is something in there,' says Lea Cloyd, the project manager. 'I really believe that. I don't necessarily think it's evil or anything, but it's there.'" Cloyd goes on to state that once as she entered a cell, she felt someone press both of their hands to her face, in an attempt to keep her from entering. "'Not violently,' she says... 'A few weeks later my husband had the exact same experience in the exact same place. He won't go back in the jail now.'"

Another renovation story related by the article was the time that workers removed some lead paint. The work kicked up a lot of dust, which was hazardous if breathed. The workers therefore wore respirators and protective suits, and then the dust was allowed to settle before proper clean-up and disposal commenced. One day Cloyd entered the cell room, which had been locked up tight for weeks. She found more than just the dust she was expecting, however: she also discovered the unmistakable impression of human footprints all over the dusty floor. Someone with very small bare feet had walked all over the floor in the locked cell, a phenomenon that Cloyd was completely at a loss to explain.

Third Floor, Cell No. 4, Entrance From Hall, Door Open. Obtained from the Library of Congress Prints and Photographs Division.

In an article which appeared a few days later in the same paper, a *Post and Courier* reporter, Bryce Donovan, volunteered to stay the night completely alone in the Old Jail. Even though he was a firm disbeliever in ghosts, he reported hearing noises coming from deep inside the building. He kept taking deep breaths and repeating to himself that he did not believe in ghosts, despite the strange, unexplainable sounds coming from within the old prison.

Tour Guides' Experiences

I sat down one evening with longtime Charleston tour guide Ginger Williams, and she filled me in about her strange experiences at the Old Charleston District Jail. "I ran tours through the Old Jail for about four years," Ginger related. "It can be a creepy place. It isn't generally creepy when you have a tour group of twenty people with you, although some unnerving things have happened then, too. But as a tour guide at the end of the night and you're by yourself to set the alarms… and you *know* that there is nobody in there to make the noises that you're hearing, but they are definitely there? I mean there's no other way to rationalize it, other than to conclude that yes, the building is haunted. I've heard doors move, and these are heavy solid iron doors weighing several hundred pounds apiece, so you know it's not the wind. It takes a real effort to move them. After six months of working there, you get very familiar with the sound that each door makes—each one has a very distinctive groan—so you know exactly which door is moving in the completely deserted jail. You know the building is empty, because you just ushered out everyone from the tour and you're the last living soul in there, and yet, the sounds are there. I've also heard footsteps, and seen unexplainable shadows moving, as well. Yes, it can be a creepy place."

I asked Ginger about the scariest thing that she ever encountered while working there. "Probably the scariest moment of my life happened in the jail. It was a night in January, I think this was 2009 or so. It was a full tour, meaning twenty other people had the same exact experience that I did." Ginger briefly recounted how the tour would unfold, namely entering the jail from the rear through the old work yard, and exiting at the same location. "Anyway, we got back to that first room that you come to on the tour where we talk about the 'crane of pain,' which was a method of disciplining prisoners during that era. We were walking back past it to exit the building out the back door, and that's when something leaned around the

First Floor, Exhibit Cel Doorways From East to West. Obtained from the Library of Congress Prints and Photographs Division.

THE OLD JAIL

Third Floor, North Section Northwest Room, Spiral Stair from Southeast. Obtained from the Library of Congress Prints and Photographs Division.

doorway, just like it was looking down the hallway at us. It was the single most terrifying thing I've ever seen in my life. It looked like a dark-colored skull, and where the eye sockets should have been there were red rings of light. It was *incredibly* frightening. The man closest to me in the tour group almost knocked me down trying to get away. We had to run past this thing, because that was the only door out. Once we were all safely outside, we all agreed what we had seen—we were describing the same thing. Some friends of mine who are paranormal investigators came in a few nights later and caught a picture of two red rings of light deep within the old jail. I think they captured his eyes in the photo." Ginger's arms had broken out in chills, but she seemed not to notice.

"There were funny things, too, where I would lose my keys. I would put my keys in my pocket when I arrived there for the first tour, and notice partway through the night that they were no longer in my pocket. At the end of the night, my keys would be sitting on the staircase right where I would have to pass on my way out when I was ready to leave. So there was some playful energy there, not negative at all." I brought up that in an old jail like that, keys would certainly draw some interest, and Ginger smiled. "Definitely! There was a 'key attraction,' and it would just seem to make sense that there was."

I asked Ginger if she had encountered any malevolent spirits other than the apparition that had been seen by her tour group. She nodded. "There was a ghost whose presence was always preceded by the smell of sweet pipe tobacco. It was really a distinct odor that just didn't belong, and it was accompanied by an oppressive vibe, a really 'not nice,' uncomfortable, heavy feeling. Well, I was once on a ghost investigation in the jail. Most of the team was setting up equipment so I had a moment to myself. I was just trying to stay out of the way of their investigation, so I was in the middle of the second-floor cellblock on the eastern side of the jail, leaning against a pole. And I began to smell it, that sort of sweet cherry smell of pipe tobacco. There were loose bricks lying all around in various parts of the room, including the windowsills. One of those bricks flew off the windowsill and landed by my foot! There were screens in all of the windows, so it wasn't like it could have been thrown from the outside. I believe that particular spirit was demonstrating that he could have really hurt me if he wanted to, and that was not exactly a friendly action. I would notice over my years of running tours that the pipe tobacco smell was sort of a warning that he wasn't happy—you know, like he was saying, 'This is your first warning.' And if that went unheeded he would move objects, like moving doors, or that one incident with the brick, as if saying, 'This is your second warning.'

THE OLD JAIL

Second Floor, Hallway from North to South of Octagonal Section. Obtained from the Library of Congress Prints and Photographs Division.

Well, I never wanted to see what that third warning would be, you know? If he can throw a brick, who knows what he might do next? He seemed to be confined to the cell blocks, which is one of the oldest parts of the Old Jail, so on the nights he would act up I would always move my tour group into the octagon, which was newer, and he wouldn't follow. It's almost as if he didn't recognize that as part of the jail, which makes me think that perhaps he was a jailer or even a warden, but not a prisoner, from the very early 1800's.

"They're not all negative spirits, though. There's one in the old jail yard that really likes me, apparently. On the right side of the property, the western side, there's an iron gate where tour groups would enter. The gate is never locked, we would just always pull it shut, but there is a heavy iron arm there for the purposes of locking it that swings down if you'd need it. We always left it down, but obviously never slipped a padlock through it. Well, I went to open the gate one night as a tour was ending and didn't realize that the arm was up, so when I opened the gate the heavy metal bar came crashing down on me. It reached my forearm and just stopped itself in mid-air, so something stopped it, almost protectively. A few members of my tour saw this, and gave me a funny look, and all I could do was shrug at them."

I asked for her overall impression of the Old Jail, and Ginger sat silently for a moment, gathering her thoughts. "Can you imagine for a moment being in that prison when it was in use? I cannot fathom how terrible it would be, with no real heating or air conditioning. I've been inside there in the late evenings in the summer on the upper floors, and even at ten p.m. it's got to be close to a hundred and twenty degrees. That's when the building is empty. Imagine it packed to capacity, and the chamber pots would be overflowing, because there was no plumbing. The sights, sounds, and smells of the place would be overwhelming. So I think it's much too easy, as a storyteller, to talk about the place as being evil or scary. But the real story is much better than the fiction. It's harder but much more rewarding to talk about how incredibly *sad* the Old Charleston Jail is, not evil or bad. I feel one hundred percent that the jail is a living, breathing entity, and an important piece of history. It's an amazing place."

"I Felt Something Touch Me..."

Longtime tour guide, Mark Jones, confirmed that he has also had several strange things happen inside the Old Jail. Two incidents stood out to him, from the multiple unexplained things he had observed while leading tours at the property.

"I was standing next to a metal cellblock door at the bottom of the iron staircase," Mark said. "I was right next to the door, which was shut. As I was speaking, I, felt a hand place itself on my shoulder, and yet no one was near me. Of course, I was mid-sentence when I felt that sensation, and if I were to jump or scream at that point, the folks on tour would think that it was staged, or all for show. So I just kept speaking and didn't mention it to anybody. I took my tour group outside and finished up the tour. Well at that point an older woman who had been on the tour, I'd guess she was fifty-five or so, approached me and asked, 'Did you have something happen to you tonight?' And I replied, yes. And she says, 'Did it happen by the staircase?' And I said, 'Yes ma'am, I felt something touch me.' And all she said was, 'I could tell.'

"Another incident involves a spirit who has been seen multiple times, both by me and other guides. The apparition is a white male, wearing a white shirt. On this particular evening I had a school group touring the jail. These were older kids, high school aged. Anyway, I had them on the first floor at the main staircase, and I was narrating. The crowd was around me, and a few of them were actually standing on the staircase to get a better view. One of these kids on the steps was a girl who was probably thirteen or so. As I glanced up, I noticed a man standing on the stairs who was not part of the school group. It was the apparition that I had seen a few times before, and he was just standing there, motionless. I guess I stared, because that girl saw me looking, followed my gaze with her eyes, and her eyes got wide. She looked back at me, kind of questioning, and some measure of understanding passed between us that we had both seen him. Keep in mind, I'm still talking this entire time, and I really must give her credit: she didn't flip out, or scream, or point. She just seemed to take it all in stride. The man vanished a few moments later. This happened pretty close to the beginning of the tour, so a little over a half an hour later, I took the group back outside and ended. They started all walking off and she turned back and asked me, 'You saw that too, right?' And I said that I did. And she says, 'I just wanted to make sure. I was pretty sure you did. Who was it?' And I told her I didn't know, but it wasn't my first time seeing him. She thought about that for a moment, got a big smile on her face, and she said, *'That is so cool!'*"

I began to ask Mark, who has been a guide for many years, how he kept his composure in both situations, even continuing to narrate uninterrupted. It occurred to me before I voiced my query, however, that experienced tour guides and jail inmates are similar in one crucial regard: both serve their sentences uninterrupted.

"...This Building Terrifies Me..."

On a blustery and unseasonably cold night in Charleston in December 2013, I stood outside the Old Jail, bundled in multiple layers of clothing, camera in hand. Despite my leather jacket, wool scarf and fingerless gloves, I was chilled to the bone. I was out at a very late hour taking photos of some of Charleston's more famous haunted landmarks, and the Old Jail on Magazine Street was my last stop of the evening. Taking long exposure photographs at night takes an inordinate amount of time, especially when dealing with a tripod and a timer to capture crystal clear images. I once overheard a professional photographer say that for every hundred photos that he took, maybe three or four were of a decent quality. I am decidedly not a professional photographer by any stretch of the imagination, so I make up for this shortcoming in training and acumen by shooting a dizzying number of photos of each location.

It was so cold, however, that my mind was already turning to thoughts of hot showers and steaming mugs of cocoa back in my hotel room, which was only a short walk away. The street and surrounding area was seemingly completely deserted, which although it made my task easier, it also gave the jailhouse an even more imposing, oppressive vibe. As I worked to frame up my shots, I became aware of a curious jingling sound from behind me. I turned around to see a young woman very quietly walking her dog, a Boston terrier, on the Magazine Street sidewalk opposite the building. The jingling sound was his collar. The dog walked up to me and introduced himself, so she stopped to talk to me; I suppose she was curious why I had chosen such an inhospitable night to take photos of old buildings. So I told her briefly what my writing project entailed, and why I was taking photos of the jail.

"That place gives me the absolute creeps," she said flatly. I agreed, and started talking about the dreadful conditions which had once existed there, and the grim history of the building. She interrupted me, however, stating, "Well, that very well might be true, but I'm talking about the present, not the past. That place makes my hair stand up just walking by it, and the only reason I go anywhere near it is because of Nomar." It took me a second to

Second Floor, Cell Room No. 2, Detail of Door from East. Obtained from the Library of Congress Prints and Photographs Division.

realize she was talking about the dog, who apparently got his name from a certain former Boston Red Sox shortstop. He was even wearing a Red Sox collar. I scratched an appreciative Nomar behind the ears, and she kept talking. "He has his usual circuit, and so Nomar insists on walking past here at least twice a day. He complains and pulls at the leash if I don't walk him here." She took a long look back up at the Old Jail and said, "But I hate it." At this point I absolutely had to inquire why.

"All my life I've been sensitive to spirits. I can hear them, usually, but sometimes I can see them, too. And this building terrifies me because of what I've seen and what I've heard. I don't like to see people suffer. I can't even watch a scary movie on TV, because even though I know that it's make-believe, I just feel so bad. But this place?" She gestured: "I've experienced such sadness from this building: sometimes there are faces looking out of the windows, calling for food, or water, or cigarettes. I've seen men in the yard over there that look like skeletons, sort of… hobbling around. Sometimes I just hear crying and wailing, or worse." I wondered aloud what could be worse than crying or wailing. She gave me a hard look.

"Well, a few of them have said some pretty obscene things to me." I thought about a bunch of men, trapped together in cells for a long time together, seeing a woman alone out on the street… yes, that would make a certain amount of perverse sense that they would harass her, I observed. "Well," she said as she and Nomar resumed their walk, "I might have to move, or Nomar might just have to find a new place to do his business. Because I can't take it anymore."

As the pair of them moved along, I found myself edging away from the building, abruptly feeling like I had taken enough photos for one evening. And my sudden bout of chills had nothing whatsoever to do with the temperature. One could feel the desperate gnaw of sadness emanating from the old structure, a permeating miasma of grief and rage which stains the location, perhaps for all time. A former burial ground turned into a prison (with a neighboring, since-demolished slave house), this site gives off a suffocatingly negative aura that must be experienced in person to truly be appreciated. In all my travels and writings, this building might exemplify the perfect cauldron of gloom and despair. I gave the Old Charleston District Jail a wide berth, physically as well as psychically, as a made my way back to my hotel.

Poogan's Porch

72 Queen Street

One of the very best restaurants serving Southern cuisine is located at 72 Queen Street in Charleston. I don't care how long the line is: when I visit the Palmetto City, I am eating at Poogan's; and yes, it's a restaurant named after a stray dog.

Built in 1888, this grand Victorian building has spent the majority of its life as a private residence. However, by the mid-1970's the area was turning increasingly into businesses due to the shifting nature of the commercial district. So in 1976 the owners sold the house and moved away, and the building became a restaurant. However, a little scruffy neighborhood dog named Poogan, who was not quite the former owners' dog yet not quite a stray, refused to leave his beloved home. So the restaurant inherited a dog, one which seemed to rule the neighborhood. He expected treats and ear-scratches from passersby and residents, and the throne-room of this canine king of Queen Street was the front porch of the restaurant. He served as official greeter, mascot, and namesake of the joint. I mean, what better to name Poogan's porch than Poogan's Porch? When Poogan passed on a few years later, the restaurant owners gave him a cherished grave (with statue) in the front yard.

A Dark Presence

Poogan's Porch is not all great food, sunshine, and puppies, however. There is another, shadowy spirit in residence at the restaurant. Some would call her a malevolent presence, and others…? Well, they just call her Zoe. I spoke to Luis, a manager at Poogan's Porch, about their resident spirit.

Luis related that a woman named Zoe St. Amand owned the house along with her older sister, Elizabeth, in the middle part of the 1900's. Neither sister ever married. The pair were almost a stereotype of spin-

"... he reported coffee cups moving on their own, and forks and knives practically dancing their way across the tables."

sters from that time period, complete with matching wire-rimmed glasses, dowdy, dark-colored, high-necked dresses, and hair cinched into the tightest bun imaginable. "The pair were inseparable," said Luis. "It was very much a 'glove fits hand' situation." Zoe was a schoolteacher, and to say that she was a rigid schoolmarm was putting it mildly. Luis continued: "Her reputation was that she was very stern and no-nonsense." Former children under her tutelage recalled her strict teaching style in a less-than-flattering light: "She made us cut the erasers off of our pencils to keep us from being tempted to make mistakes," one former student remembered, years later.

However, when Elizabeth died in 1945, Zoe, in the throes of mourning her dead sibling, went completely mad. Many oldtimers describe Zoe as a sad old woman in black looking out of her upstairs bedroom window at a world to which she had no connection. Zoe departed this life in 1954: a fall down the stairs snuffed out her already-sad existence. Or did it?

Ever since her death, it has been well documented that an apparition exactly matching Zoe's description has been seen numerous times. More often than not, people report seeing Zoe from across the street, at the elegant Mills House Hotel. The sightings are so frequent that hotel staff, upon hearing that there is a sad-looking older woman trapped after-hours in the restaurant across Queen Street, simply tell guests that they just experienced a sighting of one of Charleston's more famous ghosts. On the rare occasion that the hotel guests call the police directly, the investigating officers always find the doors locked up tight, a deserted building, and the alarms still armed and set.

Luis also revealed that many members of the restaurant staff had their own experiences with Zoe, and he was happy to relate them. "Just one example: we have a biscuit chef who has worked here for over thirty-five years. The man is a devout Christian, and has no reason to embellish. Well, he was working here at five a.m., preparing our famous biscuits, and he reported coffee cups moving on their own, and forks and knives practically dancing their way across the tables. He quite understandably found this very distracting from his job duties." Luis smiled, and then told of another strange occurrence: "We had a worker making repairs one morning. This worker was all alone in the restaurant, and he fixed himself a cup of strong black coffee. Suddenly he heard a tremendous clatter in the kitchen, sounding like all the pots and pans came crashing down at once. He set his coffee down on the first floor bannister and rushed off to see what had happened. He found everything to be in perfect order, however, and not a thing damaged or out of place. He was still shaking his head with the oddness of that unexplainable occurrence when he realized that his cup of coffee was missing from where he had set it. A search for his mug finally resulted in him finding his steaming hot beverage on the second floor bannister, not the first floor where he had left it. Even stranger was the fact that there was now a lipstick stain on the rim which had not been there mere minutes before. Someone had moved his coffee upstairs and sampled it, despite the fact that this worker was all alone in a locked building. He decided to not make the repairs while he was there by himself, and wisely waited to have others present when he worked."

Luis also told of a hostess who spotted an old woman in a dark dress who had apparently ignored the 'please wait to be seated' sign at the entrance, and had instead seated herself in an empty dining room. The hostess decided to offer to get the woman a beverage and politely try to move her to the appropriate section. Before this hostess could speak to the somber woman sitting alone, however, the older woman vanished before her very eyes.

"Zoe is sometimes seen on the second floor by patrons of the restaurant, and that would make sense, since that was Zoe's residence. She also has been known to follow women to the ladies room. Sometimes Zoe's presence manifests as a simple tickling, which would be disturbing enough considering that it is occurring in the ladies room and in theory one could not easily get away from Zoe's attentions," Luis's eyes twinkled mirthfully. "It might be a little difficult to stand to avoid it. People have even reported seeing her reflection behind them in the mirror. She does not appear to discriminate: young or old, and people from all walks of life have bolted out of that rest room, completely white-knuckled."

We both chuckled over the image for a long moment, and then Luis grew more serious. "The owners and staff here want to make it clear that we mean no disrespect to Ms. St. Amand, as funny as a few of these occurrences may be. The reality of the situation is that her presence is here, and we know and accept that. We have chosen to co-exist peacefully, and we are quite proud of our restaurant, ghosts included."

Poogan's Porch seems to have at least made peace with the fact that their establishment is haunted, even if they have not made peace with their ghost. I suppose they simply realized that Zoe was here first. Their lives and business will go smoother if they simply acquiesce to the fact that their building, which once came part-and-parcel with a small dog, also now features the shadowy form of a former schoolteacher. Ms. St. Amand is one of the most unique spirits I have ever studied: one who in life had trouble connecting, and seemed to need to depart this life in order to interact in any meaningful way with the living.

One More Encounter

Author Bruce Orr and his fiancée also once witnessed a spirit in Poogan's Porch, although he is almost positive that it was not Zoe St. Amand. They were dining together one day and noticed that there was a young boy who was playing under a nearby table, at the feet of his parents. "All of a sudden the boy starts playing with something that no one else can see. He's down on all fours, chasing something that isn't there and laughing playfully. Well, I nudged my fiancée and motioned towards the child. We watched him play with absolutely nothing for a long time, at the feet of his parents, who were completely oblivious. We both got chills up and down our spines, but it was also sort of wonderful, because we were positive that this young child was playing with the ghost of Poogan. The adults with him, of course, had absolutely no idea it was happening."

We are again confronted by a spot in Charleston so wonderful that the spirits literally refuse to depart. Whether it is the wonderful cuisine or the puzzle of ghosts which seem tied to the location, you're sure to have a memorable experience at Poogan's Porch.

The Tavern

120 East Bay

Sometimes names are misleading, and the narrow two-story structure right next to the Old Exchange and Provost Dungeon is a perfect example of when a building's history hoodwinks us. The Tavern, located at the corner of Exchange and East Bay Streets, is a bit of a misnomer: rather than truly being a tavern, it is a package shop, easily identifiable by the large red dot which all liquor stores in South Carolina display. This property has historically been a tavern for so long, though, that the owner, Gary Dow, realized that Charlestonians were going to continue to call his place 'the tavern' regardless of what he named it. Mr. Dow simply went with the flow of over two hundred years' worth of history.

Also misleading is the small size of the building in relation to the huge amount of both history and hauntings which have transpired within its walls. I sat down with the owner of the Tavern on one unusually warm December day and discussed both of these topics at length. Make no mistake, however: the ghosts here are welcome visitors, and are nothing to be afraid of. Mr. Dow, a plain-spoken, genial man with a voice vaguely reminiscent of Walter Cronkite, explained why the ghosts at the Tavern are such positive fixtures at his establishment. "I'm very respectful," Gary offered. "I like the spirits here, and I think they like me. Our spirits are happy-go-lucky, they're safe here. I feel safe, my wife feels safe, and we're protective of them. No one's running around with a crucifix or throwing holy water."

"The Fabric of the Peninsula"

There is confusion about when The Tavern was built. Jonathan Poston's book, *The Buildings of Charleston: A Guide to the City's Architecture* states that in 1806, Thomas Coates either purchased or engaged construction, in some form, on the building at 120 East Bay. There is substantial evidence

THE TAVERN

The Tavern on East Bay Street, home to friendly spirits.

that it is considerably older than 1806, however. According to a *Charleston News and Courier* article which appeared on March 10th, 1969, the building was not shown on a map of the area made in 1740, but is pictured on a 1788 fire insurance map. The article does note that a tavern, in one form or another, dated from at least 1797, when it was advertised as Mrs. Coates' Tavern on the Bay. It might be possible that the current building occupying the spot was remodeled extensively by the Coates family in 1806. However, relying on fire insurance maps to determine the age of buildings can be a wildly inaccurate way to calculate, as Gary correctly points out: "Those sorts of maps didn't even exist until the 1780's and 90's, and if you didn't have insurance, you weren't on the map. The experts I rely on come from organizations which examine the style of construction to determine the age of this building. We've had people in here from Colonial Williamsburg, the British Academy, the Tower of London, a number of academics, and even an expert from Sotheby's Auction House. And they all agree that the building is quite a bit older than the 1806 date. The man from Sotheby's, when I asked him for his best guess, said after examining the brickwork that this was a style consistent with construction in Southern England, the Lowcountries of the Netherlands and Belgium, and even Northern France in the years between 1570 and 1710. Well, Charleston was founded in 1670 and construction on the peninsula didn't begin until a decade after that, so we've narrowed it down to between 1680 and the first quarter of the 1700's."

Regardless of when it was built, the structure today exists as a narrow, simple, gable-roofed building which holds two stories: the liquor store on the bottom level and a tiny apartment above it. There is also a small wine cellar, basically a subterranean chamber, which is only accessible through a trapdoor in the floor and a rickety ladder. I can personally attest that getting into the basement is somewhat difficult, since Gary was nice enough to show me around.

And what of the history of the building? "All the records we have of this place have to do with alcohol, from the very beginning, as far back as we can go: Coates' Tavern, Tavern on the Bluff, Globe Tavern, French's Tavern, Neptune Tavern, and there are others. It was a tavern in some form or another until 1903, when it became a liquor store. It was a liquor store until Prohibition, when a couple of locals with the last name of McKenna put a phoney-baloney barbershop in here. They had a sink and a couple of barber's chairs in here, but they didn't cut any hair. No one ever had a haircut in this building! It actually was the headquarters to their bootlegging empire—bringing up rum from the Caribbean and Scotch and whiskey down from Canada. They were using it as a front and were making a fortune. I got all of this info from the granddaughter of one of the former owners. She said you'd come in and sit in the chair and they'd pour you samples, and you'd order by the case. After Prohibition ended, it went right back to being a liquor store, and it's been called the Tavern—just that, the Tavern—ever since. I first came in here as a customer thirty-five years ago, and this place has always attracted me. I bought the place back in 2004. I wouldn't have ever thought to change the name because it's a great tradition, kind of part of the fabric of the peninsula. Charleston being as steeped in tradition as it is, I wasn't going to change anything. The family histories are intertwined here; we're a real neighborhood place."

Willie

Eventually talk turned to ghosts. "My own personal experiences go back to before I even owned it," Gary said. "Before I bought the place I worked here as an employee. I was working here for about two weeks and began to notice when I was behind the counter, I would hear a sound like walking. I'd get up to investigate and there wouldn't be anybody there. I began to get that feeling that maybe I wasn't alone, you know?" Were there ever any moments where he was uneasy or scared? "No, but then again all the negative entities are gone now. We heard a bunch of stories about it when we bought the place—a ghost in the one-room upstairs apartment, a spirit they called Willie. A few people around town have told me stories about this, and all of the tales of Willie all seem to be from the 1950's through the 1980's. The stories that I've heard were all told by people who either lived up there or visited up there, and describe an entity who was very unhappy; he was sort of a poltergeist who was banging things around and would run people off." The first story involving Willie centered on a preacher, who was invited down from upstate South Carolina to perform a wedding for the then-owner and his bride-to-be. "Well, the preacher stayed upstairs and he had some strange experiences: he had extremely troubling dreams, and the bed vibrated so bad he thought there was an earthquake. The room would also get unbearably hot, and the next moment get very cold. He got up to make himself a cup of tea, and was looking for the tea when the cabinet door swung open by itself and hit him right in the face. He spun around, holding his face, and the other cabinet door popped open and smacked him in the back of the head. That's not exactly a subtle message, you know? 'Get out!' So the preacher, this man of the cloth, he'd had enough. He left, and refused to stay there.

"A few years later, the former owner's niece came to town because she was looking at enrolling at the College of Charleston. Well, she reported the bed shaking—just like the preacher did before her—and she heard the shower running. She got up to investigate and found that the shower wasn't on, and nothing was wet. After that the lights kept dimming. She only stayed the one night.

"The former owner tried to have the place exorcised. They tried it twice: once in the 1970's, and once in the 1980's. But it didn't help, and I know the reason why. More on this later." I considered pointing out that in a fair number of haunted properties I've studied where exorcisms were attempted in order to 'fix' the ghostly issues, the ceremony has had no effect. An exorcism is a religious rite intended to drive out demons, not ghosts. But I felt like I would be interrupting Gary's narrative with trivia, and besides, he was on a roll.

He continued: "At one point they tried to do some air conditioning work in the upstairs. Well, the doorbell kept going off, it was driving the workers crazy. It wasn't even hooked up to anything, but it was still going off. One of these guys got frustrated and knocked the entire doorbell unit off the wall with a hammer, and it was still ringing there on the floor. They took off. And then painters tried to work up there, too. They kept hearing people walking around, and when they'd go investigate, they'd hear the same thing from the area they just left.

"A man who was very much a nonbeliever in ghosts rented the upstairs as an office for a time. One night he came down looking very pale, and asked if we had been experiencing any electrical problems in the building. Had our lights been flickering on and off? I said no. He said the lights had been flickering and the room got extremely hot and he could hardly breathe. Then it got extremely cold in a matter of seconds. The lights in the room went off by themselves, so he stepped out to the porch where he still had lights. Well, those lights on the porch turned off, and the ones in the room came back on by themselves."

So who was Willie? "We probably figured out who he was. One afternoon a few years back, a woman came in saying she was on a genealogical search. She was looking for a reason that her great-grandfather, a man named Johan Claussen, had died back in 1886, when he was 46 years old.

This was listed as his address at the time of his death. He was Norwegian, and was a ship's chandler [a shipping supplier] and a master mariner. He had gotten work as the chandler because he spoke a half dozen languages, which was very important to the shipping business here for obvious reasons—we're an international port. One morning in September 1886, his body was found on the sidewalk right outside of this building with his head busted completely open. He was in his nightshirt. I have the police report: it states that an Officer Levy of the Charleston Police Department was on dock patrol, and headed up Exchange Street at a quarter to five in the morning. He found Claussen lying on the sidewalk with two young men leaning over him, with his blood and brains everywhere. Officer Levy asked the men what happened and they claimed that they found him like that. Levy blew his police whistle to summon other officers and the two men took off running. They never caught them. The cause of death was officially a fall from a window, but there was plenty of evidence that Claussen didn't just fall: the furniture upstairs had been knocked around, like there had been a fight. The position of ship's chandler meant that you had to have cash on hand. These guys must have found out about it, fought him, and he died that way. Well, this must have been the spirit they nicknamed 'Willie,' and we now know why he was so unhappy. Claussen was in the process of sending for his wife and kids from Norway when he was killed. He had unfinished business, see?"

At this point I had to ask the obvious question: he had mentioned that Willie's negative haunting was in the past. How did that happen? And why didn't either exorcism attempt work? Gary laughed and explained, "At the time I thought this was a little weird: the great-granddaughter I mentioned wrote her great-grandfather a letter, and left it for him, a letter which explained things to him. I guess… well, I still think it's a little strange. But she wrote him a letter in both English and Norwegian, so he'd understand, and told him that his wife came over just fine back then, his kids turned out okay, et cetera. So he wasn't an evil presence, just frustrated. That's why the exorcism didn't work. Well, we left that note around for a couple of nights, and the message was apparently received. There were no bright lights or tunnels, you know, no scrawled answer from him on the note, no blood drops. Nothing so 'Hollywood' as that. But it seemed to help. Everything negative just sort of stopped in the upstairs." Gary stopped talking for a moment, giving me chance to fully absorb that wonderful story. How many times do you get to assist a spirit and resolve their issue in such a sensitive fashion, providing answers to both the living and the dead at the same time?

Spirits and Ghosts

"When I bought the Tavern [in 2004], the area was much seedier. We had what I called 'The Outdoorsmen' as quite a few of our customers back then, you know, bums sleeping outside on benches and even behind the building in the alley. They'd come in and buy a bottle of cheap vodka or what have you. Well, we gutted the place, completely renovated it, and went back to the building's seafarer roots. I'm a former mariner myself, and so we put up all the seafaring stuff I had collected over the years, as sort of a theme. And the neighborhood changed, too, for the better. Well, it wasn't long before both my wife and I began to have experiences in here on a fairly regular basis. My wife would hear a humming sound, for instance, over in the [far southeastern] corner. Like a female humming. I mentioned hearing footsteps.

"We've had the experience where some of the bottles turn sometimes, after hours, despite the fact that we have a pretty extensive alarm. If anything moves in here while the alarm is armed, it goes off. Regardless of the security system still being activated when we arrive in the mornings, we'll occasionally find bottles turned forty degrees or so, just enough so we can see that it was intentional and not a vibration. It's very playful.

"We also have a spirit who walks through the door here," Gary gestured at the door leading to the back room, near the sales counter. "He's wearing a 1700's era salmon-colored jacket with kelly green cuffs and fronting. He has a long ponytail, dark hair and eyes, maybe in his mid-twenties, and he's always smiling. You can make him out from about mid-thigh up. He walks through, smiles, and then turns to his left and walks through the wall and disappears. I've only seen him once, but he was seen another time by a woman from Boston who came in with her sister. She said she was just drawn to the place. Once inside, she kept walking around and speaking to people only she could see. I kept looking at the sister, trying to gauge if this was a genuine psychic or just your average crazy person, but the sister seemed to take it all in stride, telling me, 'She's been doing this since she was a child. She can actually interact with the spirits.' I thought that was only something on television, but it turned out she had actually assisted law enforcement in the past, you know, the real deal.

"Anyway, the woman said that there were three men sitting around a barrel right near where the counter is now, and there was another man sitting back there—she pointed towards the back room—and he was sitting on a box and smiling at her. And then she remarked that she saw a man with a ponytail walk through, and that's when I really got interested. I asked her to describe him, and she described the apparition of the man that I myself had seen, even down to the colors he was wearing, and the smile. It was a perfect match. And then she turned to me and asked me what 'Ravenel' referred to. Well, that's a very old Charleston name, essentially one of our founding fathers. 'Well, they don't like them,' she said, meaning the spirits. She was overhearing their discussion. 'Now who is Bennett?' Well, that's another old family name here, and they actually owned the building next door a long time ago. 'Well,' she said, 'They *really* don't like them. They don't want them in the building—they hate them.' And then she giggled, and when I asked her why, she said, 'One of them thinks I'm pretty.' She looked to be about sixty years old, had very long hair, and to me she sort of looked like a witch. But at least the spirits thought she was cute! She was a really pleasant person, though, and not the least bit abnormal.

"It was very similar to a time when a lady and her husband came in. She told me, 'I came in for the spirits, and I don't mean the liquor.' I knew exactly what she meant, this place draws the seers and those sensitive to that sort of energy. Her husband stayed quietly up here by the counter, but she walked back down the aisle near the window. Suddenly she lets out an 'Oooooh!' I thought she had tripped, but she explained that someone unseen had 'goosed' her! That's happened more than once, by the way: a young lady getting grabbed like that by one of the entities in here." I pointed out that a sailor's tavern would have drawn some rough-around-the-edges types, and Gary laughed.

Adventures in Ghost-Hunting: "They're Asking For You..."

Almost universally described by those who know him as easy-going, Mr. Dow does have one topic he feels strongly about: ghost hunters. He is very particular about what sort of research team comes in to reconnoiter with the spirits in the Tavern. "I don't let just anybody investigate. I avoid the tinfoil hat types. You know, the chanters, and the weirdos. I usually have to know them before I'll let them in. But if I've met you, and know you, then sure, you can look into it. But no one coming in here is going to be allowed to provoke the ghosts. This isn't television, this is real life, and we like our ghosts here.

"There have been some good experiences, though. A while back, a local woman asked me if it would be okay if her niece, who was attending the University of South Florida, could come in and poke around in the basement. She was an anthropology major, but she was also pretty interested in ghost-hunting. I said sure, and we went down through the door in the floor. This was a typical twenty-year-old kid, kind of knew everything about everything. Well, at least until we went into the basement; then she got real nervous. I asked if she was okay, and she said, 'Yeah, I just feel a chill.' That's when it happened: the light bulb exploded right over her head. I thought she got cut at first, but other than being scared she was fine. She clambered out of that hole like a scalded cat, though! That's happened on more than one occasion, by the way, if people go downstairs and whatever is down there doesn't happen to like them, sometimes the lightbulbs explode. I've even put heavy gauge bulbs in there, and checked the fixture and the wiring, and there's nothing wrong with it. New bulb, right out of the box, *boom*. It's extremely interesting to me that she was related to both of those two families, the Bennetts and the Ravenels? I guess the spirits really don't like them in the building.

"A paranormal group from western Tennessee came in, and they turned on their EMF [electromagnetic field] readers, they got all kind of wild readings. In one of the readers, the fresh batteries lost their charge almost immediately. Another group came in from the University of Nevada-Reno, armed with the same type of device. All four EMF readers redlined immediately when they turned them on. They went out to their truck and replaced all the batteries, only to come back inside and have exactly the same results: off-the-chart readings and then dead batteries. Yet another group came in with recorders, and caught voices. They heard 'London' mentioned a lot, and 'father,' 'I've been good,' 'porter,' and 'goose.' I can tell you that when they heard the word 'goose,' I thought immediately of those ladies getting grabbed."

Gary related another great story: "When another team was in—and part of the team were friends of mine, my buddy Bill and his son Chris—they set up a recorder and two video cameras in the basement. Well, the picture went dead on the cameras right away, but the audio stayed live. They could hear someone walking, which is something we hear down here all the time, by the way, like they're walking on sand or dragging something. They said that whoever it was walking around down there would walk around the recorder and make a half-circle around and stop, and then go back again. It made a very distinct, human noise, like someone saying, 'Hmmm,' like they were saying: 'What is this?'

"Later in the same investigation, Bill and Chris were in that basement, and they turned out the lights. Bill felt his face caressed by a woman, like someone touching it, but very cold. His heart started to race, he felt completely disoriented and sick; it terrified him. We brought him outside for some air, and he stood outside while the other half of the team went in. They came outside just a few minutes later, saying that Bill was actually being summoned back by the spirits. Bill said, 'What do you mean?' and the other investigator said: 'On the recorder. Bill, *they're asking for you*. They keep asking for *the man, the man*. We have their voices on the recorder and they're asking for you.' Bill swears one of them kissed him on the cheek."

Ancient Discussions

"I had a friend in here once, one who is into paranormal research and demonology, and he told me that there are at least a dozen spirits in here. They're happy, ancient entities, according to him—and I'm inclined to agree—and that they don't know how old they are. They could be a hundred, two hundred, three hundred years old, or even older. They're in here, but they don't *stay* here. They're not trapped. They come and they go." I pointed out to Mr. Dow that that would be just as in life: taverns in Charleston during the 1600's and 1700's were social centers, even more so than today. They were more like today's coffee shops, a place for writing, reading, relaxing, and yes, for coming and going. Gary got a twinkle in his eye. "Exactly. I think the spirits here are happy because we're doing the work here that's always been done here."

Alcohol has been dispensed on that tiny yet historic corner for possibly three and a quarter centuries. Let that sink in for a moment. Uninterrupted by fire, Native American and Spanish attacks, disease, Revolution, murder, Secession, bombardment and invasion, Reconstruction, Industrialization, not one but two World Wars, Prohibition, Civil Rights, gentrification, urban renewal and even disco, this little shop, in all of its days, has served the Charleston populace precisely what they need to momentarily escape the realities of Southern life. There is nobility in that sort of singularity. Nobility, and a touch of comfort. We know that the living find great gratification in a mainstay like the Tavern, and it's nice to discover that the dead find consolation there, too. It is also quite wonderful that those entities which come and go have found such great friends like Gary and his wife. They are the rare folks who understand that there are a lot of beings, whether they are living or dead, who find the Tavern simply irresistible.

Bocci's Italian Restaurant

158 Church Street

When the sun is perfectly positioned, the narrow shadow of St. Philips Episcopal Church's steeple points directly at the front door of Bocci's Italian Restaurant. It's as if a celestial being has pointed the way to great Italian cuisine. Or perhaps that same divine hand, sensing my wish for intriguing history and hauntings, helpfully pointed this writer precisely to that same location.

And what is the story, you may be asking, with this magical spot combining delicious red sauce and great ghost tales? Well, the structure was built after the end of the Civil War, in 1868. It was constructed for the Molony family as a dual purpose building: commerce below, living quarters above. The Molonys owned the very first Irish pub in Charleston. If you look closely at the one of the brick sides of the building, you can still faintly make out the old Jax Beer signage from when it was a tavern. When the Dispensary Act was passed in South Carolina the 1890's, which essentially ushered in an era of prohibition, the pub shut down and the building became a grocery store. The clever owners, though, simply moved the bar to the back of the store, and the building moonlighted as a speakeasy (an illegal bar). When the Volstead Act passed as a national law in 1920, Prohibition caused the owners once again to operate as an illicit venue where thirsty patrons could gather. Throughout much of the 20th century, the building served as a private residence. It was a bakery and another restaurant very briefly in the late 1980's, and then in the 1990's became Bocci's Italian Restaurant.

I had eaten at Bocci's many, many times over the years (people who know me are aware of my uncanny ability to find the best chicken parmesan offered in any given city), but I was always blissfully unaware that the restaurant was haunted until a friend of mine suggested that I go in and talk to them about it. This is how I found myself on a sunny Friday late morning, talking to management about their ghostly presences.

Bocci's at 158 Church Street.

Shadows on the Bricks

I sat down with one of the managers, Jennifer, and she related several stories to me during a quiet moment in the restaurant's second-floor dining room. She exuded an upbeat disposition and an utter conviction as to the certainty of these stories about Bocci's. "As I understand it, there were two fires in the building, back when it was a house," Jennifer related. "One of the families living here on the second floor was trapped due to the intense heat. The doors swelled, and they were unable to escape. So that family did die here in the building." Jennifer paused, perhaps giving me a moment to absorb that we were sitting right in the same area where they perished in the smoke and flames, before she continued.

"It's interesting that most of the stories of ghostly activity here involve doors in some way. I've been here two and a half years, and I think most people who work here have had at least one unexplainable experience. Mostly the odd occurrences will happen up here on the second floor. I've had a number of things happen to me personally. For instance, I'll frequently discover that the manager's door, which is supposed to remain locked at all times, will be unlocked. Sometimes not only will it be unlocked, but it'll be wide open as well, when I distinctly remember closing and locking that door.

"Another story involves another door up here which is next to our server's station, a door which I've always assumed led to the old kitchen back when this was a residence. That door leads to storage today, and it remains locked as well, just like the manager's door. Well, one of my servers was in here taking inventory, and for no discernable reason, that door just slammed open by itself, really hard and really loudly. I don't think this was negative or violent activity, I honestly think that the spirits here just doesn't like the doors closed.

"There's a lot of strange activity in the downstairs, too. Not as much as the upstairs, but it does happen. One really busy Friday night, the downstairs dining room was slammed with our dinner rush. I was downstairs and happened to notice that there was a considerable line for the men's bathroom. About ten minutes later, the line had not moved at all; the same man was waiting, and he looked a little agitated. So I asked if everything was okay. Well, the man told me that he had walked into the rest room and that the door wasn't locked, but there had been a man in there—he had inadvertently walked in on him. So he waited for the person in the rest room to finish up, but he seemed to be taking forever! So I knocked a few times, got no response, and opened the door. Well, there was no one in the men's room. But the man who had been waiting insisted that he had clearly seen a man in there. I mean, why would he make a story like that up? So apparitions have been seen in the downstairs.

"Oh, here are a few more stories involving the upstairs. Our general manager, Kelly, had an unexplainable experience of her own late one evening. She was sitting in the manager's office behind a locked door doing a little paperwork. At night, we close and lock that door because we sometimes have access to cash. So on this particular night, she hears a loud knocking on the door, so she answers, 'hello?' And she gets no answer. It happens again, the knocking, her answer and no response. So she opens the door, and discovers no one there. Not only was there no one in the upstairs, *there was no one else in the entire building*. She was hearing pounding on a door in a deserted building.

"An instance involving another manager, Sadie, was probably our most famous ghostly incident. She was in the locked office doing paperwork, and she heard a loud crash that came from the nearby upstairs bathroom. Well, she went to investigate and discovered that the mirror had somehow fallen off the hook which attached it to the wall, and was now lying face-up, in the middle of the bathroom floor. Well, the hook wasn't bent, and it was still attached to the bathroom wall. The mirror would have to be lifted straight up off of the hook, and then dropped at a 45 degree angle to land where it did. And incredibly, the glass and the frame were completely intact and undamaged. She was so confused by this that she began taking pictures. In the second photo she took, there appears an unexplainable dark shape that looks like a figure standing in the bathroom with her."

I took a moment, at the end of our interview, to ask Jennifer why in her opinion Charleston was so haunted. She did not hesitate in her answer, so clearly she had given the subject a lot of thought: "I think Charleston is so haunted maybe because of our close ties to some dark history, and the fact that so many of our old buildings have remained exactly as they are for one hundred, two hundred, or even three hundred years in some instances. There's been constant activity and such upheaval here, from pirates to the Civil War to earthquakes and fires, like this building here has experienced. There's just a heightened sense of history because it is all around us at every moment. We're also a town of bloodlines, so our population is just a little more connected and attuned than most."

Jennifer's answer was as good as any that I heard while in Charleston. At nearly every turn on the peninsula, one is confronted by simultaneously great and tragic history, ghost stories, and world-class dining. It was the latter which suddenly concerned me at the end of the interview, so, stomach rumbling, I went downstairs and ordered my lunchtime usual: the chicken parmesan panini. During my brief wait I struck up a conversation with my server, an attractive girl who seemed quite competent despite not having worked at Bocci's for very long. I mentioned to her that I was in town writing a collection of Charleston ghost stories. She asked if I planned on featuring Bocci's Italian Restaurant in a chapter and I answered that yes, I was. She revealed that she was extremely happy working there, except for one thing: "I keep hearing voices, more than one person, in the upstairs. I can't quite make out what they're saying, but given the urgency of their voices, I'm not sure I really *want* to know."

Her words stayed with me all afternoon.

Fort Sumter

Flashpoint of the American Civil War

"Legions now quiet will swarm out and sting us to death. It is unnecessary. It puts us in the wrong. It is fatal."
—Letter by Robert Toombs, Secretary of State of the Confederate States of America, written to Jefferson Davis, CSA President, about the plan to bombard Fort Sumter

Tourists Jessie and Julie, visitors from Maryland and Florida, respectively, were winding down an epic vacation that they took in late winter of 2013. Meeting first in Savannah, Georgia and then moving on to Charleston, they hoped to come into contact with something authentically paranormal in either of the historic (and extremely haunted) Southern seaports. They had, as a growing number of ghost enthusiasts had before them, constructed their entire vacation around spectre-seeking. However, in all of the haunted tours and reputedly ghostly locations that they visited, they had yet to experience anything truly unexplainable. They had seen plenty of beautiful architecture in both cities, sure, and heard lots of pleasantly gruesome history. Still, one piece of their 'haunted vacation' was missing: the haunted part.

You know that old axiom that states that the moment you stop looking for something is the moment that it finds you? That was precisely what Jessie and Julie did on the last day of their trip: they gave up looking for ghosts, and instead just immersed themselves in the beauty of the day and the majesty that is Charleston. The only thing on their itinerary was enjoying some truly wonderful weather and touring a deceptively small piece of real estate, one that hugely altered the course of American history forever: the Fort Sumter National Monument, located in the middle of Charleston Harbor. As the girls took the ferry boat over to the fort on that lovely January day, ghosts were the last thing on either of their minds.

Fort Sumter, December 9th 1863, View of entrance to Three Gun Bat'y, by John Ross Key. Obtained from the Library of Congress Prints and Photographs Division.

Powder Keg in the Harbor

In 1861, South Carolina was in the early throes of Secession Fever. It was the first state to split off from Northern rule and form its own nation-state which would become the Confederate States of America, doing so in December of 1860. Charleston, South Carolina's largest city at that time, figuratively resembled a lit fuse for the coming conflict. And taking a place on the national stage was an enormous dispute over a tiny sandbar, one within easy view of Charleston's Battery.

Named for Revolutionary War hero General Thomas Sumter, the masonry fort had been built on a relatively small plot of ground as part of a series of coastal defenses in the decades following the War of 1812. Begun in 1829, Fort Sumter was still unfinished in 1861. Union Army Major Robert Anderson, who determined that it was more defensible than Fort Moultrie, moved his forces to the incomplete Fort Sumter. The tiny Union garrison of 126 men (a figure which includes 40 civilian employees of the US Army Corps of Engineers who volunteered to stay and help prepare the fort's defenses, and 8 musicians) hunkered down, in a fort designed to be defended by 650 troops, in an effort to weather the proverbial storm, menaced by the heavy guns of a hostile nation. Union attempts to resupply the fort in early January 1861 were fired upon and repulsed by South Carolina artillery forces, and on April 11th, three aides sent by Rebel General P. T. Beauregard demanded that the Union defenders of the fort evacuate. Major Anderson refused.

In the wee hours of Friday, April 12th, Charlestonians gathered on balconies and porches along the Battery, drinking toasts to the expected battle and to Secession. They were not disappointed, because at 4:30 a.m., the Confederate forces began firing on Fort Sumter from a multitude of batteries on James Island, Sullivan's Island, and Morris Island, Mt. Pleasant, and Fort Moultrie (a few local tour guides like to claim that The Battery along Charleston's southern tip also engaged Fort Sumter, but the fort is over three miles distant from the Charleston peninsula, which is completely out of range).

The bombardment lasted thirty-four hours, but Major Anderson finally surrendered to Confederate forces due to the hopelessness of his position. There were no fatalities during the attack. However, the Union forces were allowed to fire a salute the following day, and one of the Northern guns fired prematurely, killing one soldier and mortally wounding another. Union Private Daniel Hough was killed—the first of over 600,000 to die in the bloody conflict—and Private Edward Gallway died later.

The Confederate States of America had won its first engagement, and now assumed control of Fort Sumter. I was fortunate enough to secure an interview with Rick Hatcher, who has served as historian of Fort Sumter since 1992. Hatcher, an admitted skeptic on the subject of ghosts, nevertheless graciously shared his thoughts about the significance of the fort and the relation to the city it protected. "In the eyes of Southerners, Charleston and Fort Sumter have a special symbolism and meaning," Rick explained. "Sumter is looked at as the Lexington and Concord of the beginning of the second American revolution. Charleston was the most successful blockade running port, with an estimated seventy percent success rate. It was strategically important for the Confederacy to keep the port open, so they could get cotton and rice to markets and get goods back in. It's a vital lifeline. And in the eyes of the North, it is where secession, rebellion, and treason began."

If the fort's Civil War history had ended here, it would still hold a special place in the history books. As Rick astutely points out: "You can read in book after book: Charleston and Fort Sumter are addressed in the introduction or the first chapter, but then the author goes on to talk about Grant or Manassas or Vicksburg or Lincoln. All are valid topics, but time and again, we get a few scant sentences. After that opening paragraph, however, Charleston and the fort remained a great symbol, both to the North and the South, all throughout the War. At the very minimum, it was a symbolic focal point, from a morale standpoint, both for a Union victory and for the Confederacy sustaining itself. As long as the Confederate flag flew over Fort Sumter and Charleston, the symbol of the Confederacy endured. Likewise, the Union's interest in putting their colors over Charleston Harbor became increasingly important. As the war wore on, it became less strategic and more symbolic, but the relevance remained constant."

This symbolism for both North and South explains the location's deep association with bloodshed after that initial bombardment. Once they assumed control of Sumter, the Confederate forces based around Charleston scrambled to repair and finish the fort as best they could in the ensuing years (the fort was never completed). Their goal was to establish a formidable deterrent to Union attacks on the city of Charleston. Around five hundred slaves, along with Confederate Army engineers, were later tasked with repairing the damage incurred in the 1861 bombardment, and they did a very credible job in accomplishing that objective.

Their hard work would be tested in the cauldron of battle. The fort would be shelled by the Union between 1863 and 1865, mostly from US Army artillery on Morris Island. It was also attacked in a disastrous amphibious assault by US sailors and Marines in September of 1863. According to Douglas W. Bostick's great book, *Charleston Under Siege: The Impregnable City*, this Union force suddenly faced "…a barrage of musket fire, hand grenades, brickbats and fireballs. The Confederate gunboat *Chicora*… opened fire on the Union attackers with canister and grapeshot, as did the guns on Fort Moultrie and Fort Johnson. Taking on intense fire, the supporting Union ships withdrew, abandoning the sailors and marines on the rocks of the fort." The final grim tally was 124 Union men killed, wounded or captured.

Fort Sumter was subjected to a fierce pounding by the Union Army for the duration of the war. Fifty-two were killed at the fort over the years (a figure which includes Confederates and slaves). Despite enduring near-

Ruins of Fort Sumter, Charleston Harbor, S.C., by Osborn & Durbec. Obtained from the Library of Congress Prints and Photographs Division.

constant artillery barrages, the Confederacy never officially surrendered the fort.

Rick Hatcher described what life in Charleston was like during the war: "Anyone who could afford to would have left the city. The elite class and planters would have gone back to their plantations or rented a place to stay in the interior of South Carolina. The worst of the shelling would have occurred from Broad Street to the Battery. The poor and those stationed here for military service had to stay. I've only seen records of five people being killed by the Union shelling, but of course there may have been more. There was a huge fire in December of 1861 which burned about 580 acres or so, a blaze which started on the Cooper River side and almost reached the Ashley side of town. So there were a lot of abandoned houses with artillery damage, and a lot of burned ruins. There were Confederate artillery installations all along the peninsula, and the city was under martial law."

The Rebels evacuated Charleston (and the fort complex) to defend against Union General William T. Sherman's swing through South Carolina in early 1865. The Federal troops retook possession of the fort on February 18th, 1865.

When the war ended, Fort Sumter was in ruins. Partially rebuilt and reconfigured during the Spanish-American War, the structure most notably served as a lighthouse before becoming a National Monument. Today it is operated by the National Park Service, and open to touring for a modest fee.

A Fitting End to a Haunted Vacation

After the ferry ride and a short, but thorough, history narrative by a park ranger, Julie, Jessie, and the other tourists were encouraged to explore the fort on their own. The two friends were doing just that, strolling around the perimeter of the fort, and they decided to check out a bit of the complex's interior. Jessie found her thoughts turning a bit morbid as she walked. "I know that many forts have seen a multitude of deaths," she explained. But that is when something unexplainable happened to them both.

Both of them clearly saw the figure of a man, who turned and ran through a pair of doors. This struck both of them as odd. "Curious, we went to the doorway to see where it led. Much to our surprise, however, we couldn't open it. Both of us tried our hands at pushing or pulling the doors open. It surprised us when they wouldn't open, because we had just seen a man run through them so swiftly. We had even heard the doors rattle as he exited.

"Confused by what we saw, we decided to explore the other side of the doors. What we came upon was a total shock to both of us. Apparently the doors were padlocked closed on the other side! How then could this figure go running through the doors so quickly? There was no way anyone could get through these locked doors, but we were both quite sure of what we had seen."

The two friends had no way of knowing this, but they are not the first people to see a spectre at Fort Sumter. In 2006, a tourist was visiting the fort and reported seeing the image of a man wearing a dark blue coat, presumably a Union artillerist, who smartly saluted, and then vanished from sight.

So who is this strange man? Is he Private Daniel Hough, Union artillerist, the very first out of over 600,000 troops to die in the American Civil War? Or is he one of the other Union soldiers to die here in the disastrous amphibious assault in 1863? Or could he be a Confederate, one of the fifty-two killed by Union guns? Confederates, as my reenactor friends are quite fond of reminding me, often wore dark blue or charcoal grey uniforms, especially early in the war, so the fact that our apparition wears blue does not necessarily mark his identity as a Northern man. He could even be a civilian. Regardless of his true identity, he made a Southern road trip memorable for two best friends, and completed the last item on their checklist: a real encounter with a ghost. "I'll take this real ghost sighting and treasure the moment," Jessie said. "It was surreal!"

Fort Sumter, December 9th 1863, View of South East Angle, by John Ross Key. Obtained from the Library of Congress Prints and Photographs Division.

Statue in Magnolia Cemetery.

The Dare at St. Philip's Churchyard

142 Church Street

One famous and entertaining bit of Charleston folklore is the infamous 'dare at St. Philip's,' which was already an ancient story when it was recorded in print by Margaret Rhett Martin's wonderful book, *Charleston Ghosts*. I have heard countless versions of this tale over the years, and a quick scan of the archives proves that the narrative should be taken with a heaping helping of salt. However, it is an entertaining yarn, and is presented here as nothing more than an example of classic campfire storytelling.

Eleven year old Sallie lived in the spacious house nestled between St. Philip's and the Huguenot places of worship on Church Street in the very late 19th century. A pretty, popular and engaging girl, she was also blessed with a large intellect for someone so young. Seemingly her only flaw was a stubborn refusal to concede any point when she entered a discussion. A precocious child, she loved to debate and argue with her large group of friends. Even her teachers sometimes found this hardheaded tendency of Sallie's to be exhausting. Her immense ego made her unwilling to admit defeat on any contestable topic.

One cool October night after a heavy rain, she was entertaining a group of classmates when their after-dinner discussion turned to ghosts, specifically ones haunting the nearby St. Philip's Churchyard. Several in the group believed in spectres. One boy in particular, Thomas, was insistent that he had seen the ghost of Boney in the nearby graveyard. Sallie made a rude noise through plumped lips, voicing her opinion on the subject. "Anyone who believes in ghosts is a fool, and anyone who says they've seen a ghost is a liar," Sally spat out.

The boy persisted: "I did see Boney lounging on a tombstone! I'll bet you're afraid to go down and see him. Old Boneyman will get you!"

"I am not afraid because there is nothing to fear, and I'll walk through any cemetery, day or night," Sallie said defiantly. Very soon, the dare had been issued: Sallie was challenged to take a walking stick, alone and with no lantern, into the darkened burial ground. She was instructed to lay the cane on a tomb in the back corner of the churchyard, to prove that she had actually gone to the stone in question. Her friends would find the cane the next morning to verify whether she had actually done so. Within a very few moments, Sallie departed the bright, joyous party, and found herself walking through the wrought-iron gates to the burial ground, clutching the stick in the deepening gloom. She had to walk all the way around the church, from the right-hand entrance on Church Street to the left hand rear corner of the burial ground. Her lovely gown trailed behind her, getting muddier and muddier with each puddle she encountered.

There's no such thing as ghosts or goblins, she told herself as she passed the first row of tombstones. *Besides, Boney had been a good person who was rewarded for saving the church.* Boney was a slave who, close to a hundred years' previously, had famously saved the church from going up in flames during the Great Fire of 1796. It had been Boney, despite his fear of heights, who had valiantly climbed the roof and swatted burning embers away from the church with his bare hands. Boney was a hero, and for his good deeds the church took up a collection and bought his freedom. From that day forward, Boney stayed near the church as if he were charged with protecting it, until his death many years later. Many people still claimed to see his spirit at St. Philip's, saying that the old slave's devotion to the church had survived the grave.

Visions of Boney dancing in her head, Sallie ventured deeper and deeper into the pitch-black graveyard, holding the cane in front of her like a cudgel. Her heart began to pound harder. She rounded the backside of the church. Everything still dripped from the recent rain, and the sounds of water trickling seemed to be deafening to Sallie. *Even if there are ghosts, old Boney won't hurt me*, Sallie reasoned. *He's nice.* But her words did nothing to ease her growing apprehension. "H-hello? If it is you, Thomas, I am not afraid!" she called out. "I know you are there." Her only answer was a wet rustling sound. Sallie stepped off of the path, still determined to complete her mission despite her faltering resolve. She ran smack into a row of tombstones, the cold marble biting into her shins. Tears, both from the pain and her growing terror, welled in her eyes. Finally she neared her goal.

She dashed forward, found the specified tomb, and rammed the cane down into the soft damp earth with both hands. She then turned to dash back to the safety of the house and her friends. She could picture nothing but Boney's long fingers reaching out of the dripping blackness, ready to drag her away from the light forever. Suddenly, something grabbed the hem of her dress! She tugged feebly, but the iron grip held her captive. Some horrible thing had her in its clutches. She tried to scream in terror, but no sound could escape her throat. She sank to the ground, arms outstretched towards her house in the distance.

After an hour, her friends were forced to look for Sallie. Several of them insisted that they would find that stubborn girl sitting on the tombstone, laughing, where she would chastise them for believing in ghosts and phantoms. Armed with lanterns, they did indeed find her at that tombstone within the burial ground at St. Phillip's, but she was in no condition to be critical of anyone, not then or ever again. Sallie had literally been scared to death: she had driven that cane down through the hem of her own skirt, pinning herself in place. Believing that something had grabbed her, she expired at that very spot.

Many Charlestonians will tell you to be cautious of poking fun of people's ghost stories, because sometimes trying to disprove the story might just cause you to be scared to death. Local storytellers even claim that on the darkest of nights, the ghost of a little girl is sometimes seen in the burial ground, holding a cane as she walks deeper and deeper into the gloom.

The stories of Boney and the church he saved from ruin are completely true. According to a *Charleston News and Courier* article which appeared on June 6th, 1921: "In 1796… the steeple of St. Philip's was afire, and was only saved by a courageous negro, who climbed up and tore off the burning shingles; for this signal service he was given his freedom…" This story is a wonderful example of how a folklore tale can perfectly complement and highlight a true historical event.

The Old Exchange Building and Provost Dungeon

122 East Bay Street

To discuss the importance of the intersection of East Bay and Broad Streets is to actually open a discourse about two Charleston landmarks which have been located on the same spot: the Half Moon Battery, and the structure which eventually followed it, the Old Exchange Building. Both have had a huge effect on the history of the city itself, and to achieve true understanding of the ghosts which supposedly still haunt this spot, one must understand the significance and the timeline of the location. Unless you know the historical context of the site, you can scarcely conceive the strong emotions which have surged through this relatively small patch of ground. From prisoners to pirates to patriots to Presidents, this location has seen every bit of Charleston history, and offering up the very best or the worst this city has to offer. If you believe that highly-charged passions such as tragedy, heartbreaking loss, and elation can tie our incorporeal beings to those locations where such strong outpourings of feeling occurred, then there can be no doubt that this very special spot is haunted.

In Defense of Charles Town

The Battery was constructed as part of a ring of defenses, which included a wall around the town, in the very early 1700's. Edward Crisp's Charles Town map of 1704 clearly shows both the defensive battery already in place, which overlooked the water, and a small Watch House, which was a jail or workhouse for unruly colonists. The Watch House was located very close to the battery. So what, exactly, was this ring of defenses put in place to repel? Clearly, the biggest threat to Charles Town during

The Old Exchange Building at 122 East Bay Street.

that early period was England's rival, Spain, who had established themselves quite well to the south in Florida. But only slightly less dangerous were the independent operators known as pirates, who would raid the shipping which came and went from Charles Town's harbor.

In the first twenty years of the 18th century, Charles Town residents lived in real fear of pirate attack. The danger was largely seasonal, as strange as that sounds, but pirates moved through the shipping lanes as they followed the warmer weather, so pirate atrocities on the Carolina coast were much more likely to happen in the late spring through early fall, after which the buccaneers would sail south into the Caribbean. According to David Cordingly's wonderful 1995 book, *Under The Black Flag: The Romance And The Reality Of Life Among The Pirates*, there were "between fifteen hundred and two thousand pirates operating" at any one given time along the Eastern Seaboard and Caribbean during this period, which today seems to be a small number for so large an area. But Charles Town only had a population of around five thousand during this timeframe. So English authorities who wanted to put an end to piracy largely had their hands tied by numbers and geography.

And what of the pirates visiting the Carolinas during this period? To run down the list is to recite a roll call of some of the most notorious pirates in recorded history, including Charles Vane, Calico Jack Rackham, female pirates Anne Bonny and Mary Read, and perhaps the most villainous pirate of them all, Edward Teach, also known as Blackbeard. In fact, it was Blackbeard who blockaded the entire Charles Town harbor, in June of 1718, eventually demanding a ransom of medicines. Teach's associate of plunder, Stede Bonnet, was nicknamed "The Gentleman Pirate." It is Bonnet who will forever be associated with the Watch House's (and present day Exchange Building's) dungeon-basement.

The Gentleman Was Also a Pirate

Stede Bonnet was born in Barbados around 1688. According to Cordingly, he "lived in comfortable circumstances… until he suddenly tired of his life there. At his own expense he outfitted out a sloop"—a highly unusual thing to do, since most pirates stole their vessels—in 1717. He even *hired* a crew, which is again a very odd move for a pirate captain, since most pirate crews signed on for a share of each prize, "and embarked on a career as a pirate." Captain Charles Johnson's book, written in 1734, *A General History of the Robberies and Murders of the most notorious Pyrates*, mentions a nagging, shrewish wife as the reason for Bonnet's turn to piracy.

Bonnet's career as a buccaneer captain was as short as it was odd. Despite having no seafaring experience, he did manage to take several vessels. When he came across fellow pirate captain Blackbeard in late fall of 1717, the two joined forces. However, their 'merger' largely consisted of Blackbeard seizing control, which, according to the *Boston News Letter* of November 11th, 1717, Bonnet "has no command, he walks about in his morning gown, and then to his books of which he has a good library aboard." By December of that same year, the two separated.

After Blackbeard held the terrified Charles Town populace for ransom (and his crew drunkenly paraded, unafraid of any retribution, through the city's streets) in the summer of 1718, South Carolina Governor Robert Johnson, finally had enough. He encouraged several prominent local merchants, including Colonel William Rhett, to organize an expedition to capture or kill the pirates which threatened them. The force did not find Blackbeard, but in early October they did discover Stede Bonnet's pirate crew, who were refitting their ship at the mouth of the Cape Fear River.

After a furious battle in which many of the pirates were killed, Bonnet surrendered. Rhett, victorious, brought his thirty-five pirate prisoners back to Charles Town, where all but Captain Bonnet were locked in the basement dungeon of the Watch House located at Half Moon Battery. Conditions in the dungeon were lousy: at extreme high tide, brackish water could trickle into the dark dungeon area, and it was not heated in the winter nor adequately ventilated in the summer. Disease and unsanitary conditions were the norm, not the exception.

Bonnet, along with his sailing master David Herriot, was kept under guard in the home of the town marshal. It is strongly suspected that some local merchants with ties to Stede Bonnet bribed the guards and arranged for him to escape in late October, wearing women's clothing as a disguise. However, the two men were recaptured a couple of weeks later, and this time, they were cast without pity into the dungeon at Half Moon Battery with the rest of their crew. Twenty-nine of Bonnet's pirates were hanged a short time later, an event which understandably terrified their former captain greatly.

The former Gentleman Pirate pleaded with the court for mercy, at one point urging the authorities to cut off his arms and legs, but "leave me my tongue so I can forever sing your praises." Unmoved, Judge Trott replied that Bonnet faced not only "physical death… [but] everlasting burning… in fire and brimstone." After the multiple pirate raids on the area, the court was not in a forgiving mood. He was sentenced to death, and on December 10th, Stede Bonnet was led to the place of execution at White Point (a short distance away). In tears and on the verge of collapse, Bonnet was hanged, and his body (along with the other pirates in his crew) was left to swing in the breeze there for a long time, a warning to other pirates in the area.

The grisly example was incredibly effective, and pirates for the most part steered clear of Charles Town.

A New Era

In the early 1760's, talk amongst prominent Charlestonians turned to the need for a new public building. Due to the rapid expansion of transatlantic trade, a new customs and exchange house was desperately needed to oversee growth and more effectively regulate trade. The Commons House of Assembly voted a generous sum of money for that express purpose, expressing their faith in Charleston's improving commercial prospects. The site that was chosen was the location of the original Half-Moon Battery and Watch House (which had, for a short time, become a Council chamber as well). Part of the brick basement of the defensive Battery was adapted for re-use, meaning that the new building would serve multiple purposes, including economic barometer, customs house, formal meeting hall, and would still remain a jail in the basement. Begun in 1767 and completed in 1771, the Exchange Building was one of the biggest and grandest public buildings in North America when finished. According to Walter J. Fraser Jr.'s wonderful 1989 book about Charleston's history, *Charleston! Charleston! The History of a Southern City*: "In design and construction materials it was unique. Only two notable colonial American buildings preceded it, Philadelphia's Town Hall and Boston's Faneuil Hall. Yet neither of these structures matched the architectural distinction of Charles Town's new Customs House…"

The Exchange figured prominently in the patriot uprising against England. It was the location where Royal Governor Lord William Campbell met with colonists during a conflict over taxes on tea in 1773. 257 chests of tea were stored at the Exchange during this bitter disagreement. In March of 1776, South Carolinians wrote a constitution and declared it publicly on the steps of the Exchange, announcing their rebellion against the English Crown.

However, the Revolutionary War event most people would associate with the Old Exchange Building would be, for Charlestonians, the most dreadful event of the entire war: the imprisonment and subsequent execution of American patriot Colonel Isaac Hayne.

American Martyr

Isaac Hayne, and planters like him, presented a huge problem for the British authorities in the late 1770's, as the Revolution began to rage: how to keep the younger generation from rebelling against English rule? The answer was to make them sign 'loyalty oaths' pledging their allegiance to Britain and neutrality in their conflict with the Colonial forces, which, if violated, could mean a traitor's death sentence for the oath-breaker. Isaac Hayne, desperate to secure medicines for his family which could only be procured in Charleston, was forced to sign one of these loyalty oaths in order to obtain the necessary medical remedies. Later, he was told by British authorities that despite the neutrality seemingly guaranteed by the contract he signed, they planned to force him to fight for the English cause. Hayne refused, and joined the American forces instead.

Hayne was captured in July of 1781 and thrown into the Provost Dungeon underneath the Exchange Building. Much had changed in Charleston in the sixty-some-odd years between Hayne's and Stede Bonnet's incarcerations at that location, but the dungeon's horrible condition was not one of them. Rats, sickness, and filth still permeated the forbiddingly dark prison. Hayne endured much misery in his time at the squalid jail, which was tucked out of sight under the elegant Exchange.

Hayne was quickly sentenced to death by a British military tribunal. Lieutenant Colonel Nisbet Balfour, despite heavy protests from Charlestonians, refused to rescind the execution order and had Hayne executed by hanging (a traitor's death, as opposed to a military death by firing squad). Hayne went bravely to the gallows on August 4th, 1781. According to Michael Coker's great 2008 book, *Charleston Curiosities: Stories of the Tragic, Heroic and Bizarre*, "[British] soldiers escorted Hayne and his small loyal band [of friends] through the city, past the multitude watching from windows... numerous bystanders openly wept as Hayne passed." John Colcock, both friend and legal counsel to Isaac Hayne reported that a friend reminded Hayne that he hoped that the Colonel would set a good example as an American at the moment of his death. Colonel Hayne replied, somewhat peacefully, "I will endeavor to do so." And after shaking hands with his friends and pulling the hood over his own face, Hayne was hanged for treason.

Colonel Balfour thought the execution of Hayne would be an effective warning against rebellion, but the action had the opposite of the intended effect. The gallant martyr, Hayne's noble death caused a surge in those actively resisting English rule, and citizens lost all respect for Balfour. A prominent Charleston citizen even allegedly dressed his pet baboon in an exact replica of a British officer's uniform and addressed the animal as 'Colonel Balfour.'

After the Revolution ended, the Exchange Building received a prominent guest in 1791: President George Washington, as part of his famous Southern Tour. A ball was held at the Exchange in his honor. He enjoyed his visit to both the city and the building so much, he sent a letter back to the citizens of Charleston: "I beg you will accept and offer my best thanks to… the citizens of Charleston, for their very polite attention to me. Should it ever be in my power, be assured, it will give me pleasure to visit again this very respectable city."

Built originally as a public building, the Old Exchange and Provost Dungeon remains one today. The Old Exchange is run as a museum, and owned by the South Carolina Society of the Daughters of American Revolution. It offers public tours of its three floors. The exhibits and artifacts displayed highlight various facets of Charleston history during the Colonial and Revolutionary eras.

Pirate or Patriot Ghosts?

With a historic pedigree like that, the old building almost cannot help being haunted. The director of the Exchange, Tony Youmans, agrees with this assessment wholeheartedly. He even related his own personal ghost story to me. "I was opening the building to some electrical contractors on a Saturday morning," Tony related. "I got here about 6:45 and I knew I was the only one here because I unlocked the building and keyed the alarm system. We have a very elaborate alarm system, seeing as this is a historic site. As I was walking across these upper floors, I heard about ten steps behind me some footsteps. It sounded like a good, heavy leather boot. I assumed it was the contractors coming in behind me, so I called out, 'Hey Robbie, y'all are here early!' And I turned around and there was no one there! It really made me start. I searched every room, and looked behind every door, and there was no one here. It shook me up, because I know what I heard."

The director is not the only one who has experienced some strangeness. Rebel Sinclair, who leads walking tours for Black Cat Tours, has had her own experiences: "The Old Exchange and Provost Dungeon does have a presence to it. A lot of the ghostly encounters are very small. For instance, I personally have seen the chains which surround the exhibits in the dungeon start moving of their own accord. No one touches them, but they suddenly just start swaying. There's a lot of orb activity, and a lot of electromagnetic activity. The elevator, for instance, will go up and down of its own volition. A lot of the security guards have reported to me that they will see or hear this happen."

Denise Roffe, my good friend and author who wrote *Ghosts and Legends of Charleston*, related the following story to me: "One ex-staff member reported that he was in the dungeon, cleaning up and doing some of his job duties. He heard someone come into the area, but when he went to check, there was no one there. He then heard a conversation between two different people. He was sure that someone had come into the dungeon, but as he looked around, there was no one there. Understandably, he left rather quickly. Other staff members have described disembodied moans and even screams in that same area."

Personal Experiences

I personally have had two paranormal experiences while in the building, both occurring in 2008. I was part of a television pilot for a new prospective show called *Phantoms of History*. I was a producer and writer for the program, and we featured a few of the more famous ghost stories in Charleston. One of the properties that we highlighted was the Old Exchange and Provost Dungeon, which was gracious enough to give our film crew full access after-hours.

One of the days we were filming (in January of '08) was exceedingly challenging, schedule-wise. My grueling day involved getting up in the wee hours of the morning, and coordinating cast and crew all day long at three separate filming locations, the last of which was the Old Exchange. Needless to say, I was physically exhausted by the time our night shoot at 122 East Bay Street rolled around. I got everything ready, coordinating our crew and actors with Tony Youmans, who was supervising the entire filming at the Exchange. One of the sequences we were filming in the basement dungeon was winding down, and our director, Josh Jasso, turned to me and informed me that setting up the camera and positioning the lights for the next shot was going to take about 20 minutes. Seeing an opportunity to rest, if even just for a few moments, I told Josh and Tony that I was going upstairs to the deserted third floor to lie down on the floor, and they needed to come up and get me when they were ready. I ascended, and finding no one in the Great Hall, I stretched out on the old pine floor and closed my eyes, thinking about how much history those old floorboards had seen over the years.

About five minutes later, I heard the echoey sound of someone coming up the stairs. Their pace was rapid but not running, more like someone moving with a purpose, and it sounded like leather dress-shoes clicking against the floor. I both heard and felt their passage around me, the floorboards vibrated very slightly as they walked around my body, and I even felt the breeze from them walking very close to me. I laid there with my eyes closed because I was sure that this was Tony, whose office was in the direction that these feet were walking. However, rather than continuing on to his office, the footsteps stopped just past my head, and I felt the person waiting, standing within just a couple feet of me. As the seconds ticked by it became more and more awkward that this person wasn't saying anything. I finally opened my eyes, and discovered that I was completely alone in the room.

I went downstairs and asked everyone if they had just been in the Great Hall, and no one had. I suppose it would be easy to explain this away by saying that I was just dreaming about Tony's experience in that same room, but there's one problem with that thought: *I hadn't heard Tony's story yet.* Tony smiled when I related what happened to me and said, "Remember how y'all asked me for an interview tomorrow, where I am supposed to tell you my own personal ghost story? Well, that is exactly what I was going to tell you about. I've heard those same exact footsteps. Every detail matches in our experiences, even down to the leather soles. Spooky!"

My other experience in the Exchange happened a few months later: halfway through the editing process for the TV pilot we realized we didn't have any video or still photos of the Watch House, of which there is a small scale model in the Provost Dungeon. The story we were telling would flow a little better if we had that one image, so I offered to make the two hour drive from Savannah to Charleston. I recall thinking to myself that having a good excuse to grab a great meal and a tour in this beautiful city could be a wonderful thing.

I arranged things with Tony to come in right after the Exchange closed for business that day, and he ushered me down to the dungeon via the elevator. He had some paperwork to do, so he left me there to shoot a bunch of photos of the Watch House model while he went back upstairs to his office. The elevator doors closed behind him, leaving me all alone in the Provost Dungeon. I shot tons of photos, and then wandered around a little while amongst the other exhibits. It was creepy down there by myself, and I began to pity those who worked at the Exchange because they would have to spend a lot of time down there alone. I got the distinct impression that someone was down there watching me, which made me get the idea that maybe I should leave. When I walked to the elevator, it almost magically opened its doors for me, right as I approached. When I got back up to the top floor and let Tony know that I was finished, I mentioned the strangeness of the elevator opening up right as I neared it, hoping that Tony would tell me that it was motion-activated. Instead, he got that same smile as before, and said, "This is an old elevator. It only moves between floors or opens its doors if someone pushes the button, and you and I are the only two people in the Exchange right now. So it should have stayed up here, on the top floor, and it certainly shouldn't have opened its doors for you."

When I commented how strange that was, Tony simply said, "It happens all the time." And I remembered the words of tour guide Rebel Sinclair: *A lot of the ghostly encounters are very small… The elevator, for instance, will go up and down of its own volition.*

The Battery Carriage House Inn

20 South Battery

A compelling argument could be made that if a tourist only had fifteen minutes to spend in Charleston and sought to understand the city on a fundamental level in that narrow timeframe, he or she would be best served by walking the South Battery area, from end to end. Elegant mansions tell stories of a wealthy seaport, and the palmettoes, wafting in the gentle bay breezes at this southernmost point of the Charleston peninsula, indicate a temperate, balmy climate. The beautiful row of stately homes and their manicured gardens, yards away from a salt marsh where two rivers meet, speak to an idyllic, slow-paced lifestyle, while the monuments and cannons mounted in Battery Park tell of the area's deep connection to both the American Civil War and the War of 1812 (when the Battery formally earned its name). One could easily get a fairly accurate first impression of the city in about the amount of time it takes to brew a pot of tea. And maybe, just maybe, that same tourist could get an inkling of the shadowy side of Charleston's history, and her very close ties with the paranormal. Particularly if they stand at 20 South Battery, where the imposing mansion known as the Battery Carriage House Inn stands.

Pirates, Lunatics, Traitors, and Bawdy Ladies

Within a stone's throw of 20 South Battery, at an area called White Point (formerly Oyster Point) Gardens, many pirates were put to death. It was at this spot, in and around 1718, that the Charles Town authorities hanged their convicted sea outlaws, their bodies visible as grim examples to all who might be tempted to turn to a buccaneer lifestyle. According to Christopher Byrd Downey's book, *Charleston and the Golden Age of Piracy*,

This elegant mansion houses two of Charleston's most unusual spirits.

almost fifty pirates met their end at this location, including pirate captains Stede Bonnet (see his section in the chapter 'The Old Exchange and Provost Dungeon'), Richard Worley, and their crews. This area already has strong connections to tragedy and gruesome death.

The house at 20 South Battery, formally known as the Stevens-Lathers House, has had an extremely colorful history. It was originally built by Samuel N. Stevens, who was a factor, a line of work we know today as shipping agent. The three story house he built, however, looked radically different than the one we see today. Stevens sold the home in 1859 to John Blaylock, who did not live in the house very long due to the outbreak of the Civil War.

Some guides will claim that the cannons mounted on the Battery participated in the siege and reduction of Fort Sumter on April 12th, 1861, but apparently they either cannot read a map or are not aware that a ten-inch Columbiad cannon (of which the Battery had two) had a maximum range of 2.8 miles, making the Union fort a full half mile out of range. The Charlestonians did use the Battery area to throw lavish parties at the out-

"Some guides will claim that the cannons mounted on the Battery participated in the siege and reduction of Fort Sumter..."

break of hostilities, however. The Union shelled the area extensively later in the War, laying siege to the city of Charleston for 567 continuous days. During that time the South Battery became a virtual ghost town. Retreating Confederates intentionally blew up munitions and cannons to keep them from falling into enemy hands. When the Rebel soldiers detonated a large Blakely gun on the Battery, it showered many of the houses with chunks of hot cast iron and steel.

After the War's conclusion, the house was bought in 1870 by South Carolina native Colonel Richard Lathers. Unfortunately for Lathers, his military service was spent in the Union Army, and despite his honest efforts to generate goodwill between the North and South by opening up joint economic ventures, he was dreadfully unpopular amongst Charlestonians. Lathers left the South four years later. The house was repaired and renovated under his ownership, with a mansard-roofed fourth floor being added.

The next owner, Andrew Simonds, was not only a bank founder but also the owner of a phosphate company, which unfortunately involved strip-mining many of the beautiful local plantations for their minerals. Generally regarded as an unhappy man and a wild partier, Simonds eventually went insane and wound up in a Baltimore lunatic asylum. Later owners of the house converted it into Pringle's Court, which was a hotel.

The 1940's brought an influx of sailors. The outbreak of World War II saw Charleston transformed into a mighty naval shipyard, and with the sailors came the low-class ladies, plying their trade. The house was used as a boarding house which charged by the hour. By the 1960's, however, respectability returned and most of the area, the house at 20 South Battery included, became apartments.

Since the 1980's, the residence has been utilized as an upscale lodging house called the Battery Carriage House Inn. The Inn now boasts eleven tastefully decorated rooms (including one suite), which all hearken back to Charleston's history in general and the area's rich tradition in particular. Amenities include Old World touches like afternoon tea and sweets, early evening wine samples, and an in-room Continental breakfast. With creature comforts such as these, you might just forget that you live in the modern era. If the myriad of reports are any indication, the Inn offers such luxurious accommodations that many previously living residents have chosen not to leave, instead spending a free century or two forgetting all their troubles at the Battery Carriage House Inn. There are apparently many ghosts at the inn, but the two most famous are perhaps also the two most unusual spectres in all of Charleston.

The Truncated Apparition

Who hasn't heard the expression: *I'd forget my head if it wasn't attached?* Well, Room Eight at the Battery Carriage House Inn has a unique apparition who might just be the most forgetful ghost of all time. You see, if multiple eyewitnesses are correct, the fearsome entity occupying this particular room has not only forgotten to bring his head, but all of his limbs as well. His name could not be more apt: people describe him as 'the Headless Torso.'

This terrifying phantasm made his first documented appearance in late summer of 1992. An engineer and his wife were staying in Room Eight, when the man was awakened in the middle of the night. He first had the sensation of being watched. He first dismissed this perception as simply his own mind playing tricks on him, since he was trying to sleep in an unfamiliar place. However, the feeling of being observed continued. He finally opened his eyes and encountered a ghastly vision. There was a man standing in his room, making an unearthly moaning sound!

The engineer later described the being as definitely male, and just a torso, without head or other extremities. He was barrel-chested, and wearing multiple layers of clothing over his large frame. The engineer, convinced that he was dreaming, took his hand and placed it on the torso's coat. "I reached out and touched it," he later recounted. "His overcoat was of a very coarse material, like burlap. It was very scratchy." He described the clothing as an overcoat without any buttons, almost cape-like, with rough fibers sticking out of it.

The other thing immediately noticeable was the strange noises coming from the torso, like a raspy, labored breathing. The apparition made a louder sound when he was touched, as if he hated the man's hands upon him. He let out a guttural moan or growl which was distinctly threatening. "This thing didn't have an axe or a knife to kill me, but he was not happy that I was there," the engineer asserted.

Another sighting of this strange, limb-missing ghost took place in 1995, according to Denise Roffe, author of *Ghosts and Legends of Charleston*. A woman was relaxing on the bed in Room Eight while her husband showered. Suddenly she saw the exact same frightening image as the engineer had described. She saw a headless, limbless torso which wore a heavy grey coat. He approached her, causing the woman to run towards her husband in the bathroom. The Headless Torso then vanished without a trace.

Other Room Eight guests have reported that they have been awakened in the middle of the night by the sounds of heavy breathing and pitiful moaning. No apparition, they say, just the noises. One guest told me, "Most people get huge grins on their faces when I tell them about my wife and I waking up to a moaning ghost, you know, making a dirty joke out of the experience. But trust me, it was no laughing matter, and it definitely wasn't an amorous sound. I get the willies just thinking about it."

Many have speculated that this apparition is a pirate, perhaps returning from the grave for revenge, or even to protest his innocence. Most people subscribing to this theory point to the proximity to the former pirate gallows in present-day White Point Gardens as a possible explanation. The idea of a pirate still cruising the area where he died, for reasons unknown,

Photogrammetric Image: Aerial View Southeast Corner. Obtained from the Library of Congress Prints and Photographs Division.

is an intriguing one. What precisely would he be seeking, after nearly three centuries of unrest? Those condemned pirates were left to rot, swinging in the breeze until their decrepit forms were finally cut down and given to the tides and crabs along the Point. So could he be seeking a proper burial, at long last, in consecrated ground?

A more compelling theory, however, is that the ghost which haunts Room Eight was the by-product of the Confederate artillery batteries located in the area, quite possibly the explosion of the Blakely gun in February of 1865. It could very well be that this torso is all that remained of an unlucky Rebel artillerist. Was he killed in the Blakely's explosion? It is impossible to say: records from those desperate days are extremely scarce. Consider, too, that the area was pummeled by Union artillery all throughout the Siege of Charleston, so even if that specific gun's detonation did not kill the man in question, he might have been obliterated at any point during the terrible 567-day Federal barrage.

For me, a persuasive argument for The Headless Torso likely being a Confederate soldier is the engineer's exacting description of his coat material. The detailed mental picture painted by that former guest of a coarse, burlap-like material sounds like a perfect account of jean-wool, which was a blending of wool and cotton, the latter of which was plentiful and cheap in the South during wartime. This type of material was worn by many Confederates, especially late in the Civil War. Having worn jean-wool in the past, I can personally attest that it is precisely like the guest characterized, namely a very scratchy, woolen-like garment that looks and feels a bit like a burlap sack.

Whatever his identity, the Headless Torso has terrified all who have had the misfortune of coming into contact with him.

The Gentleman Caller

Room Ten at the Inn has a very different sort of ghost. Not only does he have all of his limbs, he apparently has an appetite for female company. One night in the early summer of 1992, two twin sisters were celebrating their birthday in style with a visit to Charleston, sharing Room Ten. One sister relates her experience: "I was lying on the right side of the bed, facing the door. I noticed a wispy gray apparition appearing to be floating through the closed door, and through the chair, entering the room. The configuration was of a man with no features being visible… just a gray wispy shape of a slightly built man. He moved in an upright gliding motion over to my side of the bed. He lay down… beside me on the bed. He placed his right arm around my shoulders. I didn't feel any pressure from his arm touching me. I wasn't frightened because he didn't seem threatening."

When she tried to alert her sister, the figure vanished. Rather than being alarmed or upset, the sister who had the visitation said, "I wish I had remained quiet and not spoken, because I feel I frightened him away."

Other women have reported similar sensations of having someone lay down next to them, or even caress them awake. The face of the spectral figure is never visible. The reports have one thing in common: none of the encounters are aggressively libidinous or improper. The ghost either simply lies down next to the sleeping woman or pets the female until she is awake, and then vanishes. The only time that the Gentleman Caller, as he has become known, was even remotely unpleasant was when a woman who was being lightly touched on the arm felt the ghost's skin on her own, and reported that it was freezing cold, very much like being stroked by a corpse. It was such a disturbing sensation that she screamed.

No one seems to know the identity of the Gentleman Caller. Theories usually point to a college student who supposedly killed himself on the property in the first half of the 20th century, but such reports are too vague to be substantiated. I, for one, am surprised that no one has ever latched on to the idea that the true identity of the Gentleman Caller could be Andrew Simonds, who was a former owner and also a notorious womanizer. Perhaps the mystery of the ghost's identity is preferable to establishing the ghost as a philandering man who died in an insane asylum? Given the choice of having the ghost of a nameless suicide or the ghost of Andrew Simonds creeping around my room in the middle of the night, I'm not so sure I wouldn't pick the random suicide victim, myself.

A Spirited Location

Regardless of the true identity of the spirits at the Battery Carriage House Inn, one would be hard-pressed to find a better spot to really 'experience' Charleston, South Carolina than a trip down to the South Battery. There you'll find palatial Southern mansions, warm summer breezes, pirate and Civil War history, and yes, even plenty of ghosts. It seems impossible to visit this stately location and not feel one's passions stirred: to feel the desperation of condemned pirates awaiting the noose, or of Southern families celebrating the start of a war for which they had clamored. Even many of those not particularly sensitive to psychic energy will find themselves affected by the three centuries' worth of ardor, anger and zeal for life packed into this relatively small geographic location.

Madame Talvande and the Sword Gates

32 Legare Street

Johann and Karin loved to tour Charleston, and were walking down Legare Street, site-seeing. While their English was quite good, they had particular trouble understanding the Southern dialect. Johann solved this language issue by purchasing an eBook guidebook, and they took turns narrating at each location. The shadows began to grow long as the low winter sun slipped beneath the horizon, and they decided to head back to their bed and breakfast, which was nearby. They paused briefly to get their bearings at a massively imposing gate made of swords, opening a map to orient themselves. Suddenly, an illuminated face appeared behind the gate, startling them both. Johann was so spooked that he took an involuntary step back.

Their momentary terror turned to amused embarrassment when they realized that it was just an old woman, creeping up on them as silent as the grave. "Ah, guten Abend," A slightly rattled Johann began, before trying in English: "Hello. Good evening!" The woman behind the gate said nothing in reply, only raising her lantern, as if to get a better look at the couple. She gave them a thoroughly disapproving look, and turned to walk away, disappearing into the gloom despite her lantern's light. The couple exchanged an amused look. Why was that resident so openly rude? Later, back at their bed and breakfast, the recounted the story of the incredibly strange and scary old woman to their innkeeper. He looked puzzled. "She was behind the Sword Gates? Are you quite positive?" They were.

"That property is for sale, and no one currently lives there," the innkeeper explained. "I think you just saw Madame Talvande."

"Oh, is she the owner?" Asked Karin. The innkeeper smiled and shook his head, and spoke words that chilled both of his guests to the bone.

"She gave them a thoroughly disapproving look, and turned to walk away, disappearing into the gloom despite her lantern's light."

"Not any more. She used to own it, but she's been dead for nearly a hundred and fifty years."

Swords and Bricks

Just a few scant blocks from the hustle and buzz of the downtown, a veritable Southern palace sits, shuttered to all in the outside world. To merely point out the ornately intimidating wrought iron gate, constructed in part out of swords and spears, would be to tell only a small part of the story. Drowsily smoldering behind a huge brick wall tastefully framed with stuccoed pilasters and draped with ivy, the folklore surrounding the house tells us the reason such an ostentatious and forbidding wall and gate were needed in the first place: they were designed for the unlikely purpose of keeping love out.

The three story house was built before 1810 by Solomon Legare. It was sold to the Talvande family, who were refugees from Santo Domingo, about a decade later. Ann Talvande, who was called Madame by all who knew her, converted it shortly thereafter into a girls' school. The school was the finest in the region, and Madame Talvande quickly earned a reputation as being extremely tough but fair. Affluent Charleston families took great pride in their daughters being accepted into Madame Talvande's school. During that time period, young women in institutions such as these were not only taught grammar and other academic subjects, they were also well-schooled in the art of etiquette and the social graces that were expected of proper ladies. Madame Talvande was extremely protective of her charges, since the dangers to a young woman's social standing were everywhere, especially in the form of young men. Even accepting an invitation to a formal gathering could be damaging if the young lady in question did not follow the proper protocol. This promise of purity and protection of reputation was one of the things the Madame was most renowned for, and the reason that she required any young woman who attended the school to also live on the premises. Several of her students had wound up at Madame Talvande's school specifically to avoid contact with young men who were, for one reason or another, considered by the family of the young lady in question to be an ill-suited match. This brings us to Maria Whaley, whose family insisted that she attend Madame's school specifically to avoid one particular young man named George Morris.

Forbidden Love

Maria Whaley was the sort of girl that attracted a lot of attention from the opposite sex. Barely fourteen, her good looks were legendary, and her effect on men was as instant as it was troublesome. Colonel Joseph Whaley was not eager to see his youngest daughter married off so soon. The problem was that young men for miles around their plantation on Edisto Island would find any number of excuses to come calling. If their fathers were visiting the Whaley's Pine Barren Plantation on business, their sons would tag along, eager to talk to Maria. If their horse threw a shoe while out riding, they would invariably make a beeline directly to the Whaley's, hoping to get a glimpse of the elusive (and gorgeous) daughter. The Colonel would have to shut his daughter up to keep them away from her.

She did not encourage these young men in the slightest, at least in the beginning. It seemed to her to be a mystery why the few that could endure her father's wrathful looks and stern warnings would do so, since they stammered and fumbled for word after fidgety word around her, anyway. She herself would often dismiss these young men, the ones brave enough to get close but not smart enough to engage her intellect. Eventually, the Colonel devised a rather clever rule of his own design. Any suitors who showed up seeking to engage his daughter in conversation would find their path blocked by a simple family edict: "Maria is forbidden from speaking to any man not living on this property until she reaches the proper age of sixteen." The strategy worked out wonderfully well for nearly a year; that is, until that Morris boy ruined everything.

Colonel Whaley saw sixteen year old George Morris coming, literally and figuratively, from a mile away. George approached on horseback, and the Colonel sat on the front porch, watching his approach. The Colonel knew George's family well. He was from a lesser Charlestonian family with whom Colonel Joseph had amicable business dealings. In the Colonel's estimation, he possessed neither the brawn, the good looks, or from what the Colonel remembered, the brains to successfully woo his dear sweet Maria. This would be easy to nip in the bud. George dismounted.

"Good afternoon, Colonel Whaley, I hope I am not imposing." George's strange expression, which seemed to be a sort of subtle cockeyed grin, never flickered from his face. It gave him the impression of everything he did and said being in jest.

Joseph met his gaze and barked curtly, "You *are* imposing on my time. What do you want?"

George said quickly, "Well, sir, I don't mean to trouble you. Could I perhaps have a word with Miss Maria Whaley?"

"No, you may certainly not," The Colonel said stiffly. "Maria is forbidden from speaking or corresponding to any man who does not live at Pine Barren until she is sixteen." Joseph almost expected the Morris boy to wilt and run, but George's smile never wavered.

"I see. Very well, sir, can I have your word as a gentleman that any message I leave for Miss Whaley will be faithfully conveyed?" The Colonel, somewhat stunned by the request, agreed to carry his message.

George looked him deeply in the eye and said with great conviction, "You are beautiful." The Colonel's face turned red and he sputtered with rage, but before he could interrupt, George continued, still wearing that sly half-smile: "You are beautiful, but I cannot help but wonder, dear sweet Maria, if that is all that there is to you, or is there more? Is there a powerful intellect locked up behind those azure eyes and those perfect lips? Does your lovely visage hide a wonderful wit? You deserve a man who would very much like to find out. Please, do not settle for less. That is my message, Colonel." And then George gave an odd little curtsy, adding: "Please, sir, won't you deliver my message for me?"

"I will," growled the Colonel, "Only because you tricked me into it. I am a man of my word, so I'll deliver your cursed message. Now move along before my boot delivers a message to you as well! Now move!"

George remounted his horse. "I shall move along, good sir. Just as you have requested." He left behind him a deeply troubled Colonel Whaley. He was afraid that he had underestimated George Morris, but the thing that disturbed him the most was that he was sure he had heard the faint sounds of stifled laughter coming from behind the shutters while George visited. His daughter had been listening, and George Morris, to the Colonel's knowledge, had been the very first young man who made her laugh.

The next day, a beautiful letter arrived at Pine Barren Plantation, showing elegant penmanship. It was affixed to the door, and from George Morris Esquire to Miss Maria Whaley. An incensed Colonel Whaley ripped the envelope from the door and rode down the shaded avenue of the estate, intent of returning the letter to George Morris at his home. The Colonel was going to explain things to him, and the boy's father would receive the same lesson. He was shocked, however, when he encountered George Morris at the edge of the Colonel's own property, his sly look still in place.

"What is the meaning of this?" The Colonel demanded holding up the letter. George said, "Sir, I only followed your own instructions. You told me no man could speak or correspond with Maria unless he lived at Pine Barren, am I not correct?" And with this, the Morris boy simply gestured towards something that Joseph had failed to notice: George had erected a tiny tent on the edge of the Colonel's property line. George was in fact living at Pine Barren Plantation!

"You told me to move, sir," George said, "So I did." Colonel Whaley, trapped by his own words, was forced to deliver the letter to his precious daughter. This time there was no mistaking the mirthful gleam in Maria's eye when he did so, and Joseph Whaley knew that he was in serious trouble. That odd Morris boy was outfoxing him at every turn.

A few days later, George sauntered up to the house, and again requested to speak to Maria. The Colonel drew himself up to his full height, puffed out his chest, and said, "No." When George asked why not, he was told that Maria no longer lived at Pine Barren. "She has been sent to Madame Talvande's school in Charleston, where she shall be safe from the likes of you!"

Truancy and Other Crimes

A few days later, there was a visitor at Madame Talvande's school. The young man asked if he might speak to Miss Maria Whaley. The Madame was summoned, and she gave this impertinent youth a withering glare. Many boys had cut and run from such a disdaining look, but this one only seemed to smile a little. He introduced himself, and repeated his request. "I'm sorry," she told George Morris, "School policy dictates that you may only speak to her if you have the same last name." The young man seemed to absorb this information. He thanked her, and left. Madame Talvande closed the door, confident that she would never see him again.

Later that evening, George Morris caught up to one of the young custodians as he left the school. "I have a proposition for you," George said. "All you have to do is deliver this note, and I'll pay you handsomely for your trouble…"

Madame Talvande was mildly surprised to see the same persistent young man approaching the front door the very next morning. He knocked politely, and she opened the door. "Young man, you are wasting your time. We have a long-standing policy at this school that only people with the same last name may speak to one of our students. Miss Whaley is not permitted to speak to you for this reason."

George Morris arched an eyebrow, and stated, "Dear Madame, but I am not here to speak to Miss Maria Whaley. I would never be so rude as to disregard your simple rules. I am here to see Maria *Morris*. Is she available?"

The Madame frowned. "But… we have no one here by that name. This school has no student with the last name of Morris."

George then said words which caused her heart to race: "Dear Madame Talvande, *are you quite sure*? You might want to be positive that there is no Mrs. Morris on your roll call before sending me away. After all, I personally delivered a Miss Maria Morris back to this very address late last night." And then George pulled out a marriage contract, dated the previous evening. It became obvious to the Madame that Maria had snuck off of school property just long enough to be married to this extremely clever boy. Madame Talvande, deeply embarrassed, was forced by custom to allow the new happy couple, George and Maria Morris, to depart the school together.

To prevent the same sort of episode from ever happening again (which would have positively ruined her reputation of being a reliable place to house the area's elite young ladies), Madame Talvande had a massive brick wall erected, turning her girl's school into a veritable fortress. To punctuate the penalty of attempting to sneak across the barrier, she commissioned a special iron gate, made of swords and spears. She also made it a habit to check each room several times a night, as well as walk the grounds personally, carrying a lantern. The imposing fence and gate, coupled with Madame Talvande's routine patrols, apparently did the trick: Maria Morris née Whaley was the only student the Madame ever lost in such a fashion.

"... they were designed for the unlikely purpose of keeping love out."

A Foreboding Presence Behind a Forbidding Gate

Many Charlestonians swear that they see Madame Talvande's lantern, either patrolling the grounds, or occasionally reflected in the windows of the former school, still checking to see if her charges are tucked safely in their beds after all these years. Occasionally, according to these stories, she walks right up to the gate, and then disappears. And now that list of people who believe that her devotion to her girls has survived the grave includes two German tourists, Johann and Karin, who had a close encounter with Madame Talvande one cool winter evening.

Author's Note

People always want to know: how much of a particular tale is true? Is the story accurate? Regarding this story, I can confirm that Madame Talvande (and her school) were very much real. Her most famous student was writer Mary Boykin Chesnut. The brick fence was indeed added after the school began, but evidence points to the gate at the Talvande School being made out of wood instead of iron. The famous heavy iron Sword Gate wasn't installed until 1850, after the school had closed. It was installed by George Hopley, after the property had become the British consul's private residence. It is one of the few wrought iron fences to survive the Civil War, since many of them were melted down to make cannons.

And what of the relationship between George and Maria? That is a famous Charleston love story. I leave it to the reader to decide what is factual and what is folklore in this charming tale of a clever young man and his beautiful bride.

One other bit of this chapter that I uncovered which is not connected to Johann and Karin's experience at the Sword Gates House (but is still a compelling enough story to warrant inclusion) comes from a September 3rd 1950 Charleston News and Courier article. It details the experiences of the owner of the house in 1950, Mr. Henry T. Gaud, who reported compelling evidence of another ghost in the Sword Gates House which was definitely not Madame Talvande, because the spirit was male. Mr. Gaud tells of first hearing the story from aunts and uncles some thirty-five year prior, who themselves heard the story while attending dinner parties in the home. Years later, Mr. Gaud and his family acquired the home and began to experience the spectre themselves. He was known as the 'ghost who never comes to dinner,' and apparently liked to slam the front door at a late hour, hang his silk top-hat on a non-existent antique wall-mounted rack (which Mr. Gaud himself removed when renovating) in the hall, and then vanish.

Mr. Gaud stated: "The first night we heard it was shortly after we moved in last year. It was after midnight and we distinctly heard a door, the front door we believe, slam shut. I went down and checked it but it was locked. I then put the lights on and searched the entire house but found nothing. About three hours later, we heard the door slam again. A second search also revealed nothing out of the way." Despite hearing the ghost on numerous occasions, the Gauds seemed to accept the spirit almost as if he were a member of their own family. He had never bothered the family, other than the occasional door slam. They did report that the ghost's 'routine' had scared some workmen at the home, however, who then refused to work after dark.

Gaud quite plainly stated that he never bothered the family. Was he simply an echo from the past, repeating his actions in life again in death? Or was this fashionable ghost making a snide comment about Gaud's decision to remove the hat rack, stubbornly continuing to use it even after it had been removed? If the *ghost was indeed angry about the renovations, he never gave any outward sign. The article is proof that for many Charleston families, it isn't just that having a ghost in their home is routine: the ghost's routine can even become routine. It seems at least that this ghost, whose identity Mr. Gaud never speculated, is quite content in his habit of returning home safely.*

82 Queen Restaurant

82 Queen Street

One of the very best things about Charleston is the fact that you can walk into practically any restaurant, bar, hotel or retail shop in the downtown, ask the staff if there are any ghost stories attached to the building, and almost always get an affirmative answer. In fact, many of the chapters in this volume came about from me simply (very politely) questioning the staff at a location where I was enjoying a fine meal or beverage, with no preconceived notion on my part about whether or not the building was haunted. Making inquiries with the staff if they had ever experienced anything there which they would deem otherworldly almost always yielded results. That's the beauty of a city 'blessed' by such a dark-tinged history and an effort to preserve the old buildings: you are surrounded by spots with wonderful ghost stories and legends at all times, and all you need to do to hear them is to respectfully ask the right person.

Such was the case in the short city block between King and Meeting Streets, an area which serves practically as mecca for both lovers of fine food and ghost stories. Tucked in amongst the other fine-dining establishments along this relatively small stretch of sidewalk, 82 Queen has served as one of the standard-bearers of Charleston cuisine for over thirty years. A three-time winner of the 'Best City Restaurant' award from Southern Living magazine and five time recipient of the Award of Excellence from Wine Spectator magazine, the restaurant is a must-visit for anyone interested in sampling the very best dishes the Lowcountry has to offer.

As my server delivered my lunch order, which was an impeccable grilled chicken breast and crab cake served on a bed of cheddar grits, I very casually asked him if there were any ghost stories associated with the property. He nodded, and in a low voice (acting if his answer might somehow alarm the other diners), he said, "Oh yes, of course. This is one of the oldest areas of the city. Quite naturally, we have more than a few stories of ghostly goings-on. Diners will quite often report feeling a sensation of

"I once walked through a shadow which dissipated around me like smoke," she said.

hearing or seeing things, if they're sensitive to that sort of thing. I seem to be immune, and I can't decide if that is a good or bad thing." I asked him about the stories he had heard about 82 Queen.

"I can say that I've never heard any tales involving evil ghosts. It all seems to be pleasant, or at least benign; it seems as if this area is so rich with history that the past doesn't seem to know it is in the past. Both diners and staff alike have reported hearing horses whinnying for example, when obviously there are no horses nearby, or catching small snippets of a conversation in an empty room. People catch glimpses of former events, and that sort of thing."

That sentiment was echoed by a female former server named Jenn, who said, "Charleston seems to have cornered the market on 'famous ghosts.' You know the sort I mean: like Blackbeard, for instance, or Robert E. Lee. Big names—if a particular spot is haunted then people try to tie famous personalities to them. But a place like 82 Queen doesn't have a famous ghost, even though they have several spirits in the restaurant. I worked there for about eighteen months and saw several things in my time which make me believe that, yes, absolutely, that establishment is haunted. I would round a corner and see someone in what looked like period dress, and then they would vanish. It wasn't my imagination because other servers would later describe seeing that same person, even down to the color they were wearing. Oh, and another story: I once walked through a shadow which dissipated around me like smoke. She was definitely female, but that's the only impression I could get before she was gone.

"You cannot tie a 'famous ghost' to 82 Queen. The man who built the building back in 1865, John O'Mara, was a bookseller. Well, there's no way to make a bookseller into a scary story. I've seen him, by the way, just a little pudgy bookish fellow. Like so many of us, he's not famous, and not really notable at all unless you figure in the fact that he doesn't know he's dead."

It was only well after the interview concluded did it occur to me that Jenn had described seeing an apparition disappear into a cloud of dark smoke, and the spot where she witnessed this was a location which had very famously burned, back in December of 1861. Was the haunting connected to this fire? Records of that fire do not indicate where specific deaths occurred, but several fatalities were recorded. My attempts to establish a concrete correlation between the two events simply evaporated, much like Jenn's apparition.

Charleston Orphan House

Now the Joseph E. Berry Jr. Residence Hall

80 St. Philip Street

Many ghost tours will tell you the sad tale of the Charleston Orphan House, which allegedly suffered a devastating fire in October of 1918. Just how much truth is told in these stories involving a prank gone wrong, and some poor orphans who paid the ultimate price?

Here are the facts, before delving into the folklore story: the Charleston Orphan House, which was the oldest municipal orphanage in the United States, was established by an act of the Charleston City Council in 1790. There was a need for such a facility due to high mortality rates in the area, as well as a problem of indigent families not being able to adequately care for their young. Although the Orphan House was officially created in 1790, the institution was housed in temporary quarters for nearly four years. The cornerstone of the new Orphan House, occupying the corner of Calhoun and St. Philip Streets, was laid in 1791 by President George Washington. The building formally opened in 1794. The site remained the Charleston Orphan House, with numerous additions and improvements, for nearly one hundred and fifty years, finally closing in 1951.

The folklore story about the old Orphan House, which you would likely hear from a ghost tour or other sources, is as follows:

In 1918, Charleston was, much like the rest of the world, in the deadly grip of an influenza outbreak. The pandemic, which eventually killed an estimated one hundred million people, did not leave the orphanage untouched: over two hundred of the orphans and many of the staff had been struck down by the illness. This left the orphanage extremely short-staffed, meaning many of the children had to fend for themselves. Left to their own devices, a few of the more

Orphan House, Charleston, S.C., by William Henry Jackson. Obtained from the Library of Congress Prints and Photographs Division.

mischievous children attempted to play a prank on the staff: they set fire to a bundle of oily rags and moss which they then left on the orphanage's front doorstep. They rang the doorbell repeatedly, then ran and hid a short distance away, where they waited to see which unfortunate caretaker emerged and was forced to stomp out the smoldering mess. The problem was, no one ever did emerge to put out the fire. The smoke billowed even higher and more furiously, and soon flames were shooting up from the porch. In the ensuing blaze, several children lost their lives, victims of a deadly prank gone way, way wrong.

By 1951, the venerable old building had outlived its usefulness. It was torn down to make way for a Sears and Roebuck department store, which was in turn demolished in the 1980's. In 1991, the College of Charleston opened up a new student dormitory on that location. Named the Joseph E. Berry Residence Hall, it can accommodate over six hundred students. Since the dorm opened, however, there have been constant complaints about fire alarms, which apparently will sound at all hours. The college administration and law enforcement have been completely frustrated in their efforts to catch the perpetrators of these false alarms, which continued to sound even after the college switched the fire alarm boxes to the type which, when activated, sprays a special dye. The substance stains the skin *of the person pulling the fire alarm, but despite this precaution, no offender has ever been caught. These reports have persisted, despite the college shutting down the building and renovating the entire electrical system, fire alarms included, in 2003. Students also complain of hearing the sounds of unseen children's feet running through the hallways of the dorm, and several students have reported the faint, eerie sounds of children's singing wafting through the air vents.*

Just how much truth is contained in this story? Well, we have a legend in two parts: namely, the fire in 1918, and the strange occurrences which have been experienced by students from the years 1991 to the present day. Taking them in order:

—There is no documented evidence to support the folklore version's assertion that there was a fire at the orphanage in October of 1918. There were no deaths attributed to smoke inhalation during the time period. Another (admittedly minor) technical exception that I take with this story is the fact that the so-called Spanish Flu did not typically afflict the young; that particular strain of influenza was particularly noteworthy because it tended to strike down people with perfectly healthy immune systems. Spanish Flu, unlike most other versions of that particular illness, was actually less virulent amongst children, the very old, and the infirm; so the idea of a ward full of two hundred sick children is simply not credible.

—A separate issue is whether or not students have experienced anything supernatural at the dorm. The answer seems to be a resounding 'yes.' Freshman College of Charleston student Caroline Simmel went so far as to start a petition in 2011 regarding conditions at the dorm, and one of her chief complaints was about the fire alarms: "The dorm's fire alarm system went off randomly during the day at least once every two weeks, sometimes more frequently, forcing all of the residents out of the building." Student Natasha Gehlhausen documented the phenomenon for a class paper, citing a witness: "I first heard about the hauntings from a few girls I met that lived in the dorms themselves and experienced paranormal activity on their own… 'Oh, the damn fire alarm!' joked my witness, Cara Gardner, 'I must have walked outside in my underwear fifty times in the year that I lived at Berry'…Hundreds of girls in the last decade that the Berry dorm has been open for freshmen have experienced irregular supernatural phenomenon… Even today, many girls post Facebook statuses about how irritating the false alarms are and about how they can hardly ever sleep with the voices that they hear at night."

Frequently, folklore legends are added after the fact to explain genuine ghost phenomena: disembodied footsteps on the stairs, for instance, spawn stories of a woman who used to live in the home who lost her children in the middle of the night, and now feels the need to check on them, even in the afterlife. An eerie glowing light near a railroad tracks quickly becomes explained away as the spirit of a man who was hit and killed by a train. I investigate these types of stories all the time. Even verifiable, documented events are sometimes changed to suit the ghostly happenings. I firmly believe that this is one of those cases, where a mysteriously recurring pulled fire alarm on the site of an old orphanage becomes 'explained' via some fanciful storytelling, in this case a spurious tale about a group of orphans who died in a fire. But somewhere in the midst of this overly-simplistic, fictionalized yarn about children perishing in a blaze is a very complicated truth that no one has quite managed to puzzle out yet. This plot of ground has seen Charlestonians at their very worst, from poor families giving up their unwanted offspring, and the very best, involving charity and the milk of human kindness. Imagine for a moment the very fabric of these children's lives being ripped asunder as they were orphaned at a young age. How much psychic turmoil would that generate? How much suffering and heart-rending emotions, then, has that city block seen over the years? What sort of spirit would be left behind?

The short answer is: I don't know; but whoever (or whatever) is there simply *loves* fire alarms.

St. Philip's Church.

Dock Street Theatre

135 Church Street

A short distance south of St. Philips' steeple along Church Street, a very historic building reminds us that structures can be revisited by more than ghosts; they can be 'haunted' by their former glory when the property gets repurposed. The Dock Street Theatre, located at the corner of Queen and Church streets, is the site of Charleston's first building dedicated solely to the theatre arts. As early as 1736, what was then called the New Theatre at Dock Street began hosting performances which delighted audiences of all ages, beginning with a performance of the comedy, *The Recruiting Officer*, on February 12th of that year.

Though the current structure dates from 1809 and was a lodging house instead of a theatre, that hasn't prevented the lines between the two structures from blurring, from a spectral standpoint. The common lament about old buildings is: *Oh, if these walls could talk, what stories could they tell!* Well, that might be precisely what is happening at the Dock Street Theatre. I sat down with Christopher Parham, who is the managing director of Charleston's historic Dock Street Theatre. He filled me in about the history and the ghosts of the old theatre, qualities that the old building possesses in spades.

"I've worked here for ten years," Christopher began. "I have a strong respect for both the history and the mysteries here at Dock Street Theatre. Starting at the beginning, the original building opened in 1736, and drew its name from the street which has been renamed Queen Street but at that time was called Dock Street. It runs today down to present-day Waterfront Park, and of course that used to be where the docks were located. The name of the street changed shortly thereafter, but the name stuck, and Charlestonians for many years referred to the theatre as being on Dock Street even though it was on Queen. It was the first building specifically built to be a theatre in the city of Charleston. There was a Great Fire in 1740 which took out a lot of this neighborhood. The theatre sort of dis-

Oh, if these walls could talk, what stories they could tell!

appears from the records, so we assume it burned. In that time period, theatres actually burned all the time, so it is very possible that the theatre didn't just fall victim to the fire, it could have caused it. It appears that the theatre was rebuilt by the following season and operated on the same site. The theatre operated for several years, but Charleston experienced an economic boom in the 1750's and on into the 1760's. That meant that bigger, grander, more elaborate playhouses were built, and the theatre here was eventually torn down."

Robert Armstrong Andrews, state director of the Federal Art Project, described the old playhouse in a 1937 article which appeared in 'Work News,' a monthly magazine devoted to Works Progress Administration (WPA) projects:

The interior of the Dock Street theatre was designed in the manner of London's playhouses. Facing the stage was a pit with backless benches. Flanking the walls were thirteen boxes, seating eight persons each. And in the rear of the theatre was a gallery. Candles flickered in their brackets along the panelled walls. The 18th century theatre observed class distinctions carefully. Servants sat in the pit;

their masters and mistresses looked down from the boxes. The costumes of those boxholders were dazzling; powdered wigs and brightly colored cloaks for the gentlemen; elaborate headdresses and fans for the ladies. And occasionally, if a play were naughty, a mask, or "vizard" would be worn to conceal a blush. The Charleston of this era was a carefree and happy city, secure in its bounty of indigo and rice and cotton… All this was to fade and change, leaving only crumbling walls, sea winds blowing softly through the morning glory vines.

Mr. Parham continued his narrative in our interview: "In 1809, the plot was purchased by Alexander Calder and his wife (author's note: Calder is an ancestor of the 20th century sculptor of the same name), and they opened the Planter's Hotel at this location. It was the first major hotel in Charleston, and it was an opulent place to stay. That 1809 building is the one you see today. The central façade was the front of the hotel. As the hotel grew, it absorbed the neighboring buildings, eventually forming a large 'L shaped' building that followed both Queen and Church streets. The 'planters' in the name refers to the rice, cotton and tobacco planters, the plantation owners who would stay here during the racing and gambling season. In fact, the drink 'planter's punch' was invented here, and in our upstairs pub we have a framed print of the original recipe."

Robert Armstrong Andrews' 1937 WPA article described the old Planter's Hotel:

For fifty years it stood unchallenged as the rendezvous of gentlemen and ladies from the old South. Distinguished in its cooking and wines and its liquors… Here was the center of the life of the opulent plantation days; here was the focus for wit and gallantry, romance and tragedy. And it, too, was to fade and change, falling under the shadow of the South's long trouble, falling, like the Dock Street theatre, of an earlier day, into mellow ruin.

Christopher resumed his description of the building's history. "The hotel was open from 1809 until the 1870's; of course, service was briefly interrupted during the 1860's—historians call that interruption the Civil War—and during that time frame it served as a Confederate barracks and hospital." After the time frame that Mr. Parham referenced, the hotel fell, once again, into decay. A *Charleston News and Courier* article from July 16th, 1973, noted that the former hotel was vacant by the 1930's, a sad era in which it had to be "roped off after a black delivery boy was struck by a piece of slate falling from the roof."

"It was turned back into an active theatre in the 1930's as part of the WPA," Christopher said. "So 1937 is when the theatre was rebuilt and opened." I found an old article from the *Charleston News and Courier* from that year which detailed an amazing discovery in the restoration process:

Several items of interest already have been discovered... Marks have been found where one of the [Union] shells fired in the bombardment of the city passed through the roof of the theatre, continued through the floor and two wall partitions, and landed in a fireplace in the opposite side of the building. The shell itself... [had] long since been removed, but the marks were plainly visible. A strange feature of this 'traveling' shell is the fact that although it landed in the fireplace and destroyed the arts of the fireplace, the fireplace itself was uninjured, there being no explosion.

"We've been an active live-performance theatre since 1937," Mr. Parham shared. "We are managed by the City of Charleston. The arts organization Charleston Stage, which became the resident professional theatre group at the Dock Street Theatre in 1978, produces over 120 performances each season and plays to more than forty thousand patrons annually. We were forced to renovate again in 2007, when the theatre underwent a $20 million dollar facelift. Any time a building is used on a daily basis, it is very hard on the structure. History had been rough on the theatre—for instance, we discovered that the damage from the Great Earthquake in 1886 was far greater than anyone had realized. The façade had pulled away from the building by as much as two or three inches, in essence becoming a free-standing structure. But all of that wear, neglect and damage have all been fixed now."

I asked Christopher if there were any famous ghost stories associated with the Dock Street Theatre, and he said that there were, dating from when the property was a hotel. "As larger hotels were built and competition increased later in the 1800's, smaller hotels like the Planter's were forced to change with the times." Chris seemed to be picking his words very carefully here, but fortunately I knew enough of the story that I knew where he was heading with the narrative. "Hotel staff," Christopher continued, "were inclined to relax certain standards, and allowed ladies onto the premises to make their guests more comfortable."

I tried to let him know that I understood perfectly. "Christopher, are you saying that these ladies offered a very special turn-down service? The type of service that no one was ever turned down for?"

Christopher laughed, and said, "Yes, exactly. I'm speaking of ladies of negotiable affections. Nettie Dickerson was just one such woman who was well-known by the staff. There are a number of stories told about Nettie—one goes that she turned to this line of work because she once had love and lost it, and others say that her career choice was out of sheer necessity. At any rate, she grew extremely dissatisfied with the lifestyle as time wore on. It is said that one night, at her wits end, she found herself standing on the cast iron second floor balcony, glaring up at the sky. She began to yell at God, stating that this was not the direction she wanted for her life. Witnesses say she thrust her fists in the air, angrily taunting God's wrath. Well, lightning struck the cast iron balcony, and ended poor Nettie's life.

"It is said that Nettie still roams the hotel. Most sightings are on the second floor where our dressing rooms are located today, and those would have been guest rooms when she was alive, so she is seen in an area with which she would have been very familiar. She could have even stayed in those rooms. The second floor is of course where the balcony on which she lost her life is located, and adjoining that there is a drawing room, which back during Nettie's time would have been used as a ballroom. Again, that would have been an area that she frequented and knew quite well. It is said that she appears more to men, and that seems to be the case, since every staffer here I have ever heard of seeing Nettie were all men.

"I have heard some tour guides say that when she is seen, she is only seen from the knees up—and the claim is that because she is still standing and walking on the original floor, and when the hotel was gutted the floor height rose dramatically. Well, while it is true that the floor level rose, it was not that drastic. Nettie is most frequently seen by employees in the second floor hallway."

I asked if Christopher had ever seen any apparitions during his time there. "In my ten years here," he said, "I've never seen anything like that, but I also don't go looking for anything, either. That's part of my respect towards this building. Although I've never seen any apparitions, that's not to say that I never sense anything. Plenty of afternoons and evenings, I'll just get a sense, a strong feeling, that it is time to go. I certainly know when it is time to not be here anymore. I have experienced some odd things, especially early on in my tenure here when my office was on the first floor as opposed to the second, I would hear unexplainable noises like people walking around on floors above me when I knew positively that I was here by myself. Let's just say that sometimes I calmly finish what I'm doing, turning off all of the lights, and locking all of the doors on my way out. And other times it's much more urgent: where I grab my bag, and lock the front door as quickly as I can. Like I said: respect. I've heard things,

"However, while on the first floor, I kept hearing the distinct footsteps of people—not just one or two, but of a group of six or more,"

I've had things move, and I've had papers fly off of my desk for no reason. It does seem to intensify when the city is busy, for instance during the Spoleto Festival, because during those times there is always someone here. I have noted that the building itself grows restless during those times of great activity, and that's when things start to happen. Chandeliers refuse to work, for instance, or lights flicker for no reason; papers fly off of desks, like I mentioned, or sound cables come unplugged even though you know that you've taped them together. Its times of heavy use and the fact that the building never gets to rest that it really begins to act up.

"Another ghostly visitor who is seen on a consistent basis is a male figure who is seen in either Box 'BB' or the center box balcony. What this particular spirit does is watch rehearsals. Some of our actors will see him sometimes as they're rehearsing, and he'll be in the box seats, wearing a hat and a cape. Or, as has happened occasionally, a stagehand will mistake him for another stagehand, and call out for him to do something, and grow frustrated when he doesn't respond. He has even been seen by staff members, who at first think that the door was mistakenly left open and someone wandered in, and will head up to the second floor to usher him

A spectre, thought to be Junius Booth, has been seen watching rehersals at the Dock Street Theatre.

out. But the figure always vanishes. It has been widely speculated that this Junius Booth." Christopher let the name sink in for a moment. "Junius Booth?" I asked. "Booth, as in--?"

He smiled. "Yes, I'm speaking of *that* famous Booth family. Junius was the father of John Wilkes Booth, and the Booth family was a collection of famous actors, and an even more famous collection of drunks. Junius did come to Charleston to perform. Of course, he never performed here, but it was because it was a hotel during that time period, but he did stay here. Junius certainly enjoyed alcoholic beverages, and because of that he came back here to his room one night during his visit in 1838 and suffered some sort of fit or episode. He took a fire poker from the fireplace in his room and beat his manager in the head severely, chasing the poor man down the hallway to the lobby, until he was restrained. It was reported in the papers, and everyone knew what had happened. The next night, amazingly, he was back on the stage as Richard III, seemingly without a problem."

Junius Booth had a history of erratic and volatile behavior. He penned a letter threatening the life of his friend, who also happened to be Andrew Jackson, who was then serving as U.S. President. During the same Southern trip in which he beat his manager with a fireplace iron, he also attempted suicide by leaping from a steamship. Somehow, the bizarreness of his character only seemed to enhance his performances. The next night after delivering that epic bludgeoning, the *Southern Patriot's* reviewer excitedly declared his performance as "among the finest exhibitions of histrionic power we have ever witnessed… On the whole it was the most thrilling piece of acting we have ever seen…"

"So," Chris continued, "because of the theatrical connection, people seem to think that it's Booth who lingers. Hopefully he approves!"

I asked if there were any more odd occurrences that Mr. Parham could relate. He did not hesitate, answering in the affirmative. "Another strange thing that both I and others have experienced is the random smell of pipe tobacco or cigar smoke. It's not at all unusual to be sitting by yourself and smell the very strong tobacco smell, and then it goes away. It's a very distinctive odor—you can't mistake that for anything else. You try to assume it's just a tourist who has come through who smells of it, but I've been by myself in an empty theatre and I've experienced it."

After giving me a personal guided tour of the entire theatre, Christopher finally took his leave, allowing me to take some photos. I spent some time on the upper floors, snapping frame after frame, and wandered down to the first level to do the same. However, while on the first floor, I kept hearing the distinct footsteps of people—not just one or two, but of a group of six or more, above me in the second floor box seats. I tried stepping out into the orchestra pit area to peer up and see who was there, but each time I saw no one. On my way out, I stopped at the front desk. "Has anyone else been through here when I was taking photos?" I asked.

"No," the genial woman at the front desk replied, and gestured out at the cold and rainy January day. "I suppose the bad weather has scared everyone off. Besides me out here and Mr. Parham back in his office, you had the entire theatre to yourself, and that's pretty rare. I guess you picked the perfect day to take all your pictures."

I considered mentioning the incident; instead I simply thanked her, and glanced back towards the theatre door. "Yes ma'am, I am just very lucky. I picked the perfect day."

Duelists at St. Michael's Rectory

76 Meeting Street

On occasion, we come across ghost stories where the altered nature of a building changes the fundamental characteristics of a haunting. A common story involves particularly drastic renovations on a structure which can sometimes stir up all manner of paranormal activity, either positive or negative. But an equally intriguing occurrence is when a building's purpose changes, and that modification of use seems to bring peace to the spirits that dwell within.

This brings us to 76 Meeting Street, which was built in 1785 for Judge Elihu Hall Bay at the corner of Meeting Street and St. Michael's Alley. The colorful Judge Bay, a Maryland native, demolished the Indian trading store which stood previously on the lot and erected a three story wooden house in its place. This small house dwells in the shadows of nearby St. Michael's Church. The home offers a relatively narrow profile to the street, but extends deep into the lot, making it appear deceptively tiny when viewed from Meeting Street.

A Stuttering, Irascible Figure

Judge Bay was an accomplished jurist. In fact, he was the judge that presided over the hearing which determined whether John and Lavinia Fisher had committed highway robbery in May of 1819. His verdict, which was upheld upon appeal, was one of the decisions which sentenced the couple to hang for their crimes, making it one of the most famous verdicts ever handed down in South Carolina. He did, however, have an eccentric reputation: he possessed a keen intellect, but he stuttered quite badly, and was also mostly deaf, so testimony in his court had to be screamed, rather

"... at about the hour of midnight, a sound is heard of someone walking up the stairs, dragging a heavy body such as a wounded man."

than spoken. The staunch Republican also tended to repeat himself, and had a reputation for surliness. He once had two defendants, arrested in completely separate incidents, who were incarcerated for biting. Judge Bay sentenced them to occupy the same cell, where, he said, "you have my permission to bite each other as much as you please!"

Bay's son Andrew, who contrary to his father's political leanings was a vocal member of the Democratic Party, came home very late one night in the company of two friends. The trio were obnoxiously drunk, and were not exactly quiet when they bounded up the stairs. Apparently they caused a very loud commotion with their inebriated carousing, because the next day a neighbor inquired with Judge Bay what had caused the racket. The old judge sneered, saying simply: "Drunk, drunk, and a Democrat."

Shots of Whiskey, Shots of Lead

While frequently grouchy, Judge Bay had a tender side. St. Michael's Alley, which runs along the northern edge of the house, was a location preferred by some Charlestonians to settle duels. 'Affairs of honor,' as they were called, were prohibited by law, but for the most part the practice was ignored by the law. A group of intoxicated young men got into a serious disagreement late one evening in 1786, and two of them decided to have a duel. Shots rang out a little before midnight, awakening the Judge from a sound slumber. When the smoke cleared, one of the combatants lay crumpled in the alley, writhing in pain. The wound was quite serious, and the Seconds in the makeshift duel stood over their fallen friend, loudly debating what to do. "Don't just stand there," the Judge bellowed down at them from his window overlooking the alley. "Help me get him into the house." Together, they carried the fallen man into Judge Elihu's house, awkwardly supporting his moaning, bleeding form up the stairs and putting him to bed in a second floor bedroom. Suddenly the friends of the duelist realized that, in a twist of fate, their stricken fellow had been taken into the home of a prominent Charleston judge. Fearing the legal ramifications of their actions, the cowards abandoned their compatriot, fleeing to save themselves. Judge Bay sent for the doctor, not the police, and endeavored to save the young man's life. Sadly, before medical help arrived the young duelist succumbed to his wounds.

The ghost of this fallen duelist, for many years thereafter, returned to the spot of his wounding and quick expiration, according to a 'Do You Know Your Charleston?' article which appeared in the *Charleston News and Courier* on November 19th, 1935: "The house is said to be haunted. Its present owner, averring that he does not believe in ghosts, says emphatically that on several occasions that he has heard manifestations that… others describe as being caused by ghosts. Though care is exercised not to inform servants of the ghost which is supposed to be in the house, nevertheless, sometimes they leave for this reason… at about the hour of midnight, a sound is heard of someone walking up the stairs, dragging a heavy body such as a wounded man. The wounded man's feet apparently strike each step. After the top of the stairs is apparently reached, it seems that the body is dragged into the room and thrown onto the bed."

A follow-up article a few days later (titled 'Ghost at 76 Meeting Street Conjured Up By Negro Nurse') in the same paper contained the reminisces of Mrs. B. Moroso Bellinger, who had lived in the house growing up in the late 19th century. The family knew nothing of the story of the duelist who died in the house, but amazingly, talk still centered on the sounds of a heavy body being dragged up the steps. Mrs. Bellinger related that a nurse who worked for the family began to weave an ominous narrative for the children as they tried to sleep, attributing the sounds to the ghost of a slave girl: "She literally scared us to sleep, telling us of the ghost of a slave girl who was chained in the attic, a dark place under the roof and of no use, but there is a door and inside rough steps. Naturally we believed we heard noises, chains clanking and heavy bodies dragged up the steps." Years later the family moved due to the Earthquake of 1886. "It was decided," Mrs. Bellinger related, "to move to a safer locality where there was no danger of St. Michael's steeple falling upon us. So began the exodus… when the cases of books were to be moved the attic door was opened and there we saw an anklet and chain and odd bits of leather and rags."

Spiritual Absolution

Were the ghosts at 76 Meeting the dying duelist and his delinquent companions from 1786, repeating the night of their tragic folly over and over? Or was it the slave girl, stories of whom so frightened a group of children, chained by the ankle and cruelly locked in the attic for reasons unknown? We will almost certainly never know. You see, in 1942, the Vestry of St. Michael's Church, which needed a rectory (housing for the clergy), purchased the home. By all accounts, the hauntings inside 76 Meeting Street ceased immediately upon its purchase by the nearby church. The presence of men of the cloth seem to have completely laid the spirits to rest.

The facts of this story have been neatly arranged. Now, at the very end of the story, let us engage in just a wee bit of conjecture. Consider that awful night in 1786, the events of which we are already familiar: the drunken and foolhardy duel, the agonizing wound, and the kindness of a perfect stranger to open his home. The mortally-wounded, moaning man is half-dragged, half carried, by his dubious friends, spattering the stairs with his ebbing, crimson life's-blood. The young men, fearing punishment, flee their dying companion. Now imagine that these men are condemned to repeat this awful night, over and over and perhaps forever, in the spirit world. For these young men, it is the night of their greatest sin on this earth, namely the terrible moment where they selfishly act to save themselves instead of standing by their wounded fellow. For over 150 years, they are forced to revisit that cowardly, life-altering moment, and each time the dreadful details remain unchanged. *Shooting, dragging, fleeing. Shooting, dragging, fleeing.*

Now, imagine the ghosts of these same young men, still carrying their stricken friend up the stairs, into what has, post-1942, been converted into a *reverend's* house. They are bearing their friend towards a man of the cloth. There is no judgment, no reason to flee; there is only absolution. Their dying friend suddenly experiences spiritual comfort, entering a clergyman's house. Perhaps these friends also find a strange peace washing over them. In delivering their friend to a man of God's house, they are released from their cruel loop of repeating that shameful crime against friendship. The little house at 76 Meeting has become, at long last, precisely what they needed.

The Old Citadel (now Embassy Suites)

337 Meeting Street

More often than not, to understand the hauntings in the present we must know what has come before. Never has this been truer than at 337 Meeting Street, which is currently an Embassy Suites Hotel. During the Revolutionary War, a fortification known as a 'Horn Works' was established in the vicinity of present-day Marion Square. This area was renamed 'The Arsenal' in 1829. In the 1830's, it became clear to many residents that there was a need for a military academy in the city, and the former location of the Horn Works was selected. According to Walter Frasier's book, *Charleston! Charleston! The History of a Southern City*, "after persistent urgings from Charlestonians, the state legislature chartered the South Carolina Military Academy, or Citadel, in 1842… On the site of the Arsenal… an imposing, two-story brick, fortress like building with turrets went up. Over time, two additional stories and wings were added."

The Citadel became a full-fledged military college. Citadel graduates have served in every war and major theatre of operations fought by the United States since 1842. Included in those engagements was January 9th 1861, when a Confederate battery on Morris Island which was manned by Citadel Academy cadets fired on the Federal steamer *Star of the West*. Their barrage prevented it from reaching Fort Sumter with troops and supplies; so it was Citadel graduates who fired what some consider the first shots of the Civil War. In addition, the first shot of the bombardment of Fort Sumter on April 12th, 1861 is believed by many historians to have been fired by Second Lieutenant Henry S. Farley, who was part of the Citadel's graduating class of 1860.

"... there was a guest as of several weeks ago who reported seeing an apparition and a bright light floating around his room."

For nearly eighty years, the structure served as the Citadel. When the college moved into more spacious accommodations a short distance away, the old campus sat empty for nearly seventy-five years, until it was renovated into a hotel by the Hilton Hotel Group. From the *Charleston City Paper*, October 24th, 2012:

... The thoroughly modern Embassy Suites is actually a Civil War monument—it used to be the old Citadel. Since its renovation into a hotel, scores of guests and employees reported seeing apparitions of cadets or officers in the Jacuzzi suites on the top floors, especially in the corner rooms. Embassy Suites concierge Evan Kellinger says that the top floor was originally the officer's quarters. Most of the officers stationed there died during the Civil War. When asked about the most recent sightings, Kellinger said that there was a guest as of several weeks ago who reported seeing an apparition and a bright light floating around his room. However, the guest couldn't see it very well and when he went for his glasses, the apparitions began moving from place to place and he never got a good look at them. Guess this ghost still had his sense of humor.

There have also been varied reports by guests of a male cadet being seen in the rooms, hallways, and even the parade grounds of the old Citadel building. It is believed that this recruit is the same cadet each time, because he has one key detail which is reported each time he is seen: the young man is missing part of his head. Perhaps he is lucky that the Embassy Suites does not make it a habit to charge an arm and a leg for their rooms!

Aiken-Rhett House

48 Elizabeth Street

Though not far geographically from the more touristy areas of Charleston, the Wraggborough District nonetheless feels worlds apart, especially if you use tranquility as your compass. The area north of Calhoun Street (between Meeting and East Bay) seems to have a much less insistent, frenzied pulse. Almost serving as the epicenter of all that calm feeling, the best preserved antebellum home in the entire city sits beside an intimate little green space known as the Wragg Mall. The Aiken-Rhett House serves as a beacon of historic preservation, and a testament to a time long past, but not forgotten.

The house was built in 1817 by John Robinson, a well-to-do merchant, in a then-unincorporated part of the city. Robinson's story reminds us that to do business in this era, one incurred considerable risk: he lost numerous ships at sea prior to 1825, prompting him to sell his wonderful home in that year to offset his financial losses. William Aiken then acquired the property to use as a rental unit. Aiken, already a very successful businessman, would go on to found the South Carolina Canal and Railroad Company. Ironically, Aiken was killed in a carriage accident when his horse was frightened by a train. The property passed to his son, William Jr., who inherited seven plantations along with this house. After renovations, it was the residence of Aiken Jr., who would become South Carolina governor and a U.S. Congressman. Aiken altered the floor plan significantly and added the large slave quarters located on the rear of the property.

Lords of Slaveborough Manor

It is fitting that Aiken added a slave quarters to his home in the Wraggborough District. Not only was Aiken one of the largest slaveholders in South Carolina (according to the 1860 census, Aiken owned seven hun-

The Aiken-Rhett House was built in 1817.

dred slaves in that year alone), the very district he lived in was named for the Wragg family, who had been slave traders since the earliest days of Charleston. The Aiken-Rhett House's slave quarters held accommodations for up to twenty slaves.

Aiken, a supporter of the Confederacy but an opponent to Secession, died in 1887. After the death of his wife, Harriet, the house became the property of their daughter and her descendants, the Rhetts. The house was largely sealed off by the Rhett family, who only lived in a small portion of the property until the 1970's, when the property was given to the Charleston Museum. The Historic Charleston Foundation acquired the house in 1995 and began to operate the property as a house museum. Jim Morekis' 2011 book, *Charleston & the South Carolina Lowcountry*, describes the house: "As you walk the halls, staircases and rooms—seeing the remains of original wallpaper and the various fixtures added over the years—you can really feel the impact of the people who lived within these walls and get a great sense of the full sweep of Charleston history." Indeed, what struck me as I toured the house was not the elegance, although that was very much on display. What really moved me was the feeling of stepping where two hundred years' worth of footsteps had trod before me, of their everyday existence and the sense of connectedness it gave me to do so.

Shades of the Past

Emily and Barbara, two friends from neighboring Columbia, South Carolina, were touring the house one extremely warm June day. At the beginning of their visit, they were provided an MP3 player and headset as part of their self-guided tour. An in-depth pre-recorded message played as the narrator led them through every room, describing each in detail. This format made for a most welcome respite from the heat of the day.

As they ventured out of the family kitchen in the main house back to the rear courtyard of the property, Emily became very glad for the fact that they could set their own pace, and not have to keep up with a live tour guide or a big group of people. It had been a day full of walking, and her feet were beginning to hurt. The building that their narrator urged them to enter was a long, narrow structure with bright green shutters, which he identified as the slave quarters. "Charlestonians used their slaves to imitate the servant class who supported the lifestyle of British aristocrats," the recording informed them. As they moved from room to room, he urged them to imagine themselves back in the time period. His descriptions of the smell of hot food in the air and the complex duties of the slaves in charge of the laundry fascinated them both. The audio recording instructed them to climb the narrow stairs to reach the next level.

Once on the second floor landing, the audio resumed, describing the almost dormitory-like atmosphere of the slaves' living quarters. The golden June sunlight streamed in, illuminating the long hallway which ran down one side of the slave building. Despite the somewhat distressing former use of the building, both Emily and Barbara were transfixed by the simple beauty of that area of the Aiken-Rhett complex. It was like a scene from a Dutch Master's painting. Emily could almost smell the kettle cooking up some stew, and hear the sound of hooves in the courtyard below.

While Barbara stepped into one of the former slave's rooms to take a photo, Emily spotted a slightly stout African-American woman at the other end of the hall. One moment she was seemingly alone in the hallway, she would later describe, and the next instant the woman was there. The woman wore simple, rough-hewn garb, a scarf tied around her hair, and she had a basket in her hands. In those brief seconds where their eyes met, there was no fear or negative emotion displayed. Emily remembers a moment of confusion over whether that was part of the tour experience: had the house museum hired an actor to play a slave, or was there some special event going on that she wasn't aware of? The woman looked at Emily for a brief moment, and then turned away and walked into the furthest room at the end of the hall. Emily was only then aware that Barbara had rejoined her in the hallway. Together they walked to the end of the hall, and discovered that the darkened room was completely empty. It was a dead-end. There was no way that woman could have hidden from view or slipped past her. Emily began to wonder if she had somehow imagined the entire thing—perhaps falling prey to a combination of the audio tour and an overactive imagination—when suddenly Barbara asked, "Hey, where did she go?" Emily asked Barbara to describe who she had seen, and with no hesitation, her friend listed in flawless detail exactly the same person that Emily had witnessed. Rather than being afraid or disturbed, both women were filled with a feeling of peace and a sense of wonder.

It seems fitting that a spot so dedicated to preserving the past would be a good vantage point for a tantalizing glimpse back through the ages. Who was this African American woman that these ladies saw? Her presence in the slave quarters perhaps gives us a clue as to her former station in life. The historical record, however, gives us no detailed answers. And why does she linger? We are mostly left with these unanswered questions. And yet she seemed oddly comforting to those two ladies, whose impression of the apparition was overwhelmingly positive. This amiable vibe is perhaps the only real lesson that we can draw from the encounter: not all ghosts are unhappy, especially when inhabiting a residence which has largely gone unchanged for the last two hundred years. Perhaps familiarity provides peace in the afterlife.

In this hallway two tourists experienced a ghostly encounter.

Gullah Culture: Folk Legends and Hoodoo Rituals

The Old Slave Mart Museum

6 Chalmers Street

*I*magine for a moment that you and your immediate family have been kidnapped, bound in chains, sold like property, and forcibly transported to a spot many thousands of miles from your home. The voyage is long and dangerous, and as many as twenty percent of your fellow captives do not survive the ordeal. But your nightmare is just beginning: you and your loved ones are then cruelly resold into bondage by your captors, without regard to familial ties or marital vows. Ripped from your family and/or spouse, you are forced at gunpoint to accompany your highest bidder to their home. There you are compelled, both through manacles and violence, to do manual labor for the rest of your days. You are given a new name, and encouraged to completely disregard your old life, and henceforth follow the conventions and traditions of this new culture which holds you captive.

This is an extremely simplified description of the hardships faced by Africans who were enslaved and transported to the New World. The point of this exercise is to try to imagine how incredibly important holding on to ideas and beliefs from your native land would be to a person who has been forced into servitude. After five, ten or twenty years passed, the oral traditions and folk medical beliefs, while still influenced and shaped by the culture doing the enslaving, would take on a much more personal significance and symbolism to the practitioner. Clinging to these old beliefs would literally be the only way a person who faced that horrible lack of identity could hold on to any connection with the old life.

It is this sobering perspective, among others, which is offered in the Old Slave Mart Museum. Visitors are encouraged to learn what it was like to be not only a slave, but also a slave dealer, or even a potential owner of slaves. Various venues, such as the one located on Chalmers Street, sprang up in response to an 1856 law which stated that slave sales needed to be conducted at specified locations, in an attempt to remove the stigma of the public auctions, mostly garnered in foreign press and Northern newspapers. Buildings such as this one removed the sight of families being tearfully ripped asunder from all but interested bidders. Ryan's Mart, named after the owner, was opened in 1859 and conducted its last slave sale in 1863.

The museum today is run by the city of Charleston. There are two floors: the ground floor is for learning facts about the transatlantic slave trade, viewing the building's timeline, and getting an in-depth look at how slave auctions were run. The upper floor contains documents, exhibits and tools, all which speak to the day-to-day life of a slave and the resilience of that culture.

Time and time again, I have spoken to first-time visitors to Charleston who describe a feeling of familiarity while in the area. They describe a sensation of feeling as though they have "been there before," even though they have never previously visited the Lowcountry. It was only during the research phase of writing this particular chapter that I ran across a possible explanation for this familiarity in the form of a chilling reference to Sullivan's Island, which was where the pest house (which served as quarantine for incoming vessels) was located. Sullivan's Island has been dubbed "the black Ellis Island," because an estimated 217,000 slaves were brought in through the Lowcountry (some sources put the number much higher). Close to thirty million black Americans living today can trace their lineage back to a slave vessel, most of which sailed into Charleston Harbor. Peter H. Wood wrote in his 1996 book, *Black Majority*: "Here was a thin neck in the hourglass of the Afro-American past, a place where individual grains from all along the West African coast had been funneled together, only to be fanned out across the American landscape with the passage of time." Could it be possible that the feeling of déjà vu many people report when visiting Charleston is actually a shared collective memory from a past life?

Old Slave Mart Museum on Chalmers Street.

So, Who are the Gullah?

Most visitors to Charleston only encounter the Gullah people when shopping for beautiful sweetgrass baskets, which are mostly made from sweetgrass, palmetto, and pine straw, in the Historic Market area and at stands along Highway 17. An art form in their own right, these baskets are an indication of the massive amount of oral memory retained by this culture, since the baskets are identical in every respect to ones made on the coast of West Africa. The knowledge of the art of basket-making and most of their culture, including religion, was retained through these oral traditions. Theirs is an intricate belief system involving good luck charms, terrifying spirits, and skilled conjurers (spell casters) who help protect one's spirit.

Before we get into discussions of root working, spell casting, magical amulets, hags, and goofer dust, we need to establish what is meant by the term 'Gullah,' and their belief system.

The Lowcountry slaves (and their descendants), who were moved to this area very much against their will, formed their own culture called Gullah. It is a word thought to be a corruption of the word 'Angola,' which is the country from which many of these former Africans were forcibly kidnapped. These coastal people have a style of speech and a belief system which definitely shows the influence from their African roots, yet has become something distinctly different through the proximity to mainstream American white culture and religion. Remember that they carried nothing with them as they crossed the Atlantic, and came from many different parts of Africa, so the resulting Gullah culture is a blending of what these slaves remember about the many different types of music, food, religion, stories, and even speech patterns that they were exposed to before they were sold into slavery. The hot coastal land that they tended, specifically of South Carolina and Georgia, was not unlike the climate which they had left unwillingly behind. With a relatively small ratio of white plantation owners overseeing them, these slaves existed in a fertile, creative environment which fostered the preservation of many aspects of West African culture, including folklore tales, medical treatments and superstitions.

The story and influence of the Gullah people has been largely ignored by mainstream historians until recent years. As an example, Walter Fraser's 1989 study of Charleston's history, entitled *Charleston! Charleston! The History of a Southern City*, while in all other respects is a stunning work of a master historian, almost completely ignores the Gullah people (in fact, the word 'Gullah' never even appears in its pages), and barely mentions African Americans except for references to slave importation and restrictions on their movements and liberties. I mention this not to be overly critical of Fraser's fine book, but because his omission of the Gullah culture is typical of nearly every Charleston history book available. It is especially surprising since Charleston's black population has historically outnumbered the white population since at least the 1770's, and perhaps much longer. The ties between South Carolina and slavery are striking: the 1860 national census reveals that of the top slave-owners in the country, South Carolinians occupy nine of the top twenty spots on the list. Perhaps the glaring omission is due to the fact that the slaves and freed blacks comprising the Gullah people were largely illiterate.

Even so, one would expect more space devoted to the African American history in the Charleston and surrounding areas, because their influence is far-reaching. It's not all baskets and spells. If you enjoy Southern cuisine, for instance, then you yourself have been influenced by Gullah culture. Collard greens, sweet potatoes, okra, deep fried meats (including fried chicken), shrimp and grits, oxtails, and beans and rice all have their roots with this Sea Island culture.

Gullah Beliefs

It is difficult to provide even a brief overview of an entire culture's belief system, but we must lead off with the fact that the strong West African belief in magic is evident in Gullah culture. It is important to remember, lest we slip into a flippant or dismissive mindset, to try to place these beliefs and rituals practiced by the Gullah people into a historical context. Many of the Gullah rituals have their basis in medical treatment, and have their origins during a time where one could reasonably argue that Western medicine lagged behind its African counterpart. From Roger Pinckney's great book, *Blue Roots: African-American Folk Magic of the Gullah People*:

Though it took western medicine a thousand years to realize the connection between a troubled mind and body sickness, the Gullah knew it from the beginning. And so, from the beginning, they saw no difference between faith and medicine... Mainstream [white] medical practices in the late eighteenth and early nineteenth centuries were, at best, largely ineffective and, at worst, more deadly than the maladies they attempted to cure... A medical doctor could set a broken arm, stitch up a gash, or apply salve to a skin ailment, but beyond that he was essentially helpless. Peptic ulcers, tumors, hernias, and pinched nerves led to years of degenerative misery; yellow fever, pneumonia, and cholera, to almost certain death… Many Gullah slaves noted that workings of a medical doctor might be as deadly as the disease. Most camouflaged their ailments to avoid the purging, plastering, blistering, and blood-letting a doctor was sure to prescribe and saved their complaints for the trusted herbalist… They eventually gathered an extensive pharmacopeia from field, swamp, and roadside plants… But the slave herbalist had another venue, one understood even less [by] the whites: the realm of the spirit. Traditional African medicine taught that much sickness had its origins in spiritual evil, and drugs alone would not guarantee physical health. The spirit could have been sent by an enemy or could come on its own volition because of some lingering resentment from when it had been a living being. In either case, the spirit must be placated or exorcised.

The practitioners of this blend of herbalism and magic were called 'root doctors' or 'conjurers.' Wealthy Georgia planter and Presbyterian minister Charles Colcock Jones investigated the inner workings of these root doctors in the 1830's. He wrote, with the naïve self-assured belief that anything he did not understand must be tinged with a dark purpose, that the Gullah that he observed "believe in second-sight, in apparitions, charms, witchcraft, and a kind of irresistible Satanic influence. The superstitions brought from Africa have not been wholly laid aside." Jones further reported that the charms, which are also known as fetishes or gris-gris, could allegedly "enable the possessor to make free use of any part of his owner's property without detection." He described other charms as having the power to "remove sickness" or exact "mediated revenge [on one's] enemies, or… preserve the person invulnerable."

From Erskine Clarke's chapter in the book *African American Life in the Georgia Lowcountry: The Atlantic World and the Gullah Geechee* (his chapter is entitled "They Shun the Scrutiny of White Men"):

Sometimes the charms would be placed in a little bag to be worn around the neck or buried under a door or planted along a path to keep at bay malignant forces. At other times the charms might be composed of secret roots to heal a sore or of black cat ashes and graveyard dirt, a piece of fingernail and a strand of hair to be stirred into some powerful potion… Distinct from the conjurer's charms but part of the conjurer's world were the witches who were said to roam the Lowcountry nights. They could slip into different shapes, creep into cabins at night and onto a sleeper's chest so that their victims awoke feeling not only terrified but as if they were smothering. A neighbor or an old woman who lived alone might be a witch who would wait for a moonless night to travel dark paths through swamp and marsh, to hide in dark corners of the settlements and bring sickness and trouble.

These types of witches are sometimes called 'boo hags' or 'slip-skin hags', terms which are often times shortened to 'hags.' Boo-hags—which are almost exclusively female—are capable of shedding their own skin or even stealing the skin of their victim, so that the innocent might take the blame for the hag's actions. If one is assaulted by one of these types of shape shifting spirits, it is said that the target is "being ridden by the hag." The hag is not exclusive to Gullah or even African folklore: essentially identical to the Old English 'mæra'— an evil-spirit type being which sits on one's chest while the sufferer sleeps. Nightmares are also frequently said to be sent by this type of malevolent spirit. However, set distinctly apart by Gullah believers from a skin-stealing boo-hag is the so-called 'hag-hag,' which is simply a spirit without a body, similar to a ghost.

Either type of hag has a habit similar to the *succubus* in European folklore, namely a female spirit which steals a man's sexual energy or libido. Both types of hag (boo-hags and hag-hags) are said to gain entry—and access to their victims—the same way: either down chimneys or through keyholes.

Hags, according to folklore, have several weaknesses. One such vulnerability is an aversion to salt. Someone who suspects that a hag might be riding him can leave a trail of salt around the bed, and if the hag gets it on herself it would burn, much like salt in an open wound. Another tactic involving salt is to find the hag's own skin and douse it with that substance before she can return, which will cause the hag's spirit to dissipate entirely. Another weakness of the hag is the fact that when confronted with something numerical, such as an ordinary kitchen colander or sifter (with their multiple holes for straining) left over the doorknob, she will stop to count the holes. A similar tactic is to leave a kitchen broom across the threshold: the hag will feel compelled to count the broom's bristles. Or a skilled conjurer can be hired to dissuade her from bothering her victim by magic or potions.

One aspect of the hag is actually supported by science: the phenomenon known as a 'ghost light.' Legend has it that a hag, while traveling from one point to another, will carry a glowing green lantern, and are usually seen in swampy areas. This is actually a phenomenon known as bioluminescence, where decaying swampy material will emit phosphoric gas and begin to glow. Under the right circumstances, namely on very warm, calm nights, the glowing gas can be seen drifting though the swamp. This very rare occurrence has actually been replicated under laboratory conditions.

Another Gullah legend is that of the 'plateye.' Some speak of plateyes resembling black dogs, and are distinguishable from normal canines by their immense size and a single, glowing eye in the middle of their forehead. Supposedly they are the spirits of people who were buried improperly, died unjustly, or whose graves were desecrated. From Pinckney's *Blue Roots*:

In the old days, pirates such as Blackbeard, Bluebeard, and Stede Bonnet preyed on Spanish galleons, then put ashore in Carolina to bury their booty. Typically, the pirate captain would summarily execute the men who did the burying, so he alone would know the treasure's location. Then he would throw the bodies atop the chest and cover them up. Some believe these dead sailors became plateyes and would rise from the spot to chase away interlopers. Some say they would assume the forms of animals, usually a six-legged calf or a headless hog. Others believe plateyes are permanent residents of the spirit world, coming into ours to work retribution against wrongdoers or do mischief at a root doctor's command.

Some folklorists even speak of plateyes being shape shifters. Dubose Heyward, the writer most famous for writing *Porgy*, the novel on which the musical *Porgy and Bess* is based, wrote a short story called the 'Half Pint Flask.' The story details a man who removes a grave ornament and is tormented by a plateye, which is only placated when the graveside offering is returned. Plateyes are supposed to be quite fond of the taste of whiskey, so one could elude the creature by pouring some of the spirits on the ground.

Goofer dust is graveyard dirt, and is a powerful talisman. The dirt should be gathered at midnight from a grave that is not yet too old—many sources give a span of not more than four years in the ground—and is gathered from a spot just above the corpse's heart. Not any old grave will do: the nature of the departed is vital. A devoutly religious man's grave, for instance, will yield goofer dust for working with positive spirits, and a bad man's grave will render dirt which is useful for casting evil spells. A deceased person who was a financial genius will bring goofer dust which will help one with money matters, and so on. Goofer dust needs to be tended to so it does not lose its power, usually by adding saltpeter, sulphur, salt, or sugar.

The Gullah tradition is full of hexes, taboos, beliefs, and omens. There are quite simply too many to list here, but some of my favorites include:

—Fresh drops of human blood in a pan of sugar will help overcome evil influences;

—If you see a red bird on your doorstep, count to nine and you will soon come into some money;

—Never start a new task on Friday, or you will never finish it;

—If you wake up on the first day of the month and say the word "rabbit" before leaving bed, it will be a good month;

—A hooting owl is a bad omen. To make him stop, cross your fingers, take off a shoe and turn it over, point your finger in the direction of his sound, put a poker in the fire, and squeeze your right wrist with your left hand;

—And (my favorite), never shake left hands. It curses both people.

Hoodoo vs. Voodoo

Hoodoo and Voodoo are often confused as interchangeable terms. While there are many similarities, the differences are important. The main difference can be simplified down to location: Voodoo = Louisiana and Haiti, and hoodoo = Lowcountry South Carolina and Georgia. Another main difference is the prominence of Catholicism in Voodoo: Louisiana Voodoo is considered a true religion because the central figure in that faith, 19th century New Orleans Voodoo Queen Marie Laveau, blended the African gods with Catholic saints, making the two inextricably intertwined. Lowcountry hoodoo had no comparable central figure to blend it with any other belief system, specifically Protestant Christianity. This is why Voodoo is a recognized religion and hoodoo is instead considered a belief system, and a form of folk magic. This is admittedly an extremely simplified comparison of two very complicated terms.

The difference between the two certainly escaped the Charleston press, at least judging by an article by C.S. Murray from the *Charleston News and Courier* dated October 31st, 1932, entitled 'Voodoo Gods Yet Alive on Islands.' Parts of this article's tone and wording sound offensive to our modern ears, but I have reproduced the author's words and tone intact, with only slight editing for length:

The Gods and Goddesses of the Voodoo faith are not dead—they have only changed their form. Their names have long been forgotten; their personalities have been merged with the Jewish and Christian prophets and saints, as well as the demons who live in the bowels of the earth and the devil of the Puritans; and they still give comfort to the believers and wreak vengeance on the wicked. This is the conclusion I have reached after spending years observing the religious rites of the Edisto negroes and listening to them expound their theories on mystical subjects.

Any one who has visited negro graveyards is familiar with the custom… of decorating the graves of their departed. Flowers are generally absent, but bits of gaudy crockery, glass vases and sea shells decorate the newly-formed mound. These decorations cannot be regarded as tributes of respect to the dead as in the case of floral offerings—the meaning goes a great deal deeper. For instance, when an Edisto negro of unpretentious family dies, the mourners not only place vases, pitchers and shells on the grave, but often bring cups, saucers, plates and medicine bottles and arrange these objects on the mound… They have been put there for the use of the spirits. Soon after death—a matter of about three days—the spirit of the person who has been recently buried arises and inspects his grave. He is very thirsty and hungry, and if cups, plates and pitchers are found at the grave, then all is well. He can feast to his heart's content. Human food is not provided, however, probably the other spirits furnish this. The negroes are silent on this point. If the plates and cups are missing, woe to the friends and relatives who have seen to his burial!

…The death of a wicked person has been known to cause terrible storms or else a sudden change in weather, a few days after the subject has been buried. Molsey Stoney, who is an authority on ghosts, reports that one of the worse [sic] hail storms that has visited the island in recent years was brought about by the death of a particularly wicked man, who mistreated his wife and children and had a wide reputation as a thief.

…The terror inspired by graveyards is genuine. The white man may laugh and make all manner of fun if he likes, and dismiss the matter by saying that this is only an amusing superstition which can be used to good effect in a minstrel show, but the darkies continue to regard the burial place with a feeling of awe and dread.

Lest one might sneer too much at these beliefs, the spells and potions of hoodoo men have had very real effects, even upon the United States Army. It seems that a hoodoo conjurer named Dr. Bug in nearby Beaufort County was convicted in a court of law in the early 1940's. His clever crime was rather unorthodox: he was aiding and abetting potential draft-dodgers by providing potions which caused heart flutters amongst Gullah draftees, which caused aberrations in their medical examinations prior to their induction into military service. After a rash of sudden rejections of potential recruits, the military caught wind of the scheme and had Dr. Bug arrested, bringing the sudden heart conditions to an abrupt end.

With the decrease of nearly all of our regional dialects and traditions in this country due to television and a variety of other factors, true Gullah believers are becoming rarer and rarer. A seemingly vital piece of our uniquely American heritage seems in danger of slipping away. Hopefully through the fine efforts of the curators and historians at the Charleston Slave Mart Museum, this rich Gullah culture of fine food, sweetgrass baskets, and a very rich storytelling tradition shall endure.

GULLAH CULTURE

Statue in Magnolia Cemetery.

The USS Yorktown

40 Patriots Point Road, Mount Pleasant, South Carolina

To the east of Charleston, across the harbor on the far side of the Cooper River sits a stirring memorial which celebrates the gallant maritime and airborne men and women who served our nation. Patriots Point Naval and Maritime Museum is a floating monument dedicated to these brave individuals, many of whom have paid the ultimate price to preserve liberty. The collection of ships at Patriots Point includes the World War II Allen M. Sumner-class destroyer *USS Laffey* (known as "The Ship That Wouldn't Die"), and the Balao-class submarine *USS Clagamore*; but the rightful centerpiece of the maritime museum is the World War II era Essex-class aircraft carrier, the *USS Yorktown*.

Commissioned on April 15th, 1943, the *Yorktown* participated in nearly every significant Pacific battle after that date (including Okinawa and Iwo Jima), the result of which was the defeat of Imperial Japan in August of 1945. The aircraft carrier received the Presidential Unit Citation, and earned eleven battle stars for service in World War II. In 1953, *Yorktown* was modified in order to better operate jet aircraft in her role as an attack carrier. In 1958, the *USS Yorktown* was designated an anti-submarine aircraft carrier, and would later earn five battle stars for service off the coast of Vietnam (from 1965 to 1968). The ship also recovered the capsule of the Apollo 8 astronauts, who were the first men to orbit the moon (in December 1968).

Yorktown was decommissioned by the Navy in 1970. In 1975, the carrier was towed from Bayonne, New Jersey to her new home at Mount Pleasant, South Carolina in the Charleston Harbor, where she became the star attraction of Patriots Point Naval and Maritime Museum. Patriots Point has become one of the state's major tourist attractions with more than 270,000 visitors each year. The *Yorktown* boasts one of the largest

The USS Yorktown, home to two and four legged ghosts.

education and overnight camping curriculums in the nation, with more than 40,000 school age children attending these programs each year.

A Ghost Ship's Stories

But beyond the meticulously-documented record of her illustrious seventy-plus year history, the old fighting ship has a much more shadowy, whispered reputation. Many who are familiar with the vessel at Patriots Point speak of unexplainable shapes and shadows, ones that they ascribe to the ship's tragic past. These glimpses of arcane goings-on below deck on the *USS Yorktown* by staff members are so frequent that the shadows themselves have actually been given names.

Bruce Orr, a retired criminal investigator turned author, was gracious enough to sit down and share a few of his own personal experiences, starting with a concise history of the ship. "First off, there were two carriers named *USS Yorktown*," Bruce began. "The earlier *Yorktown*, known as CV-

5, was sunk at the Battle of Midway in the Second World War, so it is not the vessel in Mount Pleasant for obvious reasons: it is currently located under three miles of water in the Pacific Ocean. CV-10, which was then under construction, was supposed to have a different name entirely, but the predesignated name was switched to *Yorktown* for propaganda reasons. The name honored the CV-5, but it also was done to confuse the Japanese. They correctly thought that they sunk the *Yorktown* six months after Pearl Harbor at the Battle of Midway, but suddenly they began receiving reports of a carrier named '*Yorktown*.'" In fact, this was part of the story that I knew: the CV-5 had been severely damaged by Japanese bombs in the Battle of the Coral Sea; the Japanese assumed that they had sunk the carrier, and in fact the U.S. Navy's initial assessment of the ship was that the vessel would need several months of extensive repair in order to be a functional fighting ship once again. However, American crews repaired the ship in a scarcely-believable two day span. Needless to say, the Japanese Navy was astounded to see the *USS Yorktown* (CV-5) opposing them again at the Battle of Midway less than one month later. Again they pounded the ship, this time succeeding in sinking the CV-5. Since the ship actually sank after the battle was largely over, however, the Americans managed to keep the confirmation of her sinking quiet. The Japanese (correctly) assumed that they had sunk the *Yorktown*, but never knew for sure. Imagine the surprise of Japanese war planners when they started seeing communiques originating from an aircraft carrier named *Yorktown*, less than a year later! Not realizing that it was an entirely different ship, to the Japanese forces it must have seemed positively supernatural—a ship that they thought that they had sent to the bottom of the Pacific not once, but twice! And yet, there was the *USS Yorktown*, launching her fighters as though nothing had happened. It was a masterful ruse by the United States Navy.

"The enemy fleet never realized that there were two aircraft carriers named *Yorktown* until long after the war was over," Bruce said, smiling. "But there were early indications that the CV-10 was going to be an unlucky ship. When the second *Yorktown* was set to be christened and commissioned, U.S. Secretary of the Navy, Frank Knox, asked First Lady, Eleanor Roosevelt, to do the honors, which consisted of breaking a bottle of champagne over the bow. The First Lady, remembering that she had done the same ceremony for the first, ill-fated carrier *Yorktown*, asked, in essence, if Knox thought that it was a good idea. He assured her that it was. The day arrived, and in the middle of the speech before the christening, the ship decided to launch itself seven minutes early. Eleanor Roosevelt, not to be denied, took aim with the champagne bottle and swung, and the bottle bounced off the hull, unbroken. Not a good early sign, they thought."

The second *Yorktown* proved to be an incredibly lucky ship, however. The uncracked champagne bottle, at the time considered an ill omen, was just the first of many blows that the big ship would dodge. "Out of nearly thirty years' worth of service, the CV-10 suffered only one hundred and forty-one casualties," Bruce stated. "Of those, only five were a result of enemy action, which is amazing. Consider that the *USS Franklin*, a similar Essex-class carrier, lost nearly eight hundred men in a single day in 1945.

"So the ship proved to be incredibly lucky. The first commander, Captain James 'Jocko' Clark, was Native American. During the christening ceremony, he invited the chief of his Cherokee Nation to attend, and it is widely believed that the chief gave a blessing to the ship, so that might explain why the ship was so incredibly fortunate during its long career."

Scrappy and Johnny Cash

I asked him about paranormal stories involving the *USS Yorktown*. Bruce Orr was definitely the right fellow to ask: in addition to writing great books about Lavinia and John Fisher, he had written ghost books about both Summerville and Berkeley County, South Carolina, as well as an entire volume devoted specifically to the ghosts, legends, and history of the *USS Yorktown*. Why, exactly, would the *Yorktown* have so many rumored paranormal occurrences? "Well, my buddy Lee Erlich with Paranormal Divers has an interesting theory, namely that if you take a big container and fill it with salt water [such as ship's ballast], now you've created salt water cells. This could become a giant salt water battery, so if ghosts are electrical like so many think, what better place to hunt them than inside a giant salt water battery? It's also sitting out here cooking in the hot Charleston Harbor sun, which makes it a giant solar panel. You have wind action, wave action, tidal action, all contributing towards that build-up of energy."

So what sort of things have people experienced on the ship? "Oh, lots of things," Said Bruce. "People have reported hearing voices, footsteps, unexplainable sounds, pots and pans rattling, shadows moving, a dog barking—" *Wait, hold on a second*, I was forced to say. *A dog barking?* Bruce laughed. "The *USS Yorktown* has their own version of Poogan, you know, from Poogan's Porch in downtown Charleston? Well, the ghost dog over here is named Scrappy. He was a little, scruffy-looking Airedale. Scrappy was walking along amongst the ruins of Pearl Harbor in Hawaii in 1943. Along came two pilots assigned to the *Yorktown*, who threw him in a trash can, sealed the lid, and smuggled him aboard the ship. So that was how Scrappy joined the U.S. Navy: he was shanghaied!"

According to the Patriots Point website, Scrappy's full name was Scrapper Shrapnel; he became the unofficial mascot of the ship, and the crew even outfitted him in a flight helmet and vest. He was present for battles, and he was beloved by all. Bruce insisted that the last assertion wasn't exactly true, however: "Some sailors were annoyed with Scrappy's presence. An aircraft carrier is a floating city: it has doctors, barbers, dentists, and what have you. But the one thing the *Yorktown* did not have was a public park for Scrappy to do his business. So Scrappy would do his business wherever he pleased, and the crew would have to clean up behind him." I nearly interrupted Bruce's narrative in order to point out that it didn't sound like the sailors minded Scrappy's presence, they were annoyed with his *presents*. Do aircraft carriers have a 'poop deck'? Scrappy's opinion was apparently that yes, it did. Bruce continued his narrative, unaware of my near short-circuit from 'bad pun' overload: "Anyway, Scrappy retired after one year. But people say that he never left the ship, and that they hear him barking on the flight deck or down on the hangar deck."

I asked Bruce if there were other notable paranormal entities besides Scrappy. There were. "There is what people call 'Shadow Ed,' which is a shadowy figure that is seen sometimes," Mr. Orr related. "Ed is not a name, by the way, it's an abbreviation. My joke is that the first sailor to see him went back to his bunk, changed his underwear, and thought up a nifty nickname for what he had seen: Shadow Enemy Designation, shortened to Shadow Ed.

"There's also Shadow Sam, so named to complement Shadow Ed. He wears a black peacoat and a black hat, and is most often seen on the hangar deck. We believe he's the spirit of a roving deckwatch, which when a ship was in port would patrol the ship while wearing a .45 caliber pistol. He has been nicknamed 'The Man in Black,' based on his attire, although now people sometimes jokingly call him 'Johnny Cash.' He's what you'd call a residual haunting, because he doesn't interact with anyone. He has been seen many times by many different people."

"I Was Looking Directly At Him When He Vanished..."

I had to ask: had Bruce ever personally seen The Man in Black? He smiled, and nodded. "You have to understand, I'm not a ghost hunter; I am a historian. I'm much more interested in finding out a historical backstory for a haunting than in being a paranormal investigator. I will tell you the documented history, but in terms of going out looking for ghosts? That's not what I do. That being said, I have absolutely had some strange experiences aboard this vessel.

"Yorktown Ghost Tours offers something called the Paranormal Experience, where you can rent out the space and bring your own ghost-hunting equipment and you can investigate the ship personally. I act as a guide and chaperone for the event. Remember, I don't conduct any investigations or operate any equipment. My role is to tell some stories and point out where things have allegedly occurred, but it is up to the client to investigate. Anyway, a mother decided to gift her daughter with a ghost investigation one cold January night. It was for the young lady's seventeenth birthday, and she brought two of her teenaged friends along on the investigation, as well. Well, we actually heard some pretty interesting sounds below decks, but once we got to the hangar deck is when things got interesting.

"It was bitterly cold that night, and the lights were pretty low on the hangar deck. Two of the young ladies pointed and said, 'Who is that down there?' And they pointed towards the fan-tail, which is the stern side of the hangar deck. We all saw an individual who was wearing a black coat and a black cap, hands in his pockets, moving towards the fan-tail, very much in a hurry. I speculated that it was one of the security officers, and even joked that he was just looking for someplace warm. But the mother said, 'That is neither of the security officers I saw tonight. I saw a young white woman and an older black gentleman.' And this fellow was a young white male. So I called out to him, and he didn't respond. He was rapidly moving on down the ship. By this point the two young ladies trained their flashlights on him and I noticed something else: his black coat did not have the words 'Security' stenciled on the back in reflective letters. Well, I realized that it wasn't good, because it meant we had a trespasser. Someone was aboard that was not supposed to be there, and if he got below deck, we'd have to shut everything down until security or law enforcement found him. I decided to stop him from getting below deck, and my law enforcement training kicked in.

I told those ladies that he was not security and that they needed to stay back, and then I called for him to stop. Again, he did not acknowledge. So I started running after him. He never changed his pace, which was sort of a fast walk. I came up from behind him. As he got close to the stairwell, I was about twenty feet behind him. Two of the girls were moving up rapidly behind me, too, with their flashlights. I was about to shift into 'super cop tackle mode,' thinking to myself that if he got any closer to that stairwell he was going to get knocked on his can, and if he resisted, I'd have to subdue him. He moved a little more to the left and I noticed that he was wearing a U.S. Navy military issue peacoat with black plastic buttons and was wearing an odd looking cap, because there was some sort of writing on it. He took one more step, and disappeared right in front of me. I mean that one second he was there and the next it was if he stepped behind an invisible wall. There was a collective gasp from the ladies behind me, and one of the young ladies started dropping enough 'F-Bombs' to sink that particular aircraft carrier, so I knew they all saw what I had just seen.

"One second he was there, the next he was gone. I've never seen anything like it before in my life. I mean, I was twenty feet away from him, and I was looking directly at him when he vanished. And even weirder, he never seemed to notice me. Security came running, too, because they heard me shouting and all of us running, and they saw no one but us the whole night. I know I saw him, though, and I had four witnesses with me that saw the same exact thing. Funny thing was, they all had cameras and equipment, but none of them thought to take a picture or anything. He looked that real. They all assumed that he was a real person, like I did.

"Interestingly enough about that hat he was wearing: one of those ladies described it as a 'chef's hat.' Well, until 1963, sailors wore what was called a Flat Hat, precisely like what Donald Duck wears. It was usually navy blue, and on the front was written in gold letters 'U.S. Navy.'"

Almost as if apologizing for having his own ghost experience, Bruce said, "Another group saw him too, about a month before. The tour guide was ushering folks out of one area of the ship, and suddenly someone asked, 'Who is that going up the other stairwell?' The guide asked them what the unidentified person looked like, and the people on the tour agreed that they had seen a young man wearing a black coat and carrying a duffel bag over his shoulder. They looked all over for him, but no one was there. Three nights later, security encountered him three separate times in the same evening on the hangar deck. So Shadow Sam has been seen by many, many people."

Bruce shared one final odd happening aboard the *USS Yorktown*: "I had given a tour on the ship a while back to some ghost hunters. Once the tour was over and we were back on dry land, I untucked my polo shirt as I was talking to them. When I did, an old penny came flipping out of my shirt. I did a double-take, because this was a really old penny, and it looked a little odd. I pulled out a magnet, and the penny stuck to it, which confirmed my suspicions. It was a steel penny, and they only made those for a little over a year, mostly in 1943. All the copper was being used to make gun and shell casings, so there was a shortage. This penny was indeed from that particular year."

1943? I didn't grasp the significance at first. "Yes, 1943," Bruce said, smiling. "The same year that the *Yorktown* was launched. I acknowledge that it all could just be a coincidence; but you have to admit that if it is a coincidence, it's pretty big one."

So What Does This Mean?

Stories of hauntings deal almost exclusively with tragedy. Prominent themes are unrequited love, suicide, duels, or senseless accidents. The *USS Yorktown* was not immune to calamities during her time spent in service to this country, as the record does reveal over a hundred casualties. When that figure is placed in context with other similar ships during that time period, however, we learn that the ship in question was extraordinarily, and yes, almost supernaturally lucky in combat. It would be overly easy (and a little false) to simply point at those deaths aboard ship as the cause of the paranormal happenings, and yet if we choose the more difficult path in the story we are left with a ghost story that is quite different than most. So what are we left with, if that normally-key value is removed from the equation?

We are discussing a ship that, almost without exception, did a phenomenal job of shielding its brave sailors from the horrors of war during combat. And perhaps that is the paranormal lesson that we are meant to draw from the *Yorktown*: not all ghosts are the spirits of those who died prematurely, and perhaps the strong psychic bonds are literally binding former sailors and airmen to the vessel because of their love for the ship. These ghosts, if the stories are judged as objectively as possible, are not unhappy in the slightest. It is entirely possible that the spirits on the ship, namely Shadow Ed, Shadow Sam, and yes, even little Scrappy are simply returning to the last place that they truly felt safe. It would be fitting that they return to honor the ship which protected them so admirably during life. Perhaps, then, they feel the need to repay the favor, standing watch over their gallant vessel in the afterlife.

Old Charleston Ghost Shop

168 Church Street

On Church Street, between South Market and Linguard Streets, sits a business with an intriguing name: the Old Charleston Ghost Shop. At first blush, it might seem the acme of foolishness to ask the proprietors of a ghost shop if their building is haunted or not, but I freely admit that I find myself asking most people I meet in the Holy City if their place of employment has any resident ghosts. I was not disappointed here. One of the co-owners, Maggy, confirmed that they have a resident spirit or two, specifically one that seems to enjoy leaving messes for them to clean up. "We've found picture frames wrenched off of the wall, with their hooks completely bent all out of shape," she related. "But the picture and frame are undamaged. We just have found them leaning on the wall when we come in to open." In one notable instance, the wall mount, which could support one hundred and fifty pounds, was wrenched and twisted by an unknown force.

The ghosts also tended to play with money left in the register. "We solved it, though," Maggy said, "because apparently these spirits are shy." She gestured to the video cameras. "As soon as the cameras were installed, the issues stopped entirely. So the ghosts in here apparently don't like their pictures being taken." I had to ask the obvious question: was that the end of the trouble? "Oh no," Maggy said. "Now they make strange, loud crashing sounds which we originally thought were coming from the clothing shop next door, but we hear the loud bangs at all hours of the day and night. It turned out to be coming from the top of our bookshelf where we display mostly items relating to zombies. It sounds as though someone is dropping a book on the shelf, but is definitely coming from inside our shop."

I asked if she had any idea who the spirits were. "No, and it seems odd to have ghosts in a building as new as the one we're in." She gestured to the late 1980's architecture. "We've had people who have come into the shop who claim that they are psychic, and suddenly they will start talking about

The ghosts of an old woman and a little boy have been reported at this ghost shop.

our ghosts. This has happened for separate times, and these are people that I don't know, understand. Each one of them has told the exact same story, describing the spirit of an older woman and the ghost of a little boy. It is always the little boy, they say, who makes all the messes and commotion. I guess little boys don't change, regardless of what time period they are from."

The identities of the ghosts at the Old Charleston Gift Shop, and even what time period they date from, are still a mystery waiting to be solved. But one clue, according to Maggy, is that at least one of the spirits seems fascinated by zombies.

The Ghost of Annabel Lee

Unitarian Churchyard

4 Archdale Street

In 1827, an eighteen year old private joined the U.S. Army and was sent to Fort Moultrie in Charleston Harbor. He was most notable for having falsified his enlistment papers: the faked documents claimed that he was twenty-two, and that his name was Edgar A. Perry. His real name, however, was Edgar Allan Poe.

Today, we know Poe as a master of literature and poetry, but at that point in his life he had met with virtually no success. He joined the army under those deceitful circumstances because of an estranged relationship with his foster family over gambling debts he accrued while at college. His first book of poems, released while he was stationed in Boston, was met with little acclaim and even fewer sales. Despite a predilection for drinking at local taverns, 'Perry' rose quickly while stationed in Charleston, attaining the rank of sergeant major of artillery. The young officer was deeply unhappy in the military, however, and sought to end his enlistment early. When he revealed his falsified circumstances to his superiors, he was granted his dismissal from service in April of 1829.

Years later, a poem was published posthumously, entitled "Annabel Lee." In it, the poem's narrator describes his love for a young woman with that same name, a devotion which began many years ago in a place he describes as a "kingdom by the sea." The nameless narrator claims that their love for one another burned with such an intensity that even the angels became envious, and it is for that jealousy that the narrator believes that the angels caused her death. Despite death separating the lovers, their bond is strong enough that it extends beyond the grave. Every night, he dreams of Annabel Lee and sees the brightness of her eyes in the stars. The poem ends with the narrator describing his nightly ritual, namely that he lies down by her side in her tomb by the sea. Many Charlestonians make the claim that Annabel Lee was a real person, and say that Edgar Allan Poe doubtlessly heard the following tale while in a local tavern, and borrowed rather liberally to construct his later poem:

A sailor from Virginia was stationed in Charleston and met a young local girl named Annabel Lee. Their chance meeting fostered a friendship, which then developed into a deep and abiding love. The two young lovers were scarcely seen apart, despite her family's strong disapproval. Annabel's father forbade her from seeing this young sailor, judging him to be unworthy of his highborn daughter. Annabel tearfully promised her father to stop seeing the boy, but the young lovers continued their trysts in secret: Annabel would meet the sailor in a secluded spot, namely the Unitarian cemetery. This worked for a short time, but Annabel's father became suspicious that she had given up so easily. One day he followed her, and caught the lovers as they held hands in the cemetery. The father was livid at his disobedient daughter, so he locked Annabel in her room for several months to prevent the pair from seeing one another. The sailor, determined to see his love again, decided that he would wait until she was ready to move out of her family home, but unfortunately the Navy transferred the sailor back to Virginia before that could happen. The lovers vowed to be reunited someday. Annabel was heartbroken.

While home in Virginia, the sailor received heartbreaking news that his beloved Annabel had died of yellow fever. The crushed sailor sent word to her family that he would be deeply indebted if he could attend her funeral, but the father refused. The sailor returned to Charleston to be at the graveside of his dear, departed Annabel. Her father, in a spiteful turn, devised a plan so the sailor would never know which grave was Annabel's. He had Annabel's grave at the family plot at Unitarian Cemetery dug to the normal depth of six feet, but then had all the other graves in the family plot dug to three feet. This would be just enough to not disturb the graves, but enough to make them all look freshly-dug. The sailor would never know the true location of his beloved's body.

When the sailor went to the cemetery every day, he would sit for hours sit by the family plot in the Unitarian Cemetery to grieve her death. He never knew exactly which grave was Annabel's, but he'd come all the same to mourn. The spot which had once given them such pleasure was now the spot of all-consuming grief. Where he once sat hand in hand with his lovely Annabel, now he sat alone, weeping, without a marker to honor her passing.

There is no record of what ever became of the love-torn sailor. There is still hope for the pair, however, in the afterlife. To this day, people claim to have seen Annabel Lee searching the cemetery for her long lost love. Perhaps this is because of the strong attachment she had and the abrupt ending of the relationship, never being able to properly say goodbye. Perhaps death has given her the strength to defy her father and try to go to her love at long last. Apparently she is still seeking him, and maybe one day they shall be united.

So Who Was Annabel?

So is Charleston the "kingdom by the sea" referred to in the poem? And did Poe use that local story as the basis for one of his most famous works? Well, the poem doesn't specify any one location, and it is impossible to know today which locale Poe was thinking of when he wrote it. It could be Charleston, or it could have been Baltimore or even Boston. Poe gave us no clues in the body of the poem. Biographers and historians still disagree over the true identity of 'Annabel.' Many women in Poe's life died prematurely, a list which includes his mother, his adopted mother, and his wife Virginia. It is probable that the character in the work is a composite character for all the lost loves of Poe's life rather than one specific person.

The folklore story is also impossible to decipher from a historical standpoint, since no year or even era was described, other than being post-Revolutionary War. I could find no burial records for anyone named Annabel Lee in Unitarian Churchyard. Due to no one being able to tie the story to a specific year, it is likely that the story was concocted well after Poe's death, and was influenced by the poem, as opposed to the other way around. I have even heard the claim that Poe actually *was* the sailor in the story, and later went on to write about his own experiences in the form of poetry near the end of his life. I can find no evidence to support this claim anywhere in the archives, so it almost certainly is not true.

I did meet a walking tour guide in Charleston who claimed to have seen a ghost she called "Annabel Lee" in the Unitarian Churchyard. If the Edgar Allan Poe/Unitarian Church connection is spurious, then who is the spectral female that this guide swears she saw? Regardless of her identity, it is but one more sighting of a ghost in a city with a hundred thousand such stories.

Andrew Pinckney Inn

40 Pinckney Street

During one of my research trips to Charleston, I had the good fortune to secure a room at the upscale Andrew Pinckney Inn at an amazingly low rate. Located downtown at the very outside edge of Charleston's French Quarter, the Inn is situated at an ideal location for both souvenir-hunting tourists and ghost-hunters (like me).

Right after a great complimentary breakfast on the terrace which provided a breathtaking view of the city's skyline, I struck up a conversation with one of the managers. I casually worked into our conversation the question: *is the inn haunted?* He looked at me uneasily, trying to gauge if I were somehow attempting to lay the groundwork for some ghost-related complaint. I reassured him that I was just curious, and he rather guardedly replied that the Pinckney Inn's official position is that it is not haunted, but after a few minutes confirmed that he had heard some stories from both the housekeeping staff and some fellow managers, specifically the third shift. "This place has all the creaks and groans which are typical of an old building," he explained. "But if you believe even just one of these stories out of the dozens that I've heard, then it also has some creaks and groans which are definitely *not* typical." He then pointed me in the direction of an online article written by a former night manager of the Andrew Pinckney, Jesse Schmitt. Mr. Schmitt detailed his own experiences at the Inn in a *Yahoo Voices* article written on July 15th, 2010:

I am reminded of some otherworldly stuff that's been going on locally at the place I call work. The Andrew Pinckney Inn is a historic Charleston, South Carolina, boutique hotel, with plenty of local character. I'd never ask anyone to feel "scared" of the Andrew Pinckney Inn, but it's haunted. I would be worried that my bosses would be furious over this admission had we all not openly spoken about it. To them, it may be a running joke, but this haunting is no laughing matter on the third shift. The Andrew Pinckney Inn is actually a relatively new property, being restored in 2001 from its numerous previous incarnations.

ANDREW PINCKNEY INN

"... it also has some creaks and groans which are definitely not typical."

The area of Charleston where the Andrew Pinckney Inn is located is the downtown French Quarter area. I'm convinced that the building we've erected here was once a burial ground. Working the night audit at this hotel, it can be very easy to lose yourself in the sounds and movements which come across. Some would offer that I'm just tired but I have been in the halls of the Andrew Pinckney Inn, delivering express checkout receipts, and I've heard and seen some spooky stuff.

While the Andrew Pinckney Inn has no bone-sucking creatures here, there are spirits. My wife Kate has been with me here once before on the overnights; she called the experience "mind bending." I have resigned myself to be surrounded by these goblins, but I'm still somewhat skittish when a noise jumps from an otherwise empty room, or things I know were there just disappear. As I've been writing this very piece, one of the unused, been-in-hibernation-for-hours computers has just revved its processors and begun spitting off an epic throttle. Some may call this technological antiquity; I'd wager it's the local spirits, shaking the tree.

For potential guests at the Andrew Pinckney Inn, these ghosts are "friendly," so there's nothing to fear. I imagine these spirits as lost, wandering souls, treading and retreading these grounds.

In an exhaustive search of the archives, I can find no positive indication that the plot of ground currently occupied by the Andrew Pinckney Inn was ever part of a burial ground, but that does not mean that it isn't true. The original city walls, which were in existence during the first third of the 18th century, extended as far as present-day Market Street, meaning that this location would have been just north of those fortifications. There does appear (on Crisp's 1704 map) to have been an Independent (Presbyterian) Church inside the walls near this location. The practice of burying the very poor and the unknown in Potter's fields to the north of existing settlements is well-documented; could this be the case here? Could the Independent Church have had a burial field outside the city walls? Or could this speculative burial site be part of the vast Native American history in the area? Perhaps this discovery, or even some previously unknown slave burial ground, awaits future historians and archaeologists. Regardless, if the numerous stories are to be believed, the Andrew Pinckney Inn appears to have some restless yet benign spirits inhabiting its walls.

1837 Bed and Breakfast

126 Wentworth Street

If you're looking for a relaxing visit, look no further than the 1837 Bed and Breakfast, located on a quiet, shady street near the College of Charleston. *The New York Times* once called the inn "a perfect place to unwind." It appears that the spirits agree with that assessment. From the *Charleston City Paper*, October 24th, 2012:

[At] the 1837 Bed and Breakfast… guests and employees have reported seeing a little boy playing around the halls, to vanish shortly after. George, as the employees there have affectionately named him, was said to have been a slave boy of the house whose parents were sold to a family in Virginia. After stealing a rowboat, George attempted to chase after the slave ship his parents were on, but tragically flipped his boat and drowned in the Charleston Harbor. The bed and breakfast was supposedly the last place George was with his parents. In rooms 2-2 and 3-1, guests and employees have said they were shaken from their beds by George or were startled by the sight of the bathroom door repeatedly slamming shut. But staff assure us there's no need to worry. Apparently even Casper can't beat George for friendliness.

I could find no records confirming the reality of this slave boy named George, but then again I did not uncover any documents which nixed the possibility of his existence, either. Slave records are notoriously incomplete, so it is possible that the story is completely accurate. However, another explanation might be that someone named the ghost George just to explain away the spirit in the house, and the moniker stuck. I can confirm, however, that numerous people have had run-ins with this ghost: most people who report an encounter with him describe seeing a rocking chair on the porch, which will rock all on its own. George has also been known to slam doors in the house, especially as people approach. Fortunately, both the staff at the 1837 Bed and Breakfast and their resident ghost seem quite content to peacefully coexist.

"... guests and employees have reported seeing a little boy playing around the halls, to vanish shortly after."

The Mills House Wyndham Grand Hotel

115 Meeting Street

This upscale hotel located at 115 Meeting Street is actually a carefully-constructed, near exact replica of a previous 1853 building on the same site. In the late 1960's, the original hotel was in such poor condition that renovation was not possible, so the owners demolished the structure and built the current building, which reopened for business in 1968. The main difference between the old and the new buildings is the addition of two more floors in the newer design.

A very interesting article (entitled 'See the Real Ghosts at These Haunted Hotels,' by Ford Dyas) appeared in the *Charleston City Paper* on October 24th, 2012, one which detailed several haunted happenings in the Mills House: "The Mills House Hotel is not... open about being a supernatural hotspot, but still has a haunted history which guests and employees can attest to. Many guests have reported seeing Confederate soldiers running up and down the halls and one apparition was said to resemble the ghost of Robert E. Lee. History buffs might recall that the hotel was used as a Confederate base during the Civil War but was damaged in the fire of 1861. Now those soldiers are said to scan the halls looking for water in order to put out the fire— which was put out for good more than 150 years ago."

Guests have reported strange knocking on the doors of their rooms in the hotel, including one man who reported that someone banged on his door several times, including while he peered out through the peephole. He saw nothing, but could both hear and feel the vibration from the knocking. Guests have also reported seeing apparitions in the hallways, and sometimes mysterious figures have appeared in photos taken within the hotel. People who rent rooms overlooking Queen Street also some-

"... the hotel was used as a Confederate base during the Civil War but was damaged in the fire of 1861."

times claim to see Zoe St. Amand next door at Poogan's Porch restaurant (please see the chapter dedicated to that restaurant located in this volume) from their vantage point at their windows.

While staff members are shy to comment 'on the record' about ghosts, one man who works at the front desk did offer a helpful tip: those looking to avoid ghostly contact (yes, those types of people do exist!) should request to stay on the top two floors. According to him, the staff has never heard of any sort of ghostly encounter on those levels, and he speculates it is because the ghosts all date from a time before those floors were added. "They don't know that those floors exist," he said with a wink.

The Jasmine House Inn

64 Hasell Street

A wealthy merchant named Benjamin Smith constructed this handsome Greek Revival house in 1843. Located in the upscale original suburbs of Charleston called Ansonborough, the area is named after early colonist George Anson. He reputedly won the parcel of land which today bears his name in a card game. The Ansonborough District runs from Hasell Street (just north of the Market) to Calhoun Street, and is bordered on either side by King and Anson Streets. Perceptive visitors to this area of the city will undoubtedly notice that very little of the architecture predates 1840. This is due to the Great Fire of 1838, which destroyed approximately a thousand homes.

After being used as a residence for a number of well-known Charleston families (including the Mazycks and the Gadsens) over the years, the building became a bed and breakfast in 1982. Since that time it has established a reputation for being one of the finest inns in the South, and is considered by architectural experts to be the finest Greek Revival house in Charleston. The structure features beautifully finished hardwood floors, plaster entablatures, fifteen foot ceilings and ornate wood and iron work. It is the very picture of Southern elegance, complete with breakfast and afternoon cheese and wine. However, if the stories are to be believed, it also played host to a bizarre incident which has been widely reported in a number of paranormal-themed books: an angry female spirit which cornered a terrified businessman, and refused to let him leave.

Then-general manager Brien Limehouse got a weird call one morning in the late 1990's. A guest staying in the Chrysanthemum Room called the front desk to report that he had awakened to find a strange woman with him in the room. She apparently had him cornered despite his best efforts to get around her. Thinking that the female was perhaps a 'lady of negotiable affections' and that there was some dispute over the man's bill for services rendered, Mr. Limehouse decided to head to the second-floor room and sort the matter out as best he could. He arrived at the Chrysanthemum Room, and walked in to find the man alone, huddled in the corner, shivering with fear. All around him were little pieces of newspaper, shredded into tiny bits.

When he was finally able to speak of the incident, he told the general manager that upon waking up in his room, he found an old woman in the space with him. When he spoke to her, he never got a response. When he tried to edge around her, she kept blocking his escape, and grew more and more agitated by the moment. When he touched his luggage, she got extremely angry, and shredded the newspaper in front of his astonished eyes in a matter of seconds. She had vanished right before Brien entered the room. Needless to say, the man's hasty exit from the Jasmine House Inn beat the standard check-out time by several hours.

No one is quite sure of the true identity of the strange, angry apparition which appeared that morning. Fortunately for subsequent guests at the fine bed and breakfast on Hasell Street, she has only been seen the one time. Perhaps her appearance was triggered by that one particular guest, or maybe it was simply a one-time haunting. Regardless of why she chose that particular morning and that particular man to vent her considerable frustrations, one thing is certain: one Charleston visitor went home convinced that this genteel, elegant city is very much haunted… and some of the ghosts there don't like newspapers.

Husk Restaurant

76 Queen Street

Not long after I announced that I was writing a collection of Charleston ghost stories and legends, I began to get questions from people through social media sites, asking about certain locations in the Holy City. One of these messages, which was from a man named Christopher, involved one of my favorite eateries on Queen Street. He wrote:

I was wondering if you knew if the restaurant Husk in downtown Charleston is haunted. My wife and I had an experience there while having dinner last night. We were seated in the upstairs dining area, in front of a window just to the left of the fireplace. The fireplace was not lit. While talking over dessert, I saw what appeared to be a small black shadow move past us. I couldn't tell if it was between us, or in back of where my wife was sitting. It happened so fast. At the same second that I jumped back in my seat, my wife got jolted forward in hers, and I heard her chair move. I said, "Did you see that?" She said, "See it? I felt it! I just felt my chair get pushed in a few inches on its own." I was so sure that I saw something fly by us that I pulled her jacket off her chair and shook it, making sure that nothing got in it, because at first I thought it was a blackbird, or something of that size, which had somehow flown into the restaurant. When I asked the waiter if anyone else had any strange experiences there, he said that two weeks ago, a perfectly healthy woman passed out at the same table.

All I could tell Christopher was a little information about the property, namely that the Graham House, which currently houses that fine eating establishment, has sat on that plot of ground since 1894. Prior to that, the residences at this location have succumbed to numerous fires, most notably the Great Fire of 1861, which ravaged most of the city. Without more clues, the identity of this dark phantom will have to wait to be revealed—perhaps by the next people affected by its presence. So those with an appetite for fine dining and as-yet unresolved ghost stories should make their

Husk at 76 Queen Street.

way to Husk, whose cheeseburger has been named one of the top dishes in its class by *Bon Appetit*, *Food & Wine*, and *Forbes* magazines.

The Phantom of the Bridge

John P. Grace Memorial Bridge

For well over half a century a terrifying sight appeared to Charlestonians who crossed the since-demolished Cooper River Bridge (which was formally named the John P. Grace Memorial Bridge, although few called it by its proper name). The people who have seen this particular apparition have reported that, in a city practically bursting with ghosts, it was unlike any other spectre that they could have possibly encountered. What is the reason for this uniqueness among Charleston hauntings? The ghost was the distinct form and shape of a green 1940's-era Oldsmobile sedan. Many of these witnesses did not know the reason for this strange encounter, and only learned of the bridge's deep association with tragedy after they related their brush with the supernatural to long-time Charleston residents.

The Cooper River Bridge, which opened in 1929, was the site of a horrific incident in February of 1946. According to the book *The Great Cooper River Bridge*, by Jason Annan and Pamela Gabriel:

On February 24th, 1946, an overcast Sunday afternoon… the 12,000 ton ship Nicaragua Victory drifted out of control during a sudden gale and slammed into the bridge. As the storm's strong winds blew, the ship drifted from its anchorage in the Cooper River. The ship's crew did not immediately realize their situation, but when they did the captain ordered an additional anchor to be dropped. It did little to stop the ship, which floated towards the bridge. The engines were off; the crew had no way to control the ship's movement. Soon the bow became stuck in the mud near the Mount Pleasant side of the Cooper River, and the stern pivoted around and slammed against the side of the bridge. One of the crewmen aboard the Nicaragua Victory described the impact the day after it occurred. "There was a thud, with little shock. There was a sickening, low grinding, groaning noise, which sharpened into a screeching tone. That was accompanied by the cracking and popping of the concrete…" Debris rained down upon the ship. The impact damaged one of the piers of the Cooper River span and carved out a 240-foot gap in the roadway.

At the time of the collision, automobiles were crossing over the bridge. According to eyewitness accounts of the accident, when the ship struck the bridge, vehicles skidded to a halt. One car could not stop in time. Elmer Lawson, a quarterman and electrician at the naval base, his wife Evelyn, his mother Rose Lawson, and his two children, Robert and Diane, were on their way to the Isle of Palms via the Grace Bridge when the collision occurred. The impact sent their 1940 dark green Oldsmobile plunging through the gap in the bridge and into the cold waters of the Cooper River. Crewmen of the Nicaragua Victory saw the car go off of the bridge and rushed to look for survivors. They observed a large bubble of air where the car splashed into the water.... One month later... the Lawsons' sedan was found, and all five bodies recovered.

From 1946 all the way to the time that they closed the bridge in 2005 to make way for the beautiful Arthur J. Ravenel Bridge which replaced it, bridge-crossers would sometimes report the strange sight of an antique auto. The strange sight was always glimpsed for a brief moment by cars heading eastbound on the old bridge, exactly as Elmer Lawson had done on that fateful day in 1946. People who claimed to have seen the ghost car reported that it abruptly slowed, and pitched forward and down into the roadway itself, as if a chasm had opened in its path. The most common sightings were in the month of February, and during intense storms, exactly like the one which forced the *Nicaragua Victory* into the bridge so many years ago.

When the old bridge closed due to structural issues, the reports of the ghostly Oldsmobile finally ceased. There have been no new reports since the new bridge opened to traffic in July of 2005. The demolition of the older bridge began a month later. Hopefully this is an indication that the Lawson family has found the peace that has eluded them for so long. Because if not, we await an eyewitness account of what would be an extremely unsettling image: a green sedan coasting down an incline of a bridge which does not exist anymore, and then abruptly dropping, trap-door style, into the dark waters below.

The Meeting Street Inn

173 Meeting Street

On Meeting Street, within a stone's throw of the Market, there sits a beautiful inn which is haunted by not one, but two spirits. The building was constructed in 1874 by German immigrant A. Tiefenthal as a restaurant and saloon. After his death in 1889, his wife sold the property to an Irishman named O'Hagan. The property was in decline, like much of the surrounding area, all through the middle of the 20th century, but was revitalized with the tourist boom of the 1980's. It opened as a bed and breakfast in 1982, and has enjoyed a reputation as a romantic and elegant inn ever since.

The Meeting Street Inn is blessed with two haunted rooms: 303 and 107. According to staff members, room 303 has a ghost with a pesky habit: it likes to lock the door's deadbolt from the inside. Once management is summoned with a master key, the ghost will even hold the door shut with a surprising amount of force. Eventually this spirit grows tired of this prank and releases the door, leaving the staff member with a thorny problem: how do they explain the locked yet completely deserted room to the guest?

The spectre in room 107 gives a completely different, yet no less puzzling display: the apparition of a female, usually at the foot of the bed, is known to appear and then disappear. The top half of this ghost is said to look completely real, and the bottom half less distinct. She simply makes her presence known, and then vanishes.

The identities of both ghosts are a mystery, even though they have been repeating their strange actions for parts of four decades.

The Meeting Street Inn.

Coda: "...You Never Feel Alone..."

*I*n a city like Charleston, it is easy to get distracted by all the tragedy when discussing hauntings. The historical record is full of truly awful events, such as great fires, terrifying storms, chronic fevers, murder, genocide, bombardment, suicide, and on and on. Even the very land on which it sits seems racked with turmoil, as seen by the horrific Great Earthquake of 1886 (and very recent geological aftershocks, one of which struck while I was visiting the city in the course of conducting research for this volume). I would be remiss in my duties as an author and historical researcher if I failed to mention the cataclysmic effects these events have had on the inhabitants of the Palmetto City. After all, a life being ended prematurely seems to be the key ingredient of a haunting, and there's no denying that the aforementioned disasters did take a lot of lives and forever carved their features across Charleston's landscape.

As interesting as these events might be, I believe to focus solely on tragic circumstances is to miss the point. When you boil the stories down to their very essence, there are two distinct elements: the ghostly entity itself, and the living person who experiences the entity's effect on the physical world. This book, then, records not only the impressions of the ghost by the observer, but their reaction to (and, by extension, their attitudes towards) the paranormal episode. The attitudes of the residents can reveal much about the character of a place. By the average person's standards, coming into contact with something not completely understood by science is the definition of a terrifying, perhaps even emotionally crippling event. I find myself, however, thinking back over the many people that I interviewed for this book—historians, authors, innkeepers, managers, servers, tour guides, business owners—and their reactions to the unexplainable events that they have experienced. The people of Charleston that I interviewed seem to be rational, thoughtful people, and very accepting of their ghostly visitors. When asked to sum up an entire city's sentiments towards the paranormal, I find myself thinking of tour guides who, in the midst of

"... to focus solely on tragic circumstances is to miss the point."

a genuinely unexplainable occurrence, merely kept speaking so as to not alarm their ghost-tour guests. That sort of thing just doesn't happen in most cities. I also find myself realizing that the owner of the liquor store on Bay Street who told me that he felt protective towards the ghosts in his establishment was not expressing his own eccentric, outlier attitude on the subject. Instead, he was expressing a pervasively inclusive Charlestonian attitude towards the paranormal that goes far beyond the expected limits of southern hospitality.

By that (or any) measure, Charleston is an extraordinary place. There is a deep connection between the residents and nearly three hundred and fifty years of history, and those ties between daily life and the distant past are strengthened by the occasional glimpse beyond the veil. "Living in Charleston has changed my life," explained tour guide Ginger Williams. "It's more than a city—it's that you can see the mark that everybody who ever lived here has made. It's a living, breathing kind of thing. You never feel alone in Charleston."

"A sense that all has ever been abides in that house forever."

Charleston has many faces. I have presented just a few of them here, but the dichotomy that is the city of Charleston is impossible to fully describe. The deep undercurrent of paradoxes and ironic contradictions run swift and deep here: this cradle of Revolutionary democracy is also one of the birthplaces of slavery in the American colonies. The hands-down winner of every prestigious 'Most Hospitable City' award is also the same town which once infamously lined their highways with the severed heads of slaves which dared rise up in opposition. The Old Exchange on Bay, symbol of financial freedom and famous host to President George Washington, was also the site of the terrible Provost Dungeon where martyr Isaac Hayne spent his last lonely night on earth. The town nicknamed 'The Holy City' was full of gambling, prostitution, and murder. And the South Battery, one of the most beautiful spots on Earth, has once-deadly cannons nestled down amongst the flowers. Charleston is all of these contradictory things and more.

I began this book with a question: why is Charleston so haunted? Well, no one, no matter how eloquent, can precisely convey the feeling that many visitors (and yes, many residents) get when walking the streets

Circular Church, St. Philip's Church, Secession Hall, Charleston, S.C., by George N. Barnard. Obtained from the Library of Congress Prints and Photographs Division.

of the city's historic downtown. I feel that Charlestonian historian and writer John Bennett comes closest to the heart of the matter in his book, *Doctor To The Dead*:

Wherever men have lived and moved and had their being, hoped, feared, succeeded, failed, loved, laughed, been happy, lost, mourned, died, were beloved or detested, there remains forever after a something, intangible and tenuous as thought, a sentience very like a soul, which abides forever in the speechless walls. No house that human lives has touched is ever after void. A sense that all has ever been abides in that house forever.

Charleston is indeed haunted, but it is now up to you to explore what that statement means. Is it the pent-up occasional flaring of energy left over from a dozen generations' worth of tragedy and romance? One simply cannot escape the inexorable tidal pull of four centuries worth of life—it, and the evidence of its passing, are all around you. With this book, I have provided an entry-point with which you, the reader, can at least gain some context for the storied and famously historic locations. You have just finished what was intended as an introduction, but now what is lacking is you. Each step on a cobblestone on Chalmers Street or a stroll through the Old City Market causes one to peel back the years with the mind's eye. Flickering gas lamps and the slow beat of horse hooves set the scene, making this narrow peninsula a blank page which only awaits your own narrative. Let Charleston seduce you. Come experience the visceral sensation of a town where passions run deep: sample first-hand the locals' ardor for the food, the culture, the history, and yes, even the ghost stories and legends.

In a life filled with uncertainty, I can offer you my guarantee that your adventure to Charleston will certainly be worth having.

Selected Bibliography

Beney, Peter. 2005. *The Majesty of Charleston*. Gretna, LA: Pelican Publishing Company, Inc.

Bennett, John. 1943. *The Doctor to the Dead: Grotesque Legends and Folk Tales of Old Charleston*. Columbia, SC: University of South Carolina Press.

Bostick, Douglas W. 2010. *Charleston Under Siege: The Impregnable City*. Charleston, SC: The History Press.

Caskey, James. 2013. *The Haunted History of New Orleans: Ghosts of the French Quarter*. Savannah, GA: Manta Ray Books.

—2013. *Haunted Savannah: America's Most Spectral City*. Savannah, GA: Manta Ray Books.

Coker, Michael. 2008. *Charleston Curiosities: Stories of the Tragic, Heroic and Bizarre*. Charleston, SC: The History Press.

Cordingly, David. 1995. *Under the Black Flag: The Romance and the Reality of Life Among the Pirates*. New York, NY: Random House.

Diamond, Jared. 2005. *Collapse: How Societies Choose to Fail or Succeed*. New York, NY: Penguin Books.

—1999. *Guns, Germs and Steel: The Fates of Human Societies*. New York, NY: W. W. Norton & Co., Ltd.

Downey, Christopher Byrd. 2013. *Charleston and the Golden Age of Piracy*. Charleston, SC: The History Press.

Eastman, Margaret Middleton Rivers, and Edward Fitzsimmons Good. 2010. *Hidden History of Old Charleston*. Charleston, SC: The History Press.

Fraser, Walter J. Jr. 2005. *Charleston! Charleston! The History of a Southern City*. Columbia, SC: University of South Carolina Press.

Jones, Mark. 2005. *Wicked Charleston: The Dark Side of the Holy City*. Charleston, SC: The History Press.

—2006. *Wicked Charleston, Volume II: Prostitutes, Politics, and Prohibition*. Charleston, SC: The History Press.

Macy, Edward B., and Julian T. Buxton III. 2001. *The Ghosts of Charleston*. New York, NY: Beaufort Books.

—Macy, Ed, and Geordie Buxton. 2004. Haunted Charleston: Stories From the College of Charleston, the Citadel, and the Holy City. Charleston, SC: The History Press.

Martin, Margaret Rhett. 1963. *Charleston Ghosts*. Columbia, SC: University of South Carolina Press.

Miller, Ruth M., and Ann Taylor Andrus. 2005. *Charleston's Old Exchange Building*. Charleston, SC: The History Press.

Morekis, Jim. 2011. *Charleston & the South Carolina Lowcountry*. Berkeley, CA: Moon Spotlight.

Orr, Bruce. 2010. *Six Miles to Charleston: The True Story of John and Lavinia Fisher*. Charleston, SC: The History Press.

Pickens, Cathy. 2007. *Charleston Mysteries*. Charleston, SC: The History Press.

Pinckney, Roger. 2007. *Blue Roots: African-American Folk Magic of the Gullah People.* Orangeburg, SC: Sandlapper Publishing Co., Inc.

Poston, Jonathan H. 1997. *The Buildings of Charleston: A Guide to the City's Architecture*. Columbia, SC: University of South Carolina Press.

Robertson, David. 1999. *Denmark Vesey: The Buried History of America's Largest Slave Rebellion and the Man Who Led It*. New York, NY: Random House, Inc.

Roffe, Denise. 2010. *Ghosts and Legends of Charleston, SC.* Atglen, PA: Schiffer Books.

Rosen, Robert. 1997. *A Short History of Charleston*. Columbia, SC: University of South Carolina Press.

—1994. *Confederate Charleston: An Illustrated History of the City and the People During the Civil War.* Columbia, SC: University of South Carolina Press.

Scott, David C. 2010. *Abode of Misery: An Illustrated Compilation of the Facts, Secrets and Myths of the Old Charleston District Jail.* Charleston, SC: Building Art Press.

Turnage, Sheila. 2001. *Haunted Inns of the Southeast.* Winston-Salem, NC: John F. Blair, Publisher.

Library of Congress Citations

Ruins of Circular Church, Charleston, S.C.. Library of Congress Prints and Photographs Division, Washington, D.C. Reproduction Number LC-USZ62-60304.

E. & H.T. Anthony (firm) Panoramic view, the ruins of Charleston, S.C., Roman Catholic Cathedral in distance, c.1865. Library of Congress Prints and Photographs Division, Washington, D.C. Reproduction Number LC-DIG-stereo-1s02465.

Barnard, George N., Graveyard, Circular Church, Charleston, S.C., 1865. Library of Congress Prints and Photographs Division, Washington, D.C. Reproduction Number LC-DIG-stereo-1s01305.

East (Front) Elevation from Northeast - Hannah Heyward House, 31 Legare Street, Charleston, Charleston County, SC. Library of Congress Prints and Photographs Division, Washington, D.C. Reproduction Number HABS SC, 10-CHAR, 306--2.

Third Floor, Holding Cell No, 3, View from Window - Charleston County Jail, 21 Magazine Street, Charleston, Charleston County, SC. Library of Congress Prints and Photographs Division, Washington, D.C. Reproduction Number HABS SC, 10-CHAR, 348--87.

First Floor, Kitchen, View from North of Dumbwaiter Shaft - Charleston County Jail, 21 Magazine Street, Charleston, Charleston County, SC. Library of Congress Prints and Photographs Division, Washington, D.C. Reproduction Number HABS SC, 10-CHAR, 348--55.

Third Floor, Cell No. 4, Entrance from Hall, Door Open - Charleston County Jail, 21 Magazine Street, Charleston, Charleston County, SC. Library of Congress Prints and Photographs Division, Washington, D.C.

Reproduction Number HABS SC, 10-CHAR, 348--84

First Floor, Exhibit Cell Doorways from East to West - Charleston County Jail, 21 Magazine Street, Charleston, Charleston County, SC. Library of Congress Prints and Photographs Division, Washington, D.C. Reproduction Number HABS SC, 10-CHAR, 348--50.

Third Floor, North Section Northwest Room, Spiral Stair from Southeast - Charleston County Jail, 21 Magazine Street, Charleston, Charleston County, SC. Library of Congress Prints and Photographs Division, Washington, D.C. Reproduction Number HABS SC, 10-CHAR, 348--75

Second Floor, Hallway from North to South of Octagonal Section - Charleston County Jail, 21 Magazine Street, Charleston, Charleston County, SC. Library of Congress Prints and Photographs Division, Washington, D.C. Reproduction Number HABS SC, 10-CHAR, 348-61.

Second Floor, Cell Room No. 2, Detail of Door from East - Charleston County Jail, 21 Magazine Street, Charleston, Charleston County, SC. Library of Congress Prints and Photographs Division, Washington, D.C. Reproduction Number HABS SC, 10-CHAR, 348--67.

Key, John Ross, Fort Sumter, December 9th 1863, View of entrance to Three Gun Bat'y, January 9, 1864. Library of Congress Prints and Photographs Division, Washington, D.C. Reproduction Number LC-DIG-ppmsca-22785.

Osborn & Durbec, Ruins of Fort Sumter, Charleston Harbor, S.C., April 1861. Library of Congress Prints and Photographs Division, Washington, D.C. Reproduction Number LC-DIG-stereo-1s02596.

Key, John Ross, Fort Sumter, December 9th 1863, View of South East Angle, January 7, 1864. Library of Congress Prints and Photographs Division, Washington, D.C. Reproduction Number LC-DIG-ppmsca-23067.

Photogrammetric Image: Aerial View Southeast Corner - Stevens-Lathers House, 20 South Battery Street, Charleston, Charleston County, SC. Library of Congress Prints and Photographs Division, Washington, D.C. Reproduction Number HABS SC, 10-CHAR, 312--19.

Jackson, William Henry, Orphan House, Charleston, S.C., 1900. Library of Congress Prints and Photographs Division, Washington, D.C. Reproduction Number LC-DIG-det-4a08846.

Barnard, George N., Circular Ch., St Philip's Ch., Secession Hall, Charleston, S.C., 1865. Library of Congress Prints and Photographs Division, Washington, D.C. Reproduction Number LC-DIG-stereo-1s01317.

ABOUT THE AUTHOR

James Caskey is a tour owner, licensed guide, historian, and author. In 2001, he founded Cobblestone Tours, a walking ghost tour based in Savannah, Georgia, where he currently resides. His tour company has always been devoted to telling the true history and real stories of Savannah. This search for accuracy naturally led Caskey to the world of writing: his first two books about the paranormal (including his second effort, 2013's *The Haunted History of New Orleans: Ghosts of the French Quarter*) have been received with strong sales and positive reviews.

He and his work in the paranormal field have been featured on the top-rated Savannah episode of *Ghost Adventures*, as well as the Travel Channel, the *New York Daily News*, *New York Magazine*, CNN, PBS, FSN, *Inflight Magazine*, the *Savannah Morning News*, WSOK Radio, and local weekly *Connect Savannah*.

OTHER TITLES FROM MANTA RAY BOOKS LLC

The Haunted History of New Orleans: Ghosts of the French Quarter
by James Caskey

New Orleans: is it the most haunted city in America? This book chronicles one writer's journey to New Orleans, LA, and his quest to find the most haunted locations in the French Quarter. Uncover the arcane and chilling aspects of ghosts and Voodoo in the Necropolis of the South. Tag along as he interviews eyewitnesses, historians, tour guides, and even a particularly spot-on fortune-teller in one of the most haunted cities in North America. Discover how he experienced the wrath of a long-dead Voodoo Queen, had an amazing revelation about one of New Orleans' most famous haunted spots, and even got to experience his very own haunting, right in the middle of an interview.

Lavishly illustrated with over 35 pen and ink drawings and photos!

Haunted Savannah: America's Most Spectral City
by James Caskey

Why is Savannah, Georgia the most haunted city in America? Historian and tour guide James Caskey answers this question and many more. This fully-revised and updated book details over forty of Savannah's most infamous ghost stories, resulting in a paranormal compilation unlike any other. Discover the truth about Savannah's haunted history as you explore spine-chilling tales about the Hostess City's shadowy "Other Side," as told by a master storyteller. This volume combines exhaustive searches of historical archives, detailed analysis, and engaging first-hand accounts of spectral activity as experienced by eyewitnesses, even by the author!

Haunted Savannah: America's Most Spectral City is not a collection of dry facts, dates and folklore; it is an enlightening and entertaining journey for anyone interested in the paranormal, from magical mystery tourist to serious ghost hunter. Containing over 50 photos and a detailed map of Savannah's Historic District, this book is the perfect 'pocket tour guide' for the do-it-yourself ghost seeker.

If Your Dream Doesn't Scare You, It Isn't Big Enough
by Kristine K. Stevens

In honor of her 40th birthday, Kristine K. Stevens sold her house, quit her job and traveled solo around the world. Carrying a backpack and the naïve belief that the trip was nothing more than a six-month long vacation, she hit the road. She braved monsoons in Zanzibar, a safari in Kenya, trekking in Nepal, kayaking in Thailand, caves in Laos, red plaid fish and lava in Hawaii, and grizzly bears in Alaska. Little did Kristine know that she was completing a pilgrimage that would change her life forever.

This Side of the River by Brayton Price

How do you discover yourself, much less life or love, in an increasingly digital age? This is one of the many questions posed by Brayton Price in this collection of over 35 original poems. *This Side of the River* explores nature, modernization, and imagination, and their effects on the human experience.